INLAND EMPIRE

INLAND EMPIRE

D. C. Corbin and Spokane

by

JOHN FAHEY

SEATTLE   *UNIVERSITY OF WASHINGTON PRESS*

FOR PEGGY AND GRACE

PREFACE

THE INLAND EMPIRE OF THE PACIFIC NORTHWEST IS A SERIES OF
plains cut by rivers, bounded roughly by the Rockies and the Cascades on the east and west and by the Selkirk and the Blue mountain
ranges on north and south. Although politically it embraces parts
of four states and one province, much of this region's history reflects the unity imposed by its geography. Commerce has flowed
through the Inland Empire with slight regard for state or national
boundaries during the area's seventy-five years of swift transition
from frontier to substantial agricultural, forest, and mineral producer.

My purpose in writing this career study of Daniel Chase Corbin
is to demonstrate the role played by early local railroads in establishing Spokane, Washington, as the center of this inland area; and
although Corbin did not build all the feeder railroads that have
served Spokane since the Northern Pacific arrived in 1881, he did
build those most useful to the city before 1900. Moreover, Corbin's
railways, unlike most of the others, were independent ventures.

Corbin was known most of his life by his initials. He signed
himself "Dan" in a few personal letters that I have located but was
rarely so addressed. He was known as D. C. Corbin. He signed
letters even to his family as D. C. Corbin and his printed checks
and business stationery identify him as D. C. Corbin.

Even in retrospect, Corbin was not a likeable or warm individual, and the awe with which he was regarded when he was alive persists. He was curt and purposeful but I do not think he should be denied a proper appreciation for delivering Spokane as a thriving metropolis to its present citizens merely because he was hard to know and hard to like. Those closest to Corbin testify that he was loyal and returned him loyalty, if not affection.

There are no recent histories of the Spokane region and few of those extant give adequate attention to its economic emergence. This lack of published material tempted me more than once to stray into beguiling legends of the Coeur d'Alenes, or to recount stories of early steamboating on the Kootenai and Columbia rivers and inland lakes, to describe the old *Galena* which was sawed in halves to be shipped overland to the Kootenai for service.

I think F. Augustus Heinze, who established British Columbia's great Trail smelter and proposed a southern railway to open the province to its coast, deserves a better biography than a few biased magazine articles and passing mention in books about more famous men, for Heinze was a promoter of amazing scope. He was a loser, and perhaps his is the appropriate fate of losers.

Rossland's momentary, glorious boom must someday be preserved in print.

But I am succumbing again to the lure of unchronicled people and places by merely suggesting the detours I tried to avoid.

Anyone who writes history depends on others. I am no exception. Among those who aided is Dr. Herman J. Deutsch, who shaped the book's purpose and offered specific suggestions for improving the rough manuscript. In a brief explanation of my annotation I credit Richard G. Magnuson with opening his files to me but I must also acknowledge his interest, suggestions, and watchfulness for material on Corbin.

The first Spokane newspapers were not available on microfilm when I began searching for items about D. C. Corbin. Harold R. Boyd, former manager of the *Spokesman-Review* library, afforded me access to the archives under his supervision, and Norman E.

Kilgore, present library manager, has continued this attention and assistance. The library staff was diligent, patient, and friendly.

Elizabeth S. Gilbert, reference librarian of the Spokane Public Library, and her staff have been attentive and helpful. David H. Stam of New York City tracked much specific information about Corbin's associates. The New York Public Library and National Archives personnel served me well. I am also indebted to Willard E. Ireland, provincial librarian and archivist of British Columbia, and to Mary K. Dempsey, assistant librarian of the Historical Society of Montana.

Two friends and members of the Gonzaga University history department, the Reverend William L. Davis, S.J., and the Reverend William N. Bischoff, S.J., encouraged me in this pursuit. Much of the economic information about northern Idaho in the chapter dealing with Corbin's Spokane International Railway was uncovered in newspaper files by Father Bischoff.

Many others helped in many ways. I regret not being able to mention each of them. Some who supplied specific detail are credited in the notes, and to the anonymous others, I extend my grateful appreciation.

The book reveals my great debt to the family of the late Edward J. Roberts, and especially to William D. Roberts of Spokane, his grandson, and Florence Morris of Madison, Wisconsin, his niece, for permission to quote from the documents cited in the notes as the Roberts papers. Without the encouragement of the Roberts family this study of D. C. Corbin would not have been written, for it began as an inquiry into the career of E. J. Roberts. I interviewed this sprightly gentleman a number of times before his death September 14, 1949, finding him clear of memory, ready for jest, and rewarding, and I will be sorry if Roberts' own contribution to Spokane does not emerge in part from this account of D. C. Corbin.

My last thanks is not least, for it is to my wife, Peggy, who spent family vacations in libraries and whose only overt revolt against my long preoccupation with D. C. Corbin was her refusal to hang a huge portrait of the old man in her living room. In its place hangs a mirror. Perhaps the mirror is more appropriate because I hope this book reflects an age whose image Spokane still bears.

John Fahey

CONTENTS

ILLUSTRATIONS

ABBREVIATIONS

C&K—Columbia and Kootenay Railway
C&PO—Coeur d'Alene and Pend Oreille Railway
C&RM—Columbia and Red Mountain Railway
C&W—Columbia and Western Railway
CKSN—Columbia and Kootenay Steam Navigation Company
CPR—Canadian Pacific Railway
CR&N—Coeur d'Alene Railway and Navigation Company
GN—Great Northern Railway
N&FS—Nelson and Fort Sheppard Railway
NP—Northern Pacific Railroad
OR&N—Oregon Railway and Navigation Company
SF&I—Spokane Falls and Idaho Railroad
SF&N—Spokane Falls and Northern Railway
SI—Spokane International Railway
W&I—Washington and Idaho Railroad

INLAND EMPIRE

CHAPTER ONE

NEW HAMPSHIRE
TO MONTANA

Seventeen years transformed Spokane, Washington, from a shanty hamlet by a waterfall to the metropolis of an inland empire that covers parts of four states and one province. In 1881, Spokane Falls was a false-front frame village on one dirt street lamenting mail delivery once a week. The town shed "Falls" from its name in 1891. In 1898, Spokane had emerged as the largest northern railroad center between Minneapolis and the Pacific Coast, sanctuary of millionaires from the mines of Idaho and British Columbia, hub of commerce—the Queen City of its Inland Empire.

In those seventeen decisive years between 1881 and 1898, rails and the mines they served shouldered Spokane past its rivals. Spokane marked two successive periods of early growth. The first followed arrival of the Northern Pacific Railroad in the village in 1881. It was augmented by the Coeur d'Alene mining rush two years later and capture of the Spokane County seat in 1886. This first distention subsided in the Panic of 1893, and the second period ensued with general recovery, exploitation of the British Columbia mines, continued richness of the Coeur d'Alenes, water power, agriculture, and timber. It lasted until perhaps 1911 when Spokane's rush of immigrants waned. During both periods, the principal mines lay in the Coeur d'Alene district of northern Idaho and the Kootenay of British Columbia, both geographically tributary to Spokane. The man who built the railroads that stitched the mines to Spokane was Daniel Chase Corbin.

Without the Northern Pacific and Corbin, Spokane might have evolved in quite a different manner. The town commanded no navigable waterway; it enjoyed less natural attraction than several of its neighbors. Spokane's gravel soil was considered inferior for farming, its water power was useful but beyond conceivable requirements, and early military trails between Walla Walla and Colville bypassed the falls because the river was easier to cross at other places.

Corbin, himself, intended at first to reach the Coeur d'Alene mines from Thompson Falls, Montana, and only a slight legal omission in Idaho's territorial constitution decided him to start from Washington. Two of Spokane's pioneers, James Monaghan and M. M. Cowley, predicted that Spokane Falls would never amount to anything and encouraged the Jesuits to locate their college, Gonzaga, at Cheney or Sprague. There were dozens of aggressive, hopeful small towns in the eighties, some with advantages that seemed to assure their futures, but only one was destined to become the inland metropolis of the Pacific Northwest.

The career of Daniel Corbin, therefore, concerns in good measure the elevation of Spokane to stature among inland western cities. His Coeur d'Alene railway "opened the marvellous treasure of the Coeur d'Alene to the world," and his line north from Spokane became "one of the chief foundations of Spokane's greatness and prosperity." In relating Spokane's history, narrators have allowed economic activity to be overshadowed by the dramatic incidents of Indian wars, labor conflicts, fire, water development, and contention over terminal rates with transcontinental railroads. When settlers came West, however, they came because Daniel Corbin and others like him dangled opportunity. Two other men talked about railways to the Coeur d'Alenes; Corbin built one. Two other roads north from Spokane languished until Corbin arrived in 1888. He was then fifty-seven, wise from nearly forty years on the unfolding frontiers of western territories.

Daniel Chase Corbin was born October 1, 1832, at Newport,

New Hampshire, the younger of two sons of Austin and Mary (Chase) Corbin. His father was a farmer and timberman, prosperous and seemingly well-educated, the son of Dr. James Corbin who received land for service in the Revolutionary War. The Corbins sent both boys to public schools, and at the age of twenty, Austin, Jr., who was five years older than Dan, worked briefly in a Boston store before his parents entered him in Harvard Law School.

"What I did in my youth didn't amount to much of interest to anyone but myself," Daniel often remarked as an old man.[1] As a young man he followed the tide of westward movement. In 1852 when he was nineteen, Daniel traveled west to Iowa to survey unallotted lands.[2]

A heavy traffic of immigrants streamed to Iowa then seeking land and freedom—Germans, Danes, French, Irish. They arrived by wagon and they came on foot pushing their meager goods in handcarts, gaunt women in sunbonnets, dust-streaked barefoot children, worn men; they cut the virgin prairie with iron plows or fished the rivers from flat scows.

Corbin saw fine native brick homes rise on the bluffs overlooking the Mississippi and riverboats gliding the broad stream; he heard the rousing songs of German societies and angry speeches denouncing slavery; he flailed against caddis fly swarms that darkened the sun and, dying, were shoveled into the river.

Perhaps Corbin passed dark Dred Scott or the young railroad lawyer, Abe Lincoln, over from Illinois to controvert the rivermen assailing the first Mississippi railroad bridge at Davenport. Railroad frenzy kindled the frontier. Ground was broken for the Mississippi and Missouri Railroad, Iowa's first, in 1853, while towns, counties, and speculators cried for money to subsidize more railways. Iowa gave the railroads four million free acres. Survey stakes sprouted on every beckoning hillside and homesteaders traded land for the stock of chimeral villages.

Corbin heard the laughter, and perhaps joined it, from sleigh rides, husking bees, and hunting parties, and he pondered the trail pounded hard into the prairie by carts and boots of Mormons and gold hunters pushing past the westward horizon.

Two years after he reached Iowa, eastern financiers who were friends of his family hired young Corbin to locate and buy desirable Iowa land for them. This occupied him twenty-four months longer.

In 1856, Austin Corbin, Jr., followed his younger brother to Iowa to establish himself as a partner in the banking firm of Macklot and Corbin at Davenport, thus becoming a member of the first national bank in the United States to open for business with a federal charter. In the frantic period of wildcat finance that accompanied the Civil War, Macklot and Corbin almost alone joined the local newspaper, the *Democrat,* in denouncing the worthless currency issued by private banks.

By the time banker Austin reached Iowa, the state had grown too settled for Daniel. In the summer of 1856, he was off for Nebraska City, metropolis of the two-year-old Nebraska Territory.

He reached Nebraska at its pinnacle of land speculation. Townsites, marked by nothing but stakes and optimistic posters, bloomed on every slope along the Missouri River. Property owners here, too, traded their land freely for town stock. Claim clubs had been organized in Nebraska, as in Iowa, to unite settlers in protecting those whose land was jeopardized by resurveys. Often the claim clubs functioned as the only local government. Frontier finance plunged recklessly after speculation. Some unchartered banks issued their own notes and occasionally insurance companies tried to operate as banks.

Nebraska's white population numbered perhaps thirty thousand when Corbin stopped at Nebraska City on the western bank of the Missouri near Table Creek where John Brown hid runaway slaves. Begun as a trading post, the city bustled with the open life of a river town, steamers plying the broad waterway, roustabouts milling among rattling wagons in the streets that led to wharves.

Corbin homesteaded northwest of Nebraska City, setting himself up as a land and insurance agent.[3] He entered politics. His attendance at city caucuses and county conventions seemed to win notice, because in 1857 and again in 1858 he ran as a Democrat for a seat in the lower chamber of the territorial legislature. He was defeated in both elections but in June, 1858, Corbin was appointed to fill a vacancy on the city council. After serving six months, Councilman Corbin resigned to visit the new Colorado mines. So enthusiastic was he about what he saw that he wrote his parents urging them to come out to Colorado, but they stayed comfortably on the family farm in New Hampshire.

Frequent passing wagon trains impressed Corbin with the increase in freighting as the borderland extended westward, and on his return to Nebraska from the Colorado country he contracted to haul government and military supplies to army posts. The army was fighting a protracted running war with the Plains Sioux to keep open the wagon and immigrant routes. In addition to his government shipments, Corbin sent consignments of blasting powder to the mines, and in the spring of 1861 erected magazines in Nebraska City, Denver, and Mountain City. To take advantage of the overland immigration, he established a ranch and stage station on the flatland west of Fort Kearney on the Platte River, halfway across modern Nebraska, on the route followed by Ben Holladay's stage coaches and the Pony Express.

"I crossed the plains to Denver and Salt Lake on mule back and by overland stage several times before the Union Pacific Railroad was built," Corbin observed years after. "I . . . enjoyed the exciting sport of chasing buffalo and being chased by Indians." [4] Corbin maintained that he laid the foundation for his personal fortune in Nebraska, dealing in land, operating his stage station, and freighting military and mining supplies.

Early in 1862 Corbin returned briefly to New Hampshire to marry Louisa M. Jackson. He took his bride to Nebraska where he continued to dispatch large trains of blasting powder to the mines, and on at least one occasion, drove out one thousand kegs himself. He was nearly thirty years old, wiry and rather short, and he must have already been businesslike to the point of reserve, forthright, a little formal in bearing, although by no means unsociable. He was simply too busy for tomfoolery.

On February 28, 1861, Congress had created Colorado Territory from what had been Arapahoe County, Kansas Territory, partly to settle a controversy stemming from a local movement to establish a

Territory of Jefferson. Again new country challenged Daniel Corbin. With his bride of a few months, he moved to Denver about the middle of 1862 where he secured quartermaster contracts to carry military goods to Fort Laramie, Wyoming. The army had moved in there in 1849 as a base for its campaigns against the Sioux which were to linger until 1881.

In the winter months of 1862 a freight driver from Montana put a milk pan of gold dust in the window of a Denver bank. Clusters of men paused to ponder it and, with them, Corbin built fancies on the reckless tales of gold strikes. While he counted flour sacks, harness, and powder kegs consigned to the army, his thoughts escaped to the magical gold fields. Everyone in Denver was talking and thinking of the gold to the north. As soon as the trails opened in the spring of 1863, thousands set off for Montana. Each dawn Corbin watched new trains muster, standing a little apart from the jubilant travelers, hearing their ebullient prophecies of fortunes, the wagons' creak and drivers' cries as they started, and yearned to go with them. When their canvas billowed out of sight, he returned to routine checking of consignment lists, captive to his contracts to supply Fort Laramie, deterred from leaving by his wife's first pregnancy. On September 24, 1863, in Denver, a son—Austin Corbin II—was born.

Denver then was a wooden city of perhaps four thousand, proud of its daily newspaper, the *Rocky Mountain News,* of its bright blue Rockies and United States mint, and fearful of rumored Indian forays. Much of the town had burned in April, 1863. Then as a result of heavy, headlong investments by New York and Boston men in dubious stock companies, the difficulty of recovering gold with the crude processes of the time, and pinching out of some diggings with promise, Colorado's gold boom collapsed a year after the fire. A general Indian uprising took place, crops failed, and grasshoppers devastated the few fields that survived the Indians and the weather. For the moment, Colorado was dismal. D. C. Corbin resolved to follow the gold seekers to Montana.

"The road [to Helena] is literally crowded with teams and packers..." observed the *Montana Post.* "Many, having no other means of conveyance, have come through on foot, carrying on their backs enough to load a common-sized mule." [5] Those lucky enough to find a stage seat, or to afford one, usually traveled without stops for rest, nine passengers inside and a tenth on top with the driver, napping as they could along the jolting way. The wagon road bumped through Prickly Pear Gulch to Helena, a lusty year-old town in the mountains of western Montana, where early in 1865 Corbin took his wife and baby son.

Helena, straggling along the steep sides of Last Chance Gulch where gold had been discovered, lived in perpetual frenzy with daily reports of new strikes. The town throbbed with mining men and their talk. It was estimated, indeed, that of Montana's 18,300 white population, sixty per cent engaged in mining. When the Corbins arrived, they found a protective association of merchants governing Helena until a formal city administration could be organized. Sunday, a holiday, passed in public auctions, drinking, gambling, and hunting gold.

Frequently miners filed claims on Main Street and dug it up, adding to the difficulty of following the trail among disordered buildings. The *Montana Post* complained the way was nearly impassable, "deplorable," filled with discarded boards and paved with rubbish. Frame buildings with false fronts, their signs painted free-hand on rough lumber, jammed against log houses and stores on Main Street—the only street—that twisted along the floor of Last Chance Gulch. From Main rose trails; after constant use, these trails acquired buildings, and then, by general consent, became side streets.

On one of these steep side streets called Grand, Corbin found a building where he opened a mercantile business—a kind of general store—and an office for the freight forwarding company Woolworth and Barton, which had commissioned him before he left Denver. He took an advertisement in the *Montana Post,* which had moved from Bannack City to Helena when the mining excitement shifted that way, announcing himself "agent for Woolworth & Barton Overland Transportation Line," connecting with the Union Pacific, offices in New York and St. Joseph, Missouri. [6]

Helena teemed with confident men. Among them was Samuel

Thomas Hauser, a magnetic Kentuckian three months younger than D. C. Corbin. Hauser had reached Montana in 1863 by way of St. Louis and Idaho after a youthful career as a railroad surveyor and miner. He was immensely popular: the *Montana Post* called him a man "of practical jokes and many friends" and already stories circulated about his exploits, his constant luck, and the good fortune of the men who gathered around him. Soon he would be described with a select group that included Marcus Daly, W. A. Clark, and C. A. Broadwater, as managers of the territorial Democratic party: "Every one of them came up from the ranks by superior merit and hard licks. . . . They are autocrats—bosses of the strongest type." [7] Hauser had been a Vigilante, and for a few years, Hauser or someone close to him seemed to be doing everything worthwhile that was accomplished in Montana Territory. By 1865 he had accumulated several thousand dollars from mining and could call on two wealthy cousins in St. Louis for more thousands.

Corbin joined perhaps a dozen other prosperous young businessmen who clustered about Hauser in mining and banking ventures. Silver had been discovered in Montana in 1865 but the emphasis remained on gold; there were fourteen gold mills but none for silver until Hauser and his partisans organized the St. Louis and Montana Mining Company, built one silver plant at Philipsburg—perhaps the first silver smelter in the United States—and a second at Argenta under the direction of Dr. George C. Swallow. The mill at Philipsburg, opened in 1865, employed a process so primitive that it produced little metal, and the German in charge at Argenta, Augustus Steitz, maintained such secrecy about his methods that no one knew at first whether he could actually turn out silver. It was Steitz who arbitrarily ordered the name of the small town where the mill located changed to Argenta, owing to the argent or whiteness in its ore. Apparently ore worth less than one hundred dollars a ton could not be smelted at a profit in the charcoal-burning plant, and part of Steitz's reticence may be blamed on the dispute among metallurgists at the time about using fire reduction to process silver ore.[8]

Steitz's air of mystery eventually became too disconcerting. The company removed him and hired a practical mill man who overhauled the equipment and solved its intricacies. Anton M. Esler, a metallurgist and miner who served as an expert consultant for Hauser, wrote Hauser that Steitz covered "the whole operation with such a mask of secrecy that I, like others, thought it impossible for any other but himself to work it, but now we learn how extremely simple the operation is." [9]

In mining's early days, rudimentary methods and ponderous transport pushed smelting costs for Montana ore fantastically high. Miners even tried to ship ore to Swansea, Wales, for proficient smelting but found the cost exorbitant. Corbin recalled that his group tried smelting abroad but found it too expensive. Mule trains hauled ore and bullion to the Missouri River for water shipment to a smelter, and occasionally a small camel caravan passed through western Montana, evidences of an attempt to transplant the beasts to North America. Fort Benton, on the Missouri, lay 140 miles east of Helena, and one legendary shipment of two and one-half tons of gold drawn there by a four-mule team in the autumn of 1866 was valued at $1,500,000!

Daniel Corbin, soon perceiving that the St. Louis and Montana Mining Company's ventures into silver would not feed his soon-to-be increased family, continued his store and his freighting. On November 5, 1866, a daughter, Louise, was born in Helena.

As an energetic merchant in the Hauser constellation, Corbin found himself involved in civic affairs. He served on a committee to establish a standard rate of exchange for gold dust, more common in Helena than minted coins. Until this group imposed its order on exchange rates, banks, stores, and saloons loosely based their individual values on the source and fineness of dust and the sobriety and reputation of its owner. On February 11, 1867, the committee placed a value of eighteen dollars an ounce on dust and published regulations for its circulation. For the first time, Helena recognized a general system of exchange, and from this and similar concerted efforts evolved the Helena Board of Trade, established in 1877.

In June, 1868, Corbin formed a partnership with James K. O. Sherwood, a bachelor fourteen years younger than he, to deal in wholesale staples. The new firm, Corbin and Sherwood, moved from

Grand into a renovated building on Broadway called the Big Barn, which it shared with another similar company. Woolworth and Barton had sold their freight forwarding business, releasing Corbin from his agency. The *Montana Post,* campaigning for reverent observance of Sunday, listed Corbin and Sherwood among stores that closed on the Sabbath, one of the few times Corbin's name was publicly connected with a function of a religious nature. That fall, the Corbins built a two-story white frame house at Seventh and Ewing, on the relatively flat land overlooking Last Chance Gulch.[10]

Early in 1869, after a February fire that consumed $75,000 worth of business property, the merchants of Helena appointed Corbin and W. S. Paynter to collect funds to organize a fire commission. The target was about $2,200 to hire fire watchers and pay two companies of fire fighters. Tramping through Helena's twisting streets, Corbin and Paynter collected $1,338 in two days by assessing property owners twenty-five or fifty cents a front foot, depending on location. From this beginning, Helena organized fire watchers and, in response to the *Montana Post's* editorials and a second fire, its first companies of volunteer firemen.[11]

As the years passed, Corbin fared well, but he had not uncovered the fortunes he had fancied as he gazed at that pan of gold dust in the Denver window seven years earlier. He was eager to improve his situation but cautious, and he did not find a real opportunity until 1871. But on May 10, 1871, John S. Atchison, the cashier of Sam Hauser's First National Bank of Helena, resigned in a huff, complaining that he had to run the bank alone six months of the year because its president and directors were usually out of town, he had not sufficient help, and was not paid enough. Corbin dissolved his partnership with Sherwood and took Atchison's place in the bank, happy to control its affairs without the directors looking over his shoulder. He bought 116 shares of the bank's stock, worth about $12,000, and then carefully lined off Atchison's name on the letterheads and wrote his own in ink.[12]

Hauser had organized the First National in May, 1866, as the pioneer bank in Montana, with a blue chip roster of the Territory's leading men, including Nathaniel Langford, T. H. Kleinschmidt (who would be twice Helena's mayor), W. B. Dance, F. L. Worden, S. M. Hall, and Julius Busch, and two Missourians, John How and L. M. Kennett of St. Louis. The redoubtable Steitz was the bank's first assayer, smelting gold dust in a small firebox in the rear of the grocery store that housed the original bank. By the middle of 1868 the First National was reported to smelt seven hundred to eight hundred ounces of gold each day, casting it in 1,682 ounce bars worth $40,000 each.

Corbin kept the directors up to date on the bank's activities by letter:

> We have a few new customers and depositors since you left. I am glad to think that my coming in here will at all events not lose any of the patrons of the institution. The dust and bullion trade is moderate and we are making a little margin on all we handle....
>
> The demand for money in the way of loans is not equal to our resources but I am taking all the good loans I can get and feel quite safe in saying that all the paper made since I came in is unquestionably good.[13]

That same year, 1871, Corbin joined eight other Montanans on September 16 in organizing the Helena Reduction Works to process silver ores. S. H. Bohm, a banker and investor, promoted the $40,000 company that included Corbin, John T. Murphy, E. G. Maclay, A. G. Clark, John Kinna, G. G. Symes, John H. Ming, and W. C. Childs. Charles Rumley, a veteran miner, supervised the plant that Bohm built. Opened December 13, it was housed in a building 65 by 100 feet, twice the size of the Imperial Hotel, until then Helena's largest structure. Ming held the contract to supply coal for the works, but there must have been difficulty with the process, for Corbin soon was sending ores to Freiburg, Germany, for treatment, using mules to the Missouri River, the Ohio to Pittsburgh, and ship to Europe. Several of the incorporators became wealthy—but not from the Helena Reduction Works. Despite an auspicious start, the firm limped and finally ceased operation sometime before 1885.

Daniel and Louisa Corbin's third child, Mary, was born in Helena on August 28, 1872. This childbearing was an ordeal for

Louisa, who never fully recovered her health and thereafter restricted her activities. Corbin put Louisa in the care of a Chicago specialist and on the physician's advice, helped her seek a more favorable climate, for her illness had been diagnosed as intermittent fever—malaria—and was to deteriorate into rheumatoid arthritis. The months after Mary's birth passed in travel: Corbin took his family to Arkansas Hot Springs, then to cities on the Atlantic seaboard, and to the deep South, and finally to France and England. The children stayed with their mother as Daniel shuttled between Montana and his latest choice of a climate that might improve the ill woman. No locale and no medicine helped. Louisa was soon imprisoned in her wheelchair.

For nearly four years during Louisa's search for health, D. C. Corbin stuck to business in his reports to the First National's president, but in a letter written during the summer of 1876 to inform Hauser of events at the Rumley mine south of Helena, he added a despairing paragraph about his wife: "I can see that she is quite helpless and dependent entirely upon a servant to look after her and the children. . . . No consideration outside of my family could induce me to leave Montana at this time." [14]

So Corbin temporarily abandoned business to devote himself to his family because, he wrote Hauser, "I feel as though it was a duty that I *cannot* avoid going to them." He was "disheartened" at leaving Montana, for after eleven years the Territory seemed to offer him money-making prospects at every hand. Corbin reflected soberly that he was forty-three, starting his career anew, departing Montana "where I am so well acquainted" to make his living "somewhere."

And truthfully, the Montana he was quitting looked attractive. With the exception of the reduction works, the projects in which Corbin had invested prospered. Silver and lead had been discovered southwest of Helena in the Alta and Montana mines, among others, and the St. Louis and Montana Company had leased the Rumley mine, among the silver claims around Jefferson City, about twenty miles from Helena on Prickly Pear Creek. The first smelting furnace, the Rutan, failed and was sold for taxes, but Esler now had taken a furnace in hand. The entire Territory thrived: in 1874 Congress had authorized an assay office for Helena; the city boasted a population of 3,800, two daily newspapers, and the territorial capitol. The next year, 1875, the Northern Pacific had answered a call to a railway convention and agreed to build across Montana. At Butte, William A. Clark had been shipping copper ores, returning a profit despite staggering costs.

Ten days after his first gloomy letter, nevertheless, Corbin wrote Hauser, "I must go to my family—I can see no other course— and find some place where my wife can live and I can be with them and give them such attention as they need." [15]

Hauser's son-in-law, E. W. Knight, who had been bookkeeper at the First National for three years, took Corbin's place as cashier on September 1, 1876, and with Granville Stuart bought Corbin's stock in the bank.[16]

Louisa Corbin and her children were again in the United States. Corbin joined them in Chicago, discovering that his wife could not travel immediately, her illness "uncertain and her recovery so far distant ... that I see no prospect of my being able to return to Montana to remain for quite a long time to come." [17] Although he had sold his interest in the bank, Corbin held and gradually increased his shares of various Hauser mines and smelters. He wrote Hauser frequently on business matters from several cities for, as soon as his wife could board a train, Corbin took his family to New York and then sent them without him to Europe.

Daniel stayed in New York to act as general manager for the New York and Manhattan Beach Railroad which his older brother, Austin, was building to connect the city with Coney Island. When the line opened at eleven o'clock on the morning of July 18, 1877, D. C. Corbin spoke briefly to the 850 spectators on behalf of Austin who was touring Europe. The New York and Manhattan Beach company campaigned to popularize Coney Island as a resort, erected the Manhattan Beach and Oriental hotels, bought the Grand Central Hotel, and built pavilions, bicycle paths, and amusements. Austin dreamed that through this company he might gain control of the floundering Long Island Railroad and use it to consolidate train service to the major resorts in the vicinity of New York.

One of Austin's associates was Daniel's former partner, James Sherwood, who had left Helena in October, 1874, commissioned by Sam Hauser to find eastern buyers for Montana property, and had gone so far as to dispatch an agent to London when he and Hauser fell out over some misunderstanding. Sherwood sued Hauser and Hauser sued Sherwood. Corbin refused to let Sherwood abuse Hauser to him, and tried to soothe Hauser, writing in 1879, "You ought to be able to settle without the aid of lawyers. . . . He [Sherwood] seemed angry and I told him I didn't care to hear about it as both you and he were friends of mine." Corbin could not entirely dodge the dispute, however, and six years later he arranged an amicable settlement between his friends.

Despite the stir of his brother's various undertakings, Daniel Corbin's interest fled more and more to his own in Montana. Hauser wrote regularly, or called to see him in New York, now urging Daniel to put money into this new scheme or that: copper claims in Idaho, the Maginnis mine in Montana (which Corbin did enter), and finally a new reduction company that Hauser planned to organize to absorb the Alta-Montana Company working the silver and lead mines southwest of Helena that sounded so encouraging.[18]

As one of the directors of the Alta-Montana since it was formed in 1879, Hauser knew the company was failing. By 1882 liens and mortgages against it totaled approximately $250,000; it slid toward bankruptcy; and Hauser invited Corbin and his other cronies to join him in organizing a new company. By early 1883 the Alta-Montana, as Hauser anticipated, abandoned its claims in the hills along Prickly Pear Creek. In four years of frustration, the original company had spent nearly a half-million dollars without turning a profit from ore deposits generally considered the richest in the area. The entire success of the Alta-Montana Company depended on making the Alta mine pay out. Unluckily, its ore turned out to be low grade. Reviewing this disaster later, a mines inspector concluded, "The ore taken from the vein had to be carefully sorted . . . and it cost more to get it ready for smelting than it was worth when run into bullion."

Hauser, apparently deciding that the Alta-Montana Company

was incapable of managing its mines profitably, brought a number of new owners into the organization to absorb it. This group, the Helena Mining and Reduction Company, was formed partly by stock transfer and partly new capital. A group of shareholders eliminated in the fusion thought Hauser's action high-handed and threatened recourse to law, but Corbin, who became vice president of the new company, conferred with Hauser's attorneys who pronounced the stock transfer legitimate, and he thereafter referred to the ousted shareholders as "blackmailers...who were left out in the cold."

Attracted by the new company, Corbin returned for another look at Montana in the fall, 1882, and during the next forty months divided his time between New York and Helena. His wife and daughters remained in Europe but Austin, now nineteen, joined his father and began to take an active interest in business.

Hauser's company imagined that better smelting methods and transportation would turn a profit where the Alta-Montana had failed. Consequently, Hauser seized the presence in Montana of Henry Villard, Thomas F. Oakes, and other influential Northern Pacific officers, to revive a plan for a long-discussed branch railway to Wickes, the smelter location. The Northern Pacific entourage had come to Montana to attend ceremonies connected with driving the last spike in the line at Gold Creek, and Daniel Corbin, there at Villard's personal invitation, some years later recalled that the featured orator, former President Ulysses S. Grant, was "about the most embarrassed man I ever saw."

The Northern Pacific men agreed to Hauser's entreaty, and books were opened on September 17, 1883, at the offices of the First National Bank in Helena for subscriptions to the stock of the new branch, to be called the Helena and Jefferson County. Hauser, Villard, and Oakes were among those who signed the notice of the stock sale. The money was quickly subscribed, Hauser was elected president of the line, and construction of the 20.1-mile road from Jefferson Junction to Wickes was finished by January, 1884, under supervision of Colonel J. T. Dodge.

With transportation assured, the Helena Mining and Reduction Company was chartered in August, 1883, with Hauser as president.

Corbin was treasurer as well as vice-president. Almost immediately the firm rebuilt the partially burned Wickes smelter, so enlarging and improving the design of the red brick furnaces and buildings that for some years Wickes was the most extensive reduction plant in Montana.

Corbin bought most of his stock in the Helena Mining and Reduction Company with a loan from the First National Bank of Helena.[19] He was the company's choice to oversee the Wickes mines and smelter, and when he returned to New York, Corbin received regular detailed reports of every operation from various superintendents, and tried to manage the venture from a continent away. Under Corbin's eye, the Helena Mining and Reduction undertook new development, driving tunnels deeper in the Alta and Montana mines in the autumn of 1883, and began building what was then the "largest concentrator in Montana. . . . By working it twelve hours each day [the company] can easily concentrate 250 tons." The concentrator was located about one mile from the smelter at a new town named Corbin, twenty-two miles from Helena on the railway. Corbin expressed frequent dissatisfaction with the superintendent, John Longmaid, perhaps simply because the two men were separated by thousands of miles and letters did not suffice for the detailed relationship necessary. The concentrator and new tunnel required a work force of a hundred men but by the following summer the company cut back to twenty-one, enough to supply the Corbin plant with 150 tons of ore a day, hauled by teams and wagons from the mines. From the outset, the Helena Mining and Reduction Company was pinched, as the Alta-Montana had been. Its ore had to be hand-sorted, a slow and expensive process, and much of it was discarded in ragged piles near tunnel portals. More often than not, wagons waited until more ore was dug and sorted before they could be loaded.

To work the Comet, four miles west of Wickes, the Helena Mining and Reduction Company installed a continuous rope tramway and a sixty-ton concentrator at the mine. The town of Wickes, flushed with activity, grew to 1,200 persons. Appearances of prosperity notwithstanding, the men close to the company were pessimistic. After reading an early report of his branch railway's income, Oakes of the Northern Pacific wrote Hauser:

> The Wickes branch was built, of course, with the idea that it would be a profit to the railroad company. The first month's operations...yielded the railroad company but $800 net...a very small return on the cost of the property.[20]

As a result of the unsatisfactory production, Corbin urged dismissal of Longmaid and had his way in February, 1885, some seventeen months after Hauser's company took over the Alta-Montana operations. Longmaid was replaced by a grave German-trained superintendent with a clipped beard and drooping mustaches, August Raht, a graduate of Freiburg's famed school of mines. In later years, Raht, as the man who was to put the Guggenheim works on their feet in 1889, would win the sobriquet, "The Prince of the Lead Smelterers." He was not yet famous when he joined the Helena Mining and Reduction Company's staff, but he was competent beyond question, and what he saw when he examined the mines and works must have appalled him. He proved, however, a classic diplomat, for he managed to tell Hauser that his ore reserves were slim, his equipment inadequate, and his outlook dismal at Wickes, in a tone almost encouraging:

> The tramway works well with the exception of a few minor details.... At present the [Alta] mine is severely taxed to supply the large demand of the concentrator as the rich ore stopes on Number Two Tunnel which furnish the bulk of the ore are as yet of limited extent.... The reduction works at Wickes do their work remarkably well and cheaply considering their inconvenient location, arrangement, and defective machinery.[21]

Hauser was in New York when Raht's appraisal of the company reached him. He showed the letter to Corbin, who occupied offices in his brother's bank. After they talked, Corbin resolved to return to Montana to run the company himself. But before he could close his business in New York, other news came which, although he did not realize it, would mortise D. C. Corbin to the West for the remainder of his life.

CHAPTER TWO

CORBIN'S FIRST RAILROAD

Ｎ
EWS THAT REACHED DANIEL CORBIN IN NEW YORK HERALDED
the buoyant prospects of a new mining district, the Coeur d'Alenes
in northern Idaho, where a gold rush occurred in the winter of
1883–84, and subsequent strikes of lead and silver spurred prospectors by the hundreds. The lead and silver ores, moreover, assured
a stable industry that would require transportation of a higher order
than muleback and wagon. Corbin went to Idaho merely to look
into the requirements of a railroad into the mountains, a look that
induced him to make a career of railroad building. Eventually he
chose Spokane as the hub of his activity, thrusting three railway
systems north, northeast, and east, the first east to the Coeur
d'Alenes. Dan Corbin ordained Spokane entrepôt of the inland
Pacific Northwest.

While he had been in New York managing his brother's railroads, the western economy had quickened, shifting the center of
intermountain commerce westward from his familiar Helena. Mining wrought change, as a Northern Pacific guidebook would say in
1915:

> Were it not for the mines, the Coeur d'Alene district would be
> nearly as complete a wilderness now as when Mullan constructed his
> road across the mountains.... It contains almost no arable land, and
> the timber, while good enough for mining purposes, would probably

not have been sufficient inducement to bring railways into the region. Mining is the one paramount industry of the district, and upon it all others depend.

The news that drew Corbin back to the West, and seemed even more arresting than management of the Helena Mining and Reduction Company on the ground, came from dour, self-seeking Anton Esler. He was in the Coeur d'Alene country scouting, as usual, for business for his small concentrator outside Helena, during the course of which he walked and rode muleback over the rough trails, talking to claim holders. Eventually he met Stephen S. Glidden, a one-time wholesale grocer who now ran a retail store while he camped on the property of his Tiger mine.[1] The Tiger lay beneath an old pack trail where the hooves of mule trains cut away the topsoil to expose a galena vein, staked on May 2, 1884, by John Carten and Almeda Seymour, two prospectors. They bonded the Tiger to John M. Burke who, in turn, sold it for $35,000 to Glidden. By the end of 1885 Glidden had driven three tunnels into the hillside and piled 3,000 tons of ore near their mouths, waiting for transportation. Some sacks of his ore were packed over the mountains to Montana for sampling on the backs of Glidden's workmen.

At fifty-eight, Glidden was considered a robust old man. His well-trimmed mustache had turned gray and he wore gold-rimmed spectacles. When snow blew into deep drifts in the mountains and the streams froze, Glidden retired to Spokane Falls to wait for springtime, where Esler found him at Christmas, 1885, measuring Glidden with his salesman's eye as a prospect for his concentrator. Esler could hardly contain his excitement when he learned what Glidden believed the Tiger could produce. Glidden declared that if Esler would erect a thirty-ton concentrator at his mine, he would guarantee 24,000 tons of silver-lead ore, pay seven dollars a ton for processing, and on top of that, give Esler one-sixth of the net profits from ore and concentrates the Tiger shipped.[2] The proposal sounded too good to be true, and Esler asked A. M. Holter and E. W. Knight what he should do. They advised him to go see the Tiger for him-self. Following their advice, Esler snowshoed to the mine. His brief inspection in the dead of winter convinced him.

Esler wrote Sam Hauser in New York an enthusiastic series of letters, which Hauser promptly showed Dan Corbin. In one letter, Esler apologized for spelling mistakes because it was "written on the run," indicating the man's agitated state of mind. In another, Esler drew a cross-section of the Tiger and penciled his evaluation of $2,400,000 in a margin, and in a third he asserted, "The contract will show a net profit of about $96,000 for us less the cost of works which won't exceed $10,000 as the motive power is water." [3] Esler's reason for bombarding Hauser with his opinions was, of course, that he wanted Hauser to put up the money for the concentrator.

As did Glidden. Glidden wanted Hauser "to take hold of it," Esler reported, because Hauser "under sufficient inducement, would put a railroad into the mines from some point near Rathdrum via Coeur d'Alene Lake which would require about thirty miles of track through a very nice easy grade." [4] Glidden learned through a friend in New York that Hauser inquired about the Tiger, and he must have reflected that transportation seemed more likely. In the event Hauser did not take his bait, however, Glidden discussed with Noah Armstrong of Glendale, Montana, the possibility of building their own railroad.

The Tiger was not the only claim on the south fork of the Coeur d'Alene River. Scores of other potentially rich locations had been staked—there was really little unclaimed ground—and competi-tion developed swiftly for the mines' traffic. In March, 1885, the Missoula County, Montana, commissioners levied a two-mill tax to build a wagon road from Thompson Falls to the Idaho border. Spokane Falls' merchants promoted a wagon route through Fourth of July Canyon, and helped to establish a Concord stage line, hailing the coaches which rattled in and out of town three days a week amid tooting horns. Stage lines sprang up, as well, from Rathdrum on the Northern Pacific main line, running fourteen miles south to Coeur d'Alene City on the lake, where two steamers picked up pas-sengers bound for the Old Mission from which they could follow the Jackass Trail into the mining region. The Rathdrum and Coeur d'Alene Stage Company operated a twenty-four passenger coach pulled by six horses.

Many prospectors from the East rode the Northern Pacific westward past Rathdrum to Spokane Falls where they outfitted, and then hitched back eastward to Rathdrum, to strike out afoot for the mines sixty-six miles off "over a trail that was a caution in summer and a holy terror in winter." Rathdrum had been founded in 1861; it was at its zenith in 1885 with a population of a thousand. Despite Coeur d'Alene City's metropolitan name, it was merely a village with a store, hotel, and a cluster of houses for perhaps one hundred fifty residents on the lake just east of the limits of Fort Coeur d'Alene. The fort, marked out in 1878 and garrisoned with five companies of the Second Infantry a year later, occupied 999 acres at a spot chosen by William Tecumseh Sherman, himself. When the old general died in 1891, the fort was renamed Fort Sherman.

Two enterprising sutlers—store proprietors who catered to the troops—named James Monaghan and Clement B. King owned the townsite of Coeur d'Alene. They had bought most of it from C. F. Yeaton, the post trader, who obtained it originally from the Northern Pacific in 1880. King was a pioneer settler and merchant; Monaghan, a veteran wagon train and store man for the army at Walla Walla, then at Fort Colville, and in 1882, at Fort Spokane. The two men opened their store and gambling and dance halls to the pleasure of the soldiers who regarded Coeur d'Alene City as their oasis in a desolate land. King and Monaghan platted their townsite shortly after buying it. King bought a two-story frame hotel from a homesteader, Tony Tubbs, moved it to the lake front, and renamed it The Lakeside in 1884. When the gold rush began, Coeur d'Alene City glittered like a nugget in the human stream that flowed toward the camps.

King and Monaghan commissioned Captain C. P. Sorenson to build them the second steamer on Lake Coeur d'Alene, the *General Sherman,* which they would employ to haul passengers and freight from Coeur d'Alene City sixty miles to the Old Mission. The first steamer was a federal boat, the eighty-five foot *Amelia Wheaton,* named for the daughter of the second post commandant; it cost $5,000, was launched in 1880, and hauled cordwood and hay for the military. A Norwegian by birth, Sorenson came to Idaho from Portland, Oregon, and as the first professional pilot on the lake, named most of its bays and points. Monaghan, a Roman Catholic, was said to have secured exclusive permission to land at the Old Mission. There the Indians earned their fares by cutting cordwood for the steamer and by treaty were allowed to bring their ponies on board. In 1885, King and Monaghan scratched a road from the Old Mission to Murray, one of the temporary seats of Shoshone County, in which the Coeur d'Alene mining district lay.

Excepting the spider-web trails that wound through the punishing mountains grown over with brush and evergreens, the boat line was the highway to the mines when Esler wrote Hauser that Glidden hoped Hauser would build a railroad. Esler had no sooner mailed his letters to Hauser, however, than he bumped into a voluble Irishman, James F. Wardner, who carried in his pocket the lease on the most fabulous strike of all in the Coeur d'Alenes, the Bunker Hill. Wardner, like Glidden, had Hauser in his sights and he also grasped his opportunity to reach Hauser through Esler.

Since he was to make mining history, it is worth pausing to examine how Wardner obtained control of the Bunker Hill. The Bunker Hill was discovered on September 10, 1885, by Noah S. Kellogg who had been grubstaked to hunt for gold by Dr. John T. Cooper and Origin O. Peck of Murray. After looking for sixty days, Kellogg returned with samples from an old iron-capped quartz ledge. Cooper and Peck wanted only gold, and to make matters worse, Kellogg had lost the donkey they loaned him. They were resounding in their scorn, but Phil O'Rourke, a veteran of the Colorado camps, recognized Kellogg's samples as galena bearing silver and lead. O'Rourke abandoned his partner, Con Sullivan, to return with Kellogg and post the ledge with a new grubstake from the proprietors of a Murray saloon, Dutch Jake Goetz and Harry Baer. The revelation of their find set off a roaring sprint over the mountains in a driving rainstorm by prospectors from Murray contending to be next after Kellogg in uncovering galena. Con Sullivan suc-

ceeded in staking the claim adjacent to Kellogg's, naming his the
Sullivan, not for himself but in honor of the prizefighter, John L.
Sullivan. Cooper and Peck, claiming a share in the Bunker Hill because they grubstaked Kellogg, went to court to obtain it and won
one-quarter of the location. The judge's decision was appealed,
O'Rourke owed most of his share to pay old gambling debts, and
nobody was sure who eventually would own the Bunker Hill when
Jim Wardner rounded up the probable owners and talked them into
leasing him both the Bunker Hill and the Sullivan. The locators
were anxious to have the mines in production, for they gamboled
through the mountain towns spending borrowed money, playing at
being as rich as they expected to be some day.

Wardner spent his own money rapidly and borrowed $3,000
more to undertake the barest development. When he ran through
his borrowed capital, he cadged $300 to travel to Spokane Falls, Port-
land, and San Francisco, where he hoped to find investors to help
him. Most listened politely but none would risk the capital required
to prove out two trenches in the north Idaho wilderness. The mon-
eyed men of the Pacific Coast knew about the Coeur d'Alene district
but were daunted by the investment needed to wrest a profit from
the mines, and by the formidable opposition of the Northern Pacific
Railroad which claimed most of the region as its land grant.

The determined Wardner had been an optimist, however, since
the day in 1883 when he walked from Thompson Falls to Murray
with two hundred packages of butterine [margarine] to peddle. Now
he turned toward Montana. He talked to William L. Austin, the
metallurgist at a small plant at Toston, Montana, who recalled that
Wardner walked up to his door dragging a sack of ore. Austin advised him to see Sam Hauser who had money, railroad connections,
and a smelter at Wickes. When Wardner showed Hauser his samples,
Hauser gruffly turned him away, but directed his own people to
look into the Bunker Hill and the Sullivan. It was then, early in
1886, that Wardner encountered Esler and tried a second time to
attract financial backing from Hauser. Wardner proposed a contract that paled Glidden's: he would provide 50,000 tons of ore for
concentrating, pay five dollars a ton, and allow Esler to reject any

ore he believed too low grade for concentration, "making it abso-
lutely safe to depend on the ore for ... pay," in Esler's opinion.[5] For
his part, Esler must contract to erect a fifty-ton concentrator near the
Bunker Hill and Sullivan by June first of that year, 1886.

Esler dragged Holter over the trails to see the Bunker Hill, and
they agreed it represented a bigger opportunity than Glidden's Tiger.
Esler added some clauses to his agreement with Wardner: one permitted more time to complete his concentrator if "delayed by bad
roads, bad weather, or unforeseen circumstances or accidents," figur-
ing this extended his contract thirty days because the roads unde-
niably were bad. He consented to rebate Wardner one dollar a ton
in return for one-tenth of the gross income from concentrates and
ores, and secured an option on production of the mines over Wardner's 50,000-ton guarantee.

Esler, reckoning he could move his concentrator from Helena
and reconstruct it for not more than $9,000, estimated his net profit
from the Wardner contract at about $40,000. Once his contract was
signed, Esler wrote Hauser a long factual letter on March 16, 1886,
urging Hauser to "stand in with me and move ... [my] machinery
over there." Sam Hauser had been enthusiastic about the Coeur
d'Alenes for some months, although he had not let Wardner realize
this, and had discussed the district with Oakes of the Northern Pacific
as much as twenty-four months previously. Furthermore, the Helena
Mining and Reduction Company sorely needed a source of rich ore
to turn a profit. If the Coeur d'Alenes were going to make money,
Sam Hauser wanted it.

Thus Hauser agreed to stand in with Esler and asked Esler to
write D. C. Corbin in New York to see whether Corbin thought
they could expect a railroad to the mines to pay out. Corbin was
packing to move West, anyhow, and Hauser was too busy to supervise a concentrator or a railroad personally. He was, at the moment,
governor of Montana, president of the Helena and Jefferson County
Railway, rancher, banker, and had committed to build four new
Northern Pacific branches: the Helena, Boulder Valley and Butte;
the Helena and Northern; the Drummond and Philipsburg; and
the Missoula and Bitter Root.

Esler prepared to dismantle his concentrator and move it to Milo Gulch beside the Bunker Hill. As he studied the route, he discovered that J. C. Davenport and Company were laying out a fourteen-mile horse tramway from Old Mission to the mines. He also uncovered Glidden's plan to organize a railway with Noah Armstrong, and learned that Armstrong and his son-in-law, C. W. Turner, were nearer actual construction than generally supposed. Esler had written Corbin on April 11, and he now fired a second letter on the same day to Hauser:

> If you seriously contemplate a movement I would advise you to make some demonstration for business very soon, for I believe that if a bold bluff is made that it will silence action by them [Glidden, Armstrong, and Turner]. Should you take action upon a railroad proposition, it would be ... very gratifying to have my name among the incorporators and I would contribute sufficient money to pay for laying one tie, for grease to lubricate one train, and brains and energy to supply an abundance of ore to load the cars and promote general good to the scheme.[6]

Corbin had little time to consider a railway, he had never seen the country where Esler suggested he build, but he and Hauser did not dally. They solicited the Northern Pacific for support in constructing a railway to the Coeur d'Alene mines. From the Northern Pacific they learned that John J. Browne, an attorney and businessman from Spokane Falls, already was organizing a railroad to connect the Northern Pacific main line with Coeur d'Alene City, and a steamer connection with a second rail line from Old Mission up the south fork of the Coeur d'Alene River to the mines. An obligation existed between Hauser and Tom Oakes, vice president of the Northern Pacific, however, so Oakes handed Browne a letter to deliver personally to Hauser in which he recommended consolidation of the two proposed railways, leaving Browne little doubt that the Northern Pacific favored Hauser. Oakes also urged that Corbin and Hauser exclude S. S. Glidden from their company because "we do not feel he is essentially identified with the interest of the N. P. Ry." [7] Behind Oakes's comment lay his suspicion that Glidden and Armstrong in-

tended to connect their projected line with the Union Pacific, which
had run preliminary surveys in the area. Glidden wrote Hauser
denying any allegiance to the Union Pacific, to no avail.

Browne had undertaken no construction because he believed he
needed congressional authorization for a railway. Perhaps this was
due to his misinterpretation of the law of 1875 that granted railways
right of way through public lands, but neglected to assign regula-
tory powers. For whatever reason, Browne frittered two and one-half
months in the national capital trying to lobby a bill through Congress
that would permit him to build, then returned to Spokane Falls and
was waiting still when Corbin and Hauser encroached on his backing from the Northern Pacific. There had been an understanding for
a time between Browne and Glidden, but Glidden could not wait
for Congress to creep to any business concerning him, so he personally paid the cost of surveying a route and, with Armstrong and
Turner, quit Browne.

Now that Corbin and Hauser had won the blessing of the
Northern Pacific, Corbin came to inspect the ground for himself.
He used what he euphemistically called later "some leisure time,"
and Jim Wardner, remembering their first meeting, said that a
"gentleman on a good-looking mule" rode into the village of Kentucky in Milo Gulch, introduced himself as Dan Corbin, and politely
inquired about the Bunker Hill and Sullivan ores. Wardner was
working the two from open slashes in the brushy hillside. Corbin had
ridden the Northern Pacific to Rathdrum, then boarded a stage to
Coeur d'Alene City where he spent a day sizing up the growing
hamlet. After that he had taken the steamer to Old Mission, and the
mud-wagon stage up the south fork.

Wardner introduced Corbin to the boys—O'Rourke, Sullivan,
Kellogg, and Baer—and then he and Corbin set off with a sack to
collect samples. In a short while the sack grew so heavy that they
dumped it for sorting, and out rolled a stick of giant powder that
could have detonated at any instant as the two blithely thumped ore
into the sack!

After his tour with Wardner, Corbin proceeded to Colonel W.
R. Wallace's clearing in a cedar grove, where Wallace ran a store

and had two houses, met Glidden, and after fallen trees were cleared from the trail to the Tiger, inspected it and other nearby claims. Next, back to Kentucky for another examination of the Bunker Hill and Sullivan. "It all impressed me forcibly," Corbin declared, "and I concluded a connection with the Northern Pacific . . . would pay." [8]

Corbin returned to New York where on May 20, 1886, he outlined for the Northern Pacific directors a tentative route: He would commence at some point in Missoula County, Montana (probably at Thompson Falls) and build west into the Coeur d'Alene mining district to the Bunker Hill and Sullivan, thence down the south fork to Lake Coeur d'Alene, establish steamers from Old Mission to Coeur d'Alene City, and from there, build a second line of railroad to the Northern Pacific near Rathdrum. His projected line thus followed closely the ones visualized by Glidden and Browne. Corbin asked the NP directors to underwrite the portion of his railway between their main line and Coeur d'Alene City. He could not induce them to answer quickly; the railway's president, Robert Harris, seemed to think his proposition "cheeky," as Corbin observed to Hauser; and the directors rejected outright his petition for a rebate on shipments his road would deliver to the Northern Pacific.

While he awaited his answer from the NP directors, Corbin went about organizing the section of railway between Montana and the Old Mission. His Helena attorneys, Bullard and Barber, filed an application for a Montana charter for a company to be called the Coeur d'Alene Railway and Navigation Company, capitalized for $500,000, with main offices in Helena. Its petition indicated the Corbin line would construct a 140-mile track from Thompson Falls, and that it might build branch lines as far south as Nez Perce County, Idaho. Directors of the company were Corbin, Hauser, Holter, Esler (who got his wish to be an incorporator), Glidden, Wardner, and Monaghan. [9]

Then something occurred that changed the fortunes of Spokane. The Northern Pacific attorneys told Corbin they did not believe he could build legally in Idaho Territory with a Montana charter. They reasoned that Idaho's laws referring to commercial corporations failed to mention railroads specifically. So Corbin went to Washington, D.C., seeking support from Idaho's delegate whom he hoped to influence with "a fee of $1,000," but came away from the capital convinced that "if the carrying out of the enterprise depended upon any action of Congress, I might as well quit." [10] Doubtless he and J. J. Browne, when next they met, exchanged acid comments on the nation's conduct of its business. An omission in Idaho's laws, however, had worked to the benefit of Spokane, for D. C. Corbin determined that his line must appear to start from Washington Territory, and he would build eastward to the Coeur d'Alenes rather than westward from Montana as he originally intended.

Time also became a compelling factor, for the Spokane and Palouse, building southward from Spokane Falls to Genesee, Idaho, surveyed a line to the mines running south of Lake Coeur d'Alene, using Northern Pacific field crews, and its president, Anthony M. Cannon, petitioned the NP to finance construction. Corbin scoffed that this "don't and won't amount to anything," because the route was long and expensive. Apparently the Northern Pacific directors agreed, for they threw their support to Corbin. A more formidable threat was the newly organized Washington and Idaho, supported by the Union Pacific, which had surveyors in the field south of Lake Coeur d'Alene and on the Coeur d'Alene Reservation, scouting a way to the Old Mission. [11]

While Corbin struggled with Congress and with the Northern Pacific to launch his railroads, Esler moved his concentrator by wagon from Helena to Milo Gulch, installed new jigs and trommels, and got it running. A company was organized to finance it, and share in its profit, named the Helena Concentrating Company, including Hauser, Holter, Esler, W. E. Cox of Helena, and Corbin. Crushing the ore and separating it from rock cost about fifty cents a ton, and the operating profit at five dollars a ton, minus the one dollar rebate to walrus-mustached Jim Wardner, provided the company a handsome return. As events would have it, the men who actually owned the Bunker Hill and Sullivan were the last to make money on it: they were paid after the concentrator operators, the railways, and the smelter. The mine owners did have one recourse. They badgered Esler for money, and Wardner frequently asked for an advance to pay the expenses of digging ore. By May, 1886, the Bunker Hill and Sullivan were shipping ore to Wickes by wagon, boat, and the Northern Pacific.

"The mine owners are a little hostile because no returns from the ore sent to Wickes as they are very clamorous for money," Esler told Hauser in a typical letter. "Consequently today as a panacea I advanced them some, for it won't do to antagonize them." [12]

As it was reconstructed in Milo Gulch, Esler's concentrator reputedly cost about $30,000, was contained in a thirty by sixty-foot building four stories high, and displayed "the latest and most improved machinery from Fraser & Chalmers, Chicago. The ore bins [had] a capacity of 350 tons.... The concentrator, run by steam, requires only five men to the shift." [13] Robert Cheyne, who came from Helena to supervise the plant, was to follow mining around the world, return to Idaho, and eventually become mill superintendent for the Bunker Hill and Sullivan company. Esler had started up his machinery without ore on June 24, and wrote Hauser happily that it "worked like a charm." Five days later in a modest dedication ceremony his daughter turned on the steam and the concentrator ran its first ore batch, the first Coeur d'Alene ore concentrated right in the district. From then on, the machinery processed twenty-four hours a day for some months. By August ninth, Esler reported:

> The mill is working from 60 to 65 tons per day and if we had another jig we could easily run the daily capacity up to 75 tons.... We shipped from the mill and mine last week 164 tons, including 42 tons of lump ore, all from the Bunker Hill. The concentrates assay 33 ounces silver, 68 per cent in lead.[14]

Now two south fork mines, the Bunker Hill and the Sullivan, actually were producing commercial ore, and others would produce as soon as they had mills and transportation. The Coeur d'Alenes were emergent. There were perhaps eight thousand prospectors in the mountains. The trails to Belknap, Montana, and Thompson Falls, on the Northern Pacific, and the Jackass Trail to Old Mission, were well worn. To satisfy postal authorities, the village of Kentucky, ugly, poorly built frame houses strewn in tumbleweed disorder along

the trail up Milo Gulch, had been renamed Wardner. No matter
what the post office called the town, its mail deliveries were slower
and slower. Private contractors carried the mail, charging up to fifty
cents a letter, but as the camps overflowed with newcomers, the
contractors could not be persuaded or bribed to take on more cus-
tomers. The district was ripe for a railway, and every man asked
when it would come. D. C. Corbin, the formality of organizing his
railways completed, fumed as he waited for the Northern Pacific
directors to ratify the contract Sam Hauser had drawn. Corbin wrote
Hauser in the middle of August that "the work should now be underway but instead nothing has been done. The season is slipping
away" and he was "getting d——d tired" of waiting.

CHAPTER THREE

OPENING IDAHO'S MINES

In order to serve the Coeur d'Alenes with the route he had chosen, Daniel Corbin needed to build two railways and to acquire or organize a steamer line on the lake. One railroad would link the Northern Pacific main line to Lake Coeur d'Alene and be underwritten by the NP; the second would begin near the Old Mission at the head of navigation on the Coeur d'Alene River and wind eastward along the river's south fork to the mines. Between these two railways, steamers would ferry passengers, freight, and ore. Corbin had organized his course from the Old Mission up the south fork as the Coeur d'Alene Railway and Navigation Company, and he and Sam Hauser would have to finance it and the steamboats from their own pockets and the sale of stock.

For their part, the Northern Pacific directors, in July, 1886, sent Corbin and Hauser identical telegrams agreeing to do most of the work on the railway connecting their main line with the lake. This was to be called the Spokane and Idaho Railroad. Although the NP would locate the route, Corbin insisted that he select its terminus on the lake. After receiving his telegram, Hauser drew a formal contract. While the NP directors deliberated this, Corbin did what he could—and fussed. He contemplated abandoning the Spokane and Idaho to confine his effort to the south fork line and steamers, writing Hauser from Coeur d'Alene City:

If it was not greatly to our interest it [the Spokane and Idaho]
could go to the devil, and anyway, if it is delayed much longer I shall
arrange to get my rolling stock and rails over by wagon and let this
end of the line take care of itself.[1]

Corbin, building two railways at the same time, separated by
sixty miles of waterway, was a study in harassment, for he always
seemed to be needed at some trouble spot hours away. Morever, two
sections of less similar construction would be hard to imagine: the
line to Coeur d'Alene City would cross fairly level terrain through
farms and sparse timber, but that up the south fork would climb
constantly through rocky, steep mountains so thick with brush and
trees that a man had to fight his way through them. Although Corbin
managed both in the summer, 1886, his two projects are easier to follow taken singly.

In July, a surveying party was withdrawn by the Northern
Pacific from the Spokane and Palouse and assigned to lay out the
Spokane and Idaho route, finding that some farmers along the way
regarded them as a tool for annexing Kootenai County, Idaho, to
Washington Territory. The surveyors were directed by Paul F. Mohr,
chief engineer of the Spokane and Palouse. Corbin thereupon let
contracts for clearing and grubbing the right of way, as it was determined, and for ties, and decided to use local labor because that
would be as cheap as bringing men from Montana. Obviously he still
felt foreign to Idaho, and considered, at first, importing men whose
capacities he could estimate. With a start made on the railway,
Hauser extracted a promise from the Northern Pacific traffic manager, J. M. Hannaford, "to give ... ample protection" on freight and
ore rates to the Spokane and Idaho. The NP finally was stirring after
a delay occasioned by a dispute with James J. Hill of the Great
Northern over station rights in St. Paul which had taken the directors' whole attention.

Corbin had settled on Coeur d'Alene City as the terminus of
the Spokane and Idaho after a careful investigation of the Spokane
River, flowing westward from Lake Coeur d'Alene, to learn whether
the river might be navigable as far as Post Falls, Idaho. Corbin urged
the Northern Pacific's chief engineer, General Adna Anderson, to

inspect the river for himself, but the general declined. He was a soldier, not a sailor, and although he traveled the land route in person, he refused to trust the river's swift currents. Navigation of the river proved too expensive. Corbin closed consideration of it because he "would not feel safe in undertaking the job with less than $30,000 or $40,000 and if I am right in this, I conclude it would be best to build the road to the lake direct." [2] Accepting his estimate, clearing the Spokane for steamers would have doubled the construction cost of the Spokane and Idaho.

The next year, a stage proprietor, Nelson Martin, unwittingly corroborated Corbin's judgement that the Spokane was not navigable without costly improvements. Martin scheduled a thirty-seven-foot passenger boat between Post Falls and Old Mission, but it capsized, his passengers were lucky to escape alive, and Martin abandoned his service. Not only cost but time dictated against steamers on the Spokane because the Washington and Idaho now had surveyors locating the first section of a definite line toward Old Mission and its negotiators courted the Coeur d'Alene tribe for permission to cross its reservation. And ore waited for shipment. Corbin determined to run his trains before the close of 1886.

In the middle of August, the Northern Pacific approved a formal contract, leaving Corbin two months of good weather to build the Spokane and Idaho, which he hoped to finish by October 1. He let a grading and tracklaying contract to John Burns of Spokane Falls, to be supervised by Mohr, whose surveyors had drawn a route entirely within the land grant claimed by the Northern Pacific, beginning at a point on the NP main line 21 miles east of Spokane Falls, a place named Hauser Junction, and running 13.6 miles to the Coeur d'Alene City waterfront. Work near Hauser Junction appeared "very light" to Corbin, and the contractor promised to "have the grade ready to commence laying track in 10 days." [3] Burns' contract, however, called for the grading to be done in thirty days at costs varying from seventeen cents a yard for earth moving, $1.25 for solid rock, fifty cents for loose rock, and clearing and grubbing at cost plus fifteen per cent. Corbin felt that "it will be done cheaply." Another slight delay: only after he had signed, contractor Burns advertised in the *Spokane Falls Review* for fifty teams with scrapers to start the railroad. It would also fall to Burns to dicker for right of way with private property owners along the route, who may have settled on land claimed by the Northern Pacific.

In the meantime, Corbin reached an "understanding with the owners of the townsite" of Coeur d'Alene City, Monaghan and King, for water transport on their steamers and a right of way through the town to the lakefront. The Spokane and Idaho would end on a dock thrust from the shore between the Lakeside Hotel and Tubbs Hill, a rounded pine-furred promontory that formed the east arm of a bay before the town. There the railway would meet steamers from Old Mission.

Daniel's son, Austin, retired from the First National Bank of Helena, came to Coeur d'Alene City, bought a time book for twenty-five cents, and went on his father's payroll at $2.50 a day as time-keeper.

When maps of the route of the Spokane and Idaho were ready to file with the land office at Coeur d'Alene City for transmittal to the Secretary of the Interior, Corbin discovered one of the short-comings of his railroad. Until this time, it apparently existed only through the arrangements he had concluded with Hauser and the Northern Pacific. He wrote Hauser urgently, asking Hauser to elect some officers for the company and to have a company seal made be-cause the railroad's president would have to sign affidavits to ac-company the maps, the secretary must witness the president's signa-ture, and the company seal be affixed. Until that moment, the Spo-kane and Idaho had not required a president, a secretary, or a seal. Under the federal laws of 1875, the railroad was obligated to file maps of its route, articles of incorporation, and proof of legal organi-zation, in order to receive its approval of right of way through public lands. Corbin feared that prowling agents of the land office might interfere with construction unless his maps were filed. A few days later, he needed money. "Have you arranged to get the money we require . . . at six per cent?" he wrote the busy Hauser. "We shall only require $30,000 to $35,000."

Corbin's original deadline for running trains, October first,

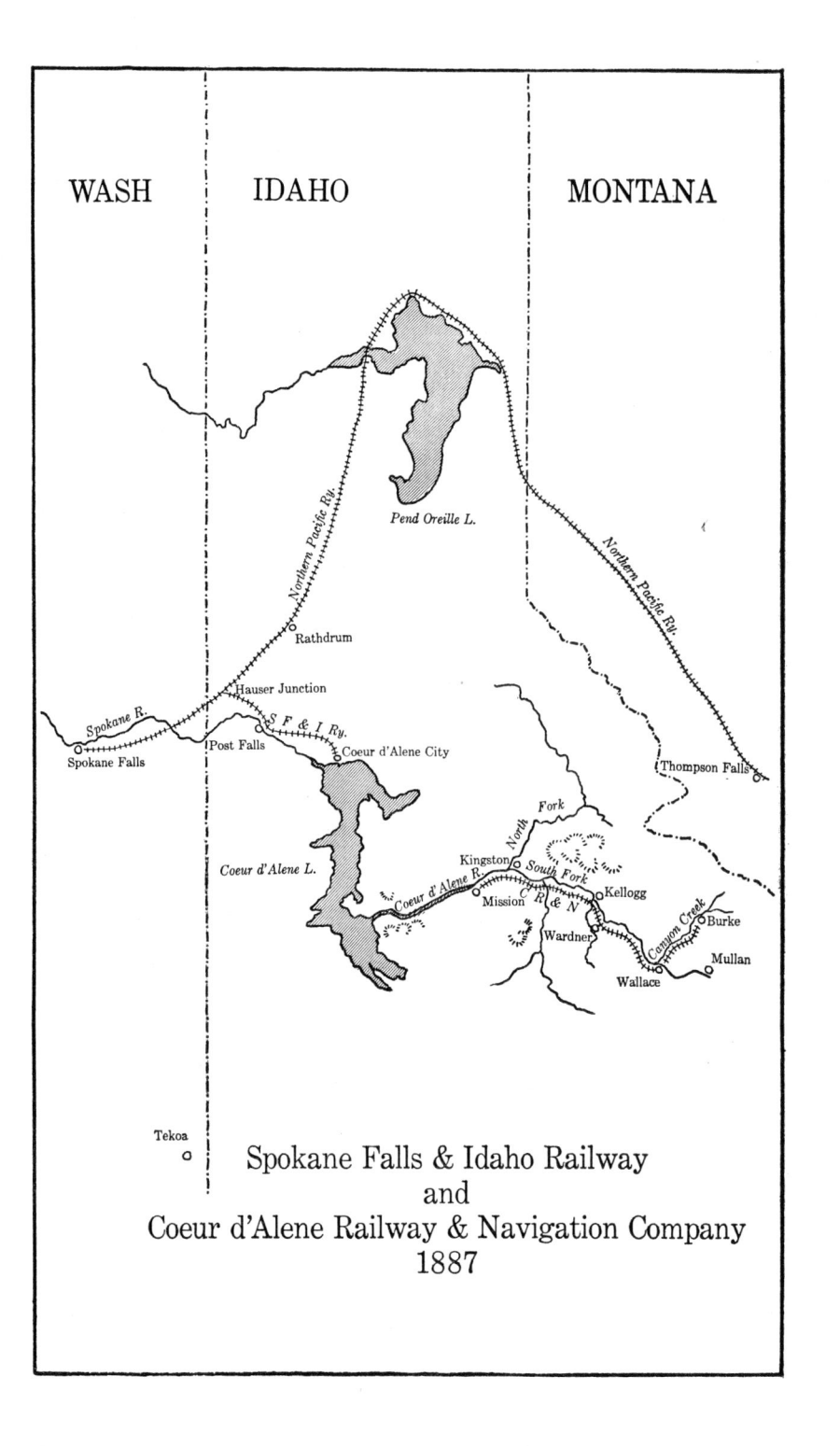

Spokane Falls & Idaho Railway
and
Coeur d'Alene Railway & Navigation Company
1887

slipped past before a rail was laid, but "a large force of workmen" hewed the countryside, and the *Spokane Falls Review* predicted, "Cars will be running to Coeur d'Alene City by November 1." Track-laying began October fourth along a course "nearly straight from the main line to the Little Falls [Post Falls] of the Spokane River and from there follows the river to the lake," said the *Review*. Once begun, laying the track required only twenty days, but at the lake-front, construction stalled while the builders waited for iron ordered to finish the dock. Despite the lack of landing facilities, trains began running to the waterfront at Coeur d'Alene on October 24, 1886, and when the iron arrived, Burns' men pushed a wooden dock, braced with iron, into the lake the length of fourteen freight cars.

Completion of the dock in the first days of December ended construction of the Spokane and Idaho. Its building had cost $52,496.59 including the wooden wharf and payments to eight land owners for rights of way, in addition to those negotiated by John Burns. Most of the railway's right of way deeds were filed during November, 1886, although some were not signed until the following April. Of the total cost, Burns received $14,849.90 for grading, from which he paid his subcontractors. Morning and Wright of Rathdrum were paid $8,992.75 for 35,971 crossties, and lumber for trestles and road crossings cost $6,474.09. The railroad's demand for wood sent a shock of prosperity briefly through Rathdrum, so soon to be punctured by the railway's diversion of its traffic to Coeur d'Alene City. The dock contained 9,229 feet of piling and cost $7,402.49, including Austin Corbin's timebook, and $9.75 spent for telegrams to and from the engineer in immediate charge of construction.[4]

Some weeks before the dock was done, on the date the first train ran, October 24, a party of Northern Pacific officers, a railroad attorney, H. E. Cullen of Helena, and D. C. Corbin met in the Spokane and Palouse offices in Spokane Falls to organize the company that until this time had had only a president, a secretary, a seal, and a contract with the NP. The group dropped Montana men, and changed the road's name by adding "Falls," so the line became the Spokane Falls and Idaho Railroad Company, incorporated in Spokane County, capitalized at $500,000, to "build, equip, run, and operate a railroad from the City of Spokane Falls to the village of Coeur d'Alene." [5]

The clear reference to terminals established the Spokane Falls and Idaho incontestably as a Washington corporation, which was necessary, in the attorneys' view, to avoid a conflict with Idaho law. In its operation eastward from Spokane Falls, the company used Northern Pacific trackage, and it shared offices and shops in Spokane Falls with the Spokane and Palouse. Its own construction lay wholly within Kootenai County, Idaho, between Hauser Junction and Coeur d'Alene Lake.

The officers of the Spokane Falls and Idaho included the Northern Pacific chief engineer, General Anderson; Anthony Cannon, president of the Spokane and Palouse, whose involvement apparently mollified his rejection in favor of Corbin; Arthur A. Newbery, NP land agent in Spokane Falls; James M. Buckley, assistant superintendent of the NP western divisions; Paul Mohr, Sam Hauser, and Corbin. Glidden was conspicuously absent, as was J. J. Browne. Corbin was elected president, Hauser, vice president, Newbery the secretary, and Cannon, treasurer.

While Corbin had been building, the Coeur d'Alenes unfolded: the Bunker Hill and Sullivan shipped ore in increasing amounts by wagon and boat. So did Esler's little concentrator. Corbin joined Colonel Wallace and Richard Lockey of Helena as an incorporator of the Wallace townsite at the cedar grove. The Washington and Idaho completed its survey to Old Mission on October 22, 1886, and started running a line up the south fork, its way through Indian land eased by Congress' precedential act allowing the Kansas City, Fort Scott and Gulf Railway a right of way through a reservation. And almost overnight, completion of the Spokane Falls and Idaho "gave impetus to a tie and pole industry...supplying needed shipping facilities for both the mining and lumber industries." [6]

Corbin had not been occupied solely with the Spokane Falls and Idaho, however, for during these same months he had pushed construction of his Coeur d'Alene Railway and Navigation Company from Mission up the south fork of the Coeur d'Alene. The Spokane Falls and Idaho was standard-gauge; this line from Old Mission was narrow-gauge, three feet wide, to save money. Such narrow trackage was common, and a congressional committee in 1876 had actually predicted that narrow-gauge railroads would become important in providing an inexpensive national transportation system. Narrow lines were cheaper to build and to run than standard, and in 1886 did not suffer the disrepute that, within a few years, made their stocks impractical to sell. As Corbin did not intend to run the cars of one line over the trackage of the other, transferability was of no consequence, because there was not a boat on the lake that could carry a train, so that freight would need to be transferred from railcar to boat and back to railcar in any event.

So unfamiliar was Corbin with his new role as railroad builder that he had to write Sam Hauser to ask:

> I intended to ask you, but forgot to do so, if you obtained any permission or authority from any source to cut ties and timbers... or do you just go on and do it on the assumption you have the right? [7]

Corbin's surveyors, directed by his chief engineer, George P. Janes, began the Coeur d'Alene Railway and Navigation line at a landing on the Coeur d'Alene River approximately a half-mile down-stream—toward the lake—from the mission, itself, a white-washed frame church built by Roman Catholic Indians over a period of years between 1848 and 1867. The railway's landing lay near the furthest point upstream that steamers could navigate, about thirty-six miles from the lake, overlooked by the mission church from a gentle hill between the river and a thick evergreen forest. On either side of the church, a grassy prairie sloped toward the placid river, 130 feet wide at this point, meandering through meadowland and hay farms, its water clear, and its current imperceptible. The church had been fastened together with hand-made wooden pegs, and had six white pillars at its entrance, a pitched shingle roof, and an ornate sunburst, surmounted by a cross, carved on its facade. Although this Mission of the Sacred Heart once was surrounded by outbuildings and two hundred cultivated acres, it was no longer staffed or maintained when Corbin began his railroad.

Either as a result of haste or inexperience, the station grounds at Old Mission, twenty acres approved by the land office, were located too far from the river to be useful during low water, and a spur had to be built to the river's bank. Some years later, the railway was extended one and four-tenths miles west to a station called New Mission, more favorably located.[8]

As laid out, the route wound entirely on unsurveyed public lands, following the main stream and south fork of the Coeur d'Alene, crossing and recrossing the sluggish river with perhaps a score of trestles.[9] The Northern Pacific regarded most of the lands along the river as falling within its forty-mile limit, so as far as anyone could tell, the Coeur d'Alene Railway and Navigation Company was on NP land. On August 4, 1886, Corbin awarded a grading and track-laying contract to W. L. Spaulding, and another for bridge construction to J. L. Bayley, both of Spokane Falls. Each man now recruited workmen while August dwindled into September.

Their way lay upward through unrelenting country, with the only natural pathway along the river which narrowed quickly above Old Mission, and Corbin goaded his contractors and their crews. Grading was finished by the middle of October, six miles of it hacked through heavy forest with a lane barely wide enough to let trains progress, and a portion so close to rocky cliffs that the Washington and Idaho soon was to contend there was not space enough for a second track. Corbin regarded the grading as "some light and some heavy work," although it was far heavier than the level passage of the Spokane Falls and Idaho. He estimated the construction cost of the thirteen-mile road from Old Mission to Wardner Junction at $43,000, give or take a few thousand as he added unexpected or forgotten items in subsequent accountings.[10]

Tracklaying was begun November first, using forty-pound steel rail, lighter than usual mountain construction, and Corbin hoped all the tracks would be down in twenty days. But after nine miles were placed, one of Jane's subcontractors forcibly stopped the work until his men were paid. Corbin was in Coeur d'Alene City, fretting about ironwork for the Spokane Falls and Idaho dock, when he heard that construction had halted upriver, so away he dashed, as he had to so many times, to smooth the difficulty.

In his haste to operate his railroad, Corbin ignored ordinary practice that graded roadbed should lie unused for a year to settle, or "green." Perhaps he knew no better, or perhaps George Janes pointed out the bed was too new for track and Corbin overruled him because ore was waiting and the Washington and Idaho active. For whatever reason, the Coeur d'Alene Railway and Navigation Company's tracks went down on fresh, unballasted bed, and the hardwon passage up the south fork abused its builder's innocence, for he was beset by troubles.

The weather turned "the worst possible . . . raining and snowing most of the time," Corbin wrote Hauser. The roadbed wrenched with frost and dampness. Wagon roads bogged, "practically impassable for freighting—the worst you ever saw." Nevertheless Corbin insisted that the final four miles of track to Wardner Junction be laid, and the crews went grimly to work while the December wind whipped snow into their faces. As they approached open hillside, snow slides menaced them. The men stopped often to stomp circulation into their freezing feet around slash-timber fires. Two engines that had ridden to Old Mission on steamers heaving across the turbulent gray lake now stood idle on the track waiting for the road to open. By Christmas Day, 1886, it was ready. Corbin wrote Hauser triumphantly:

> I have the road finished to Wardner Junction, and expect to commence hauling ore, etc., in three days from this time. . . . There is quite a large accumulation of ore at the junction and I expect to commence delivering it at the rate of fifty to sixty tons a day.[11]

Had the weather been better, he added, the railroad would have been running a week earlier. Perversely the weather changed again. It warmed, the streams rose, the ground softened, and the unseasoned roadbed trickled from under its tracks. Adam Aulbach's *Murray Sun* explained:

> It seems that much of the iron was laid during the first cold snap. . . . At the time, the embankment was frozen and looked solid enough. Later the Chinooks came, and they have literally melted

away much of the roadbed, the black loam soil without gravel for ballast, readily yielded. The road, such as it is, is ironed to Milo, but as it stands it is useless.[12]

One engine stalled sodden on the track between Pine Flat and Mud Prairie, the *Sun* went on, and another between Kingston and Old Mission, neither able to move. Again freight dispatched by wagon, travelers by cayuse. The *Spokane Falls Review* reproved, "The Coeur d'Alene railroad has hardly been a success this winter owing to imperfect construction." Nothing could be done to start the trains. The ground froze again, snow piled deeper over the silent tracks and drifted against the fireless engines. Anton Esler wryly pondered his stockpile of ore, perhaps five hundred tons, piled along the tracks near Milo, all frozen into a solid mass that could not be moved until a thaw. The Coeur d'Alene River closed over with ice ten inches thick. So D. C. Corbin had run his railroad in 1886, for approximately one week, and then it stopped in the grip of winter. He went unhappily off to New York to attend to other business.

CHAPTER FOUR

THE NORTHERN PACIFIC
TAKES OVER

WHILE HE HAD BEEN BUILDING BOTH THE SPOKANE FALLS AND Idaho and his railway from Old Mission to the mines, Daniel Corbin had been elected president in November, 1886, of the Woodruff Sleeping and Parlor Coach Company, formed in 1871 to manufacture and operate a railroad sleeping car designed by T. T. Woodruff, master car builder of the Terre Haute and Alton Railroad. Corbin held stock in the company, probably acquired during his period of service as manager of his brother's New York railways, and when he left Idaho for New York in the first days of 1887, expected to increase his interest "to a considerable extent." He found the sleeping car field busily competitive, however, and sensed that mergers soon must occur. In less than three years, the Woodruff was purchased by the Pullman Palace Car Company.

Corbin advanced his interest in the Woodruff company to Sam Hauser as his excuse for rejecting Hauser's suggestion that he buy one-sixth of the Drummond and Philipsburg Railroad, one of the four that Hauser was building for the Northern Pacific. He needed his money, Corbin explained, and offered to sell his shares in the Spokane Ranch and the McClellan Ditch, near Helena. At this time, Corbin began going his way separate from Hauser. Foremost in his mind was his Coeur d'Alene project, and Corbin used his days in New York to try to wheedle concessions, perhaps an allowance on timber structures, from the Northern Pacific but he failed to budge that company's hard-headed directors. As soon as weather allowed, Corbin returned to northern Idaho, preparing to operate his Coeur d'Alene Railway and Navigation Company.

Spring came early in 1887. Before the middle of March, Corbin's narrow-gauge line had been properly ballasted. The ice broke on the river, steamers again ran to Old Mission, and freight shipments were resumed March twentieth after a slide had been shoveled from the tracks above Kingston at the last moment. Once more, Corbin had to hurry, for in February a senator recommended approval of the Washington and Idaho's petition for a right of way through the Coeur d'Alene Reservation.

Construction began again to extend the Coeur d'Alene Railway and Navigation Company's track from Wardner Junction to Wallace over right of way claimed also by the Washington and Idaho. Corbin was quoted as telling the New York *Mining Record* that if the St. Regis, Montana, mines proved out, he might extend his road down the St. Regis River as far as Missoula. And Stephen Glidden, encouraged by the approach of Corbin's railway, now organized his own Canyon Creek Railroad Company, to build from the vicinity of his Tiger mine to a point near Wallace, where it would connect with the Coeur d'Alene route. Glidden's railway was a family affair, including his son, Harry M.; his mine manager, Frank R. Culbertson; another employee of the Tiger, Alexander H. Tarbet; and the Wallace attorney, Charles W. O'Neil. Its articles of incorporation provided that it might run "by steam, horse, or other motive power," and its headquarters was to be in the "office of the Tiger mine, on said Canyon Creek." [1] As Corbin's men graded toward Wallace, the Glidden railway began building, too. The Bunker Hill also built to meet Corbin, clearing its own loading area beside the tracks at Wardner Junction, connected to the mine by a wagon road.

This season Corbin gave his roadbed more attention, building slower, taking time to ballast his track and brace his embankments. By August 22, the first train entered Osburn; on September 10 the line reached Wallace. Its progress had attracted general interest, and the *Spokane Falls Review* believed that "it would be almost impossible to overestimate the advantages which Spokane will derive from

direct railroad connection with the mining district." [2] The Coeur
d'Alene Railway and Navigation Company erected a twenty-four
by eighty foot frame depot at the head of Sixth Street on the north
side of the river, and a few months later, Corbin provided the material, Wallace's citizens the labor, to construct two wooden sidewalks along Sixth from the depot to the Wallace hotel.

The five hundred residents of Wallace planned to observe the
arrival of the railway with an outdoor celebration, and to invite the
populace of Murray and Mullan, on Friday, September 30, but a rainstorm drove the crowd and speakers indoors to the first floor of the
Carter Hotel. Despite the inclement weather, the *Wallace Free Press*
counted the day a success:

> The first attempt by the people of Wallace to celebrate an impor-
> tant event may, in the beginning, be set down as a complete success. It
> was four o'clock when the train arrived bearing the greater part of
> the crowd....People came from all along the line of the road and
> the two cars were well filled. [3]

Colonel Wallace welcomed the visitors with what the editor considered a "neat speech." D. C. Corbin was introduced, although he
hardly could have been flattered by the speaker of the day, the attorney Albert Hagan, who referred to Corbin as "a little man from
Montana," in his flowery tribute to the railway builder. Corbin
smiled through it, and the signal day ended with a grand ball at
the Carter. Almost immediately a controversy arose, however, over
whether Wallace should continue to observe sun time or adopt railroad time, thirty minutes slower, and this was never satisfactorily
settled so long as the railroad ran.

About ten days later, the Coeur d'Alene Railway and Navigation
Company trains stopped running to Wallace as the result of a petty
dispute with the Washington and Idaho. The two companies had
bickered all summer over a mile and a half of right of way between
Osburn and Wallace, and finally Corbin's chief engineer, George
Janes, had written the Washington and Idaho on July 11 that his
company intended to lay its tracks on the route approved by the
land office. On August 23, Janes received a written reply ordering

him to "desist from occupying any portion whatever of the Washington and Idaho's right of way."[4] It was a comic spat, for by law neither railway could be granted land until the area was surveyed by the federal government, and the maps filed with the land office conveyed no title. Moreover, the Northern Pacific claimed the ground, and when the Washington and Idaho resorted to the district court, it faced Northern Pacific attorneys. Corbin's railroad was enjoined from serving Wallace during most of October, until Judge Norman Buck, peering through his tiny oval gold-rimmed glasses, dissolved the Washington and Idaho's injunction.

Glidden had not completed his 6.57-mile Canyon Creek road when the Washington and Idaho halted Corbin's trains, so Glidden stopped construction to await the outcome of the contention. Once Corbin resumed service to Wallace, Glidden took heart and continued laying his track, also on unsurveyed land, and connected it with the Corbin line on December 23, 1887, which was the occasion for another celebration, attended by delegations from all the mining towns of the district who gathered this time at Burke, the village growing up about the Tiger mine and adjacent claims. Glidden, himself, drove a silver spike commemorating the junction of the two railways. The Murray brass band played, and among the spectators was John Carten, one of the discoverers of the Tiger.

The depot at Wallace, and the branch to Burke, marked the end of the Coeur d'Alene Railway construction under Corbin's management, although he surveyed eastward to Mullan and often mentioned plans to build those few additional miles. But there was far more to railroading than laying the track. The Corbin line hummed with commerce. A steadily enlarging stream of ore was flowing from the Coeur d'Alene mines over the Corbin railways and lake steamers. The first carload from any point on the line above Wardner consisted of thirteen tons from the Granite on Canyon Creek. The Bunker Hill, Sullivan, and Esler concentrator, which previously freighted at most twenty tons a day by wagon, now consigned an average of sixty tons each day by rail. The road handled 1,340 tons of ore and concentrates each week in good weather. Its capacity increased as Corbin added to the first equipment: three wood-burning locomotives, twenty-four freight cars, two passenger coaches, and a combination car. From March 20 through May 17, 1887, the Coeur d'Alene Railway and Navigation Company recorded a gross income of $25,603, with operating expenditures of $8,300. Bar none, the Corbin railway was the busiest in Idaho.

Moreover, during March, 1887, when he established service to the mines and began extending toward Wallace, Corbin also consolidated his route by buying the Coeur d'Alene Steam Navigation and Transportation Company, which operated the lake steamers.[5] This, the survivor of three private steamboat companies on Lake Coeur d'Alene, was controlled by Monaghan and King, and two steamer captains, I. B. Sanburn and Abner Haines. Both captains had come from Portland to operate the sternwheeler *Coeur d'Alene* for Oregon investors during the gold rush of 1883–84, and stayed when the company sold to one organized by Monaghan, James Glover of Spokane Falls, and Thomas Graney, which sold out, in turn, to Monaghan, King, Sanburn and Haines. Under this management, the steamer line made its first run between Coeur d'Alene City and Old Mission on June 18, 1886, charging three dollars for passengers, and ten dollars a ton for freight. In addition to the *Coeur d'Alene,* the company also ran the propeller-driven *General Sherman,* and advertised "a good wagon road from Mission to the mines," a statement not likely to be supported by anyone who had been over the trail. Because it had no competition, the steamer company was believed to net as much as $2,000 on good trips.

Corbin realized that he could not run through the winter with his steamers, and he consequently authorized Sanburn to build the *Kootenai,* a powerful screw-driven steamboat with a heavy plank and boiler-plated hull designed to break ice twenty-two inches thick. Sanburn contracted with the Willamette Iron Works of Portland for an icebreaker 110 feet long, which was not much longer than the *Coeur d'Alene,* and with a 480 horsepower engine, four times stronger than any other boat on the lake. The *Kootenai* would draw eight feet of water, requiring the river channel to be deepened, and the railway extended another mile downstream from Old Mission to a point where the sturdy boat could land. In design, the *Kootenai*

was modeled on icebreakers that churned the Great Lakes, and reduced the time between Coeur d'Alene City and Old Mission to
four hours in good weather with a speed of more than fourteen
miles an hour.

At eleven o'clock on the morning of December 13, 1887, the
Kootenai was to be launched without ceremony at Coeur d'Alene
City, where she had been assembled. After the boat was in the water,
the boilers and smokestack were to be installed. For some reason,
the *Kootenai* failed to respond to cutting the moorings and roosted
motionless on the launching track while Corbin and a select group
watched from a steamer on the rain-swept lake. In an hour the
boat moved only ten feet, then suddenly lurched into the water.

Even the powerful *Kootenai* did not always get through: she
was stuck nearly a month in lake ice during January and early February, 1888, when record low temperatures were reached, and this
caused actual hardship in the mining towns where residents had
neglected to lay in their customary winter stores anticipating that
the *Kootenai* would deliver all through the cold weather. Once she
had been chopped free early in February, Captain Sanburn managed to smash a channel through the ice by repeatedly backing the
Kootenai and then ramming full speed ahead. Nevertheless, from
1887 to 1890, the *Kootenai* carried the bulk of the mines' winter
traffic, often towing as many as four barges loaded with ore.

Perhaps here it is well to recall that Corbin's first purpose, when
he undertook the two railways to the mines, had been to secure a
steady source of profitable concentrates for the Wickes smelter.
Only by chance had his plan benefitted Spokane Falls, albeit soon
a magazine would remark, "Thus is Spokane Falls encircled by a
jeweled ring [of mines], the crowning ornament of which is the
famous Coeur d'Alene." [6] Even so, the Coeur d'Alene Railway and
Navigation Company remained a Montana corporation and its projected line crossed the territorial border between Idaho and Montana.
Had not competition developed so swiftly, Corbin doubtless would
have extended the line eastward. His water route was dictated by
the necessity to reach the mines fast by the easiest and cheapest way.

Now that all-weather transportation had come, a half-dozen

mines shipped regularly: the Bunker Hill and Sullivan, of course, and the Stemwinder, Tyler, Sierra Nevada, and from Canyon Creek, the Tiger, Poorman, and Granite. The Bunker Hill and Sullivan were worked alternately and their ores mixed at the direction of Jim Wardner, who carefully recorded every pound of ore or concentrates shipped, exercising special vigilance because he sensed that Sam Hauser had grown to distrust him. Hauser had been warned that Wardner sought more profit for himself, perhaps by diverting ore to a smelter that would rebate secretly.[7] Wardner's records show, however, that Wickes processed more Coeur d'Alene ore than did any other smelter at the time. To choose a month at random, August, 1886, Wardner reported that Whittier Fuller and Company of San Francisco took 368,293 pounds of Bunker Hill and Sullivan ore. The Selby Smelting and Lead Company, San Francisco, received 30,111, and Wickes, 1,262,584 pounds. Indeed, in 1887, thirty per cent of Wickes' total production was Coeur d'Alene silver and lead.

Wardner recorded the date, waybill, sacks, car number, and net weight for every shipment. One typical carload of 303 sacks, for example, cost $498.67 to ship and treat, and the gross return amounted to $850.84, demonstrating that more than half the value of every pound of Coeur d'Alene ore found its way into the pockets of the men who ran the railways and the smelters.

Furthermore, the railway rates imposed by the Northern Pacific encouraged mine owners to ship their output to Wickes as the cheapest destination. The Coeur d'Alene Railway and Navigation Company charged from five to six dollars, depending on the length of haul, to deliver a ton of ore from a mine to Coeur d'Alene City, and the Northern Pacific demanded eight dollars more to carry the same ton to Helena, $8.50 to Wickes, $10.40 to Portland, $17.00 to Omaha, and $18.00 to Denver. Such elastic rates, common as they were to all railroads and all commodities, so incensed the Portland Board of Trade that it threatened to boycott the Northern Pacific for "rate discrimination," and openly asserted that Jim Wardner "and others" colluded to favor Wickes and share in its profits. When some mine owners patronized Denver and Omaha, the NP raised its rates to Garrison, a division point west of Helena, to $8.30

a ton, thus charging more to carry ore to Garrison than eighty-six miles farther to Helena, and effectively increasing the cost of shipment to Denver and Omaha.

Corbin's all-weather transportation system not only increased ore shipments; it actuated a second period of development in the Coeur d'Alenes. The first period may be said to have been the days of prospecting and location, 1883–87; the second, the era of transition from prospector-owner to stockholder-owners, marked by labor wars, 1887–1903; and the third, large-scale corporate development using machinery. The invasion of outside capital began within a month of the day that Corbin established regular train and steamer schedules, when the diverse owners of the Bunker Hill, the Sullivan, and adjacent fractional claims optioned their holdings to Simeon Gannett Reed of Portland, lumberman, merchant, and vice president of the Oregon Railway and Navigation Company, suzerain of the Washington and Idaho in the Union Pacific system.

Reed naturally knew a good deal about Coeur d'Alene district mines. He was solicited to buy the Bunker Hill by Jim Wardner, who communicated with Reed in cipher, referring to Corbin as "Kate" and Hauser as "Elsie." On March 5, 1887, Wardner signed over his own interest in the Bunker Hill, the Sullivan, and the Esler concentrating plant, and was authorized by Reed to represent him in further purchases. On April 18, Wardner obtained an agreement from Hauser to sell Reed the Helena Concentrating Company, and two days later telegraphed Reed in code that he had acquired options from the owners of the mines involved.[8]

Before consummating a contract, Reed wanted to see what he was getting. Consequently, Wardner had William Lee, the Bunker Hill superintendent, draw a map of the properties and showed the map to Reed and Reed's agent, Bernard J. Goldsmith, at a meeting in Spokane Falls. At this meeting, Reed learned for the first time that Wardner's options were valid only until April 30—about seven days away—and required a down payment of $200,000. To assure himself of the mines' value, Reed had Patrick Clark steal samples of Bunker Hill and Sullivan ore under cover of night. The samples assayed fourteen per cent lead and twenty-two ounces of silver. Certainly the mines seemed worth the price asked, and Reed launched into a mad week during which his bankers, Laidlaw and Company of New York, delayed granting his request for $200,000, and, as his options ran out, Reed drew on Laidlaw and Company without their authorization through the First National Bank of Spokane Falls.[9] Thus Reed took up the options, and made peace with his bankers later. The mines, concentrator, ore on hand, and equipment, cost him approximately $731,765. When his purchases became final in August, he asked Wardner to recommend a competent engineer, and among those he suggested, Wardner named Marcus Daly of Montana.

Goldsmith told Reed:

> The mines look first rate and bigger than ever, but the expenses on account of want of system are much more than they ought to be ... but I do not want to cast any reflection on Wardner—he did well enough, considering the large amount of work piled onto him, the newness of the country and the hard crowd he had to deal with.[10]

Corbin was part of the "hard crowd," in Goldsmith's opinion, for as soon as he inspected the mines he wrote Reed appalling accounts of the railway's rates and methods of handling ore, declaring that sacks were strewn from Coeur d'Alene to the concentrator, "laying out in the mud and rain and everywheres," with wagons driving over them. Wastage at the Bunker Hill was "scandalous, fearful," ore was spilled between the mine and the railroad and then spilled along the right of way, and the railway dumped ore without regard for its ownership into leaky, unlined cars, and sent the sacks back to the mines because sacks were scarce. "The waste amounts to almost as much as the transportation," complained Goldsmith. "By emptying sacks at Coeur d'Alene all shipments lose their identity and you can never keep control or track of it."

When Reed began doing business with the Wickes smelter (the first receipt was dated June 27, 1887) he lamented its procedures, too. In the manner of alchemists, the smelter operators whisked Reed's ore out of sight inside the red brick walls, and eventually offered him a statement supposed to represent the results of their treatment of his ore. Reed wrote Hauser many letters disputing reports of moisture in his ore, because moisture lowered the value, or arguing the payment, which was based on New York rates. Weeks passed following one of Reed's scorching missives, but no answer came, and the railway and smelter operated as they had. "I telegraphed and wrote your private secretary, but he has never replied," Reed scolded. Again he wrote, concerning moisture in the ore:

> The ore in question was delayed on the road fully six weeks in dry summer weather.... I think the correct solution is as I have been informed, viz., that your men have been in the habit of selecting a few of the wettest sacks from the bottom of the car for the sample.[11]

Reed had vested his holdings in a new firm, the Bunker Hill and Sullivan Mining and Smelting Company, organized as an Oregon corporation on July 29, 1887, and his new superintendent, Victor M. Clement, was able to advise Reed in December that an agent he had assigned to the Wickes smelter had the run of the works and the Bunker Hill company was "getting the best of it."

The Coeur d'Alene Railway and Navigation Company had been making money so fast that Reed's complaints probably seemed merely ungrateful. The faulty Wickes smelter, on the other hand, paid only small, infrequent dividends, and perhaps defied accurate accounting due to its clumsy process, even under the supervision of August Raht. Within a year, Hauser and his Montana friends gave up the Wickes enterprise to form the Helena and Livingston Smelting and Refining Company, which absorbed the Helena Mining and Reduction, and built a more suitable works at East Helena. D. C. Corbin traded his Wickes stock for shares in the new company, but he was no longer as close to Hauser as he had been, was not active in the new company, and felt that he had been ignored during its formation.[12]

Early domination of the Coeur d'Alenes by Montana men was ending while Corbin was drawing away from his earlier business associates, perhaps committing himself again to newer country without a conscious decision. Corbin's railway had been the "entering wedge" to the Coeur d'Alenes in 1886, and by 1889 the district was one of the major lead-producing regions in the United States, with an annual aggregate output valued at nine million dollars in cash. At the same time, the burgeoning district outgrew Corbin's one-track railway with its leaky cars, its frequent transfers, its small steamboats, and its frenzied bustle to keep pace with expanding production. Moreover, substantial new money entered the district.

Wardner had arranged the terms whereby Reed bought the Helena Concentrating Company for $88,000, of which $50,000 represented the company's contract with Wardner, and $38,000, the plant and its stockpile. Reed estimated that in twenty-three months and twenty-six days, Esler's little plant had produced 15,255 tons of concentrates worth more than $1,353,008, or an average of more than $56,000 worth of concentrates a month! Oregon investors showed growing interest in the mines; a number of them wrote their congressmen urging that the Coeur d'Alene Indian tribe's land be returned to the public domain because it contained valuable minerals and timber.

In August, 1887, the Washington and Idaho, taking a delegation of Indians to Washington, D.C., headed by Steve Liberty, had been successful in securing its right of way through tribal land with a direct appeal to President Grover Cleveland, who by law had to satisfy himself that the grant would not harm his Indian wards. With an all-land railway near at hand, the days of Corbin's screeching "chippy" engines, as the miners called them, were numbered. Approval of the Washington and Idaho's right of way through the reservation prompted the Northern Pacific to take direct control over the Spokane Falls and Idaho section of Corbin's system, which the NP did on October 1, 1887, by leasing the railway for fifty years and paying off $270,000 in outstanding bonds. Northern Pacific crews began renovating the Spokane Falls and Idaho trackage, and frequently shifted to help maintain that of the Coeur d'Alene Railway and Navigation Company. Surveys were instituted to find an overland route north of Lake Coeur d'Alene to the mining district.

Corbin may well have leased his Spokane Falls and Idaho to the Northern Pacific as a result of the quest for an overland way, for after the NP had completed its search and appointed new trustees, the railway's directors voted on July 16, 1888, to construct a branch line from one and one-half miles north of Coeur d'Alene City eastward approximately sixty-seven miles to Mullan. The proposed route would follow the northern shores of Lake Coeur d'Alene to Wolf Lodge Creek, trace the creek to the summit of Fourth of July Canyon, and then proceed along the general course of the old Mullan road to Mullan, a route today utilized for the federal highway through the region.[13] This decision, foreshadowed by the surveys, would have terminated the Northern Pacific's support to Corbin for any extension of his Coeur d'Alene Railway and Navigation Company route eastward into Montana. He doubtless concluded properly that, in any event, the Northern Pacific intended to assume direct command of its destiny in the Coeur d'Alenes.

Nevertheless, for the time remaining to him, Corbin sent his railway clattering busily through the timbered mountains, now dotted with three new concentrators, an experimental smelter, and new mining companies as numerous as wild flowers. Some days as many as sixty passengers rode, sitting in the caboose or on benches nailed to flatcars when the two passenger cars were filled. "The capacity of the Corbin railroad is taxed to the utmost to transact the quantity of ore now being shipped," declared the *Spokane Falls Review* in April, 1888, so Corbin added twenty new boxcars, and by June, the newspaper observed that "many mines are comparatively idle because the railroad cannot handle all the ore." Even though the district's production increased faster than his narrow-gauge could handle it, Corbin prowled for more cargo, saying he would extend the line to Mullan "as soon as the output of the mines in that vicinity will guarantee a fair amount of freight." Next to the military post, Corbin's railway payroll of $6,000 a month was Coeur d'Alene City's biggest.

The major railroads continued to close in. Under engineers J. R. Stevens and R. E. Brown, two hundred and fifty Northern Pacific workmen invaded the route of the Coeur d'Alene Railway and Navigation Company, widening the roadbed in preparation for standard-gauge tracks. "That the Northern Pacific and the OR&N railway companies mean business is now beyond a question. Both are in the field," announced the *Wardner News* in July. By the middle of that month, more than fifteen hundred men were at work on two overland routes to the mines: the Oregon Railway and Navigation Company, on behalf of the Washington and Idaho, its subsidiary, clearing from Farmington, Washington, toward Wallace, and the Northern Pacific grading from Thompson Falls toward Wallace and improving the twisting roadbed from Old Mission up the south fork. Labor pirating became commonplace. "As fast as men are brought in by one contractor, they are bought up and put to work on the other road," said the *Review*. The Washington and Idaho again appealed to the courts to secure uncontested right of way. At one interval a bloody railroad war seemed inevitable, as both companies moved all the men they could muster onto the ground they disputed, ready to fight with guns, tools, and axes. Jim Hill, extending to Butte via the Montana Central, released "a large force of men ... to aid the OR&N in the Coeur d'Alenes." [14] Luckily both sides blustered and delayed, so the battle choked in threatening talk and the two forces returned to uneasy construction.

Signs that the Northern Pacific was tightening its control of the Corbin railways continued to appear. When Kootenai County, Idaho, served the Spokane Falls and Idaho with a notice of taxes due, the Northern Pacific had intervened. It had happened this way: the county assessor, a tenacious man, John J. Costello, interviewed Corbin on the value of the railway, but Corbin referred him to Arthur Newbery, secretary of the road, who refused to list the company's property on the ground that the Spokane Falls and Idaho operated wholly with Northern Pacific equipment. Costello thereupon evaluated the railway from his own observation at $74,250, and posted notices that he would auction off the railway at Rathdrum on February 6, 1888, for nonpayment of taxes amounting to $1,967.63. That brought Northern Pacific attorneys on the run to enjoin the sale, and Judge Norman Buck issued the injunction, after ordering the railway to file a "legible" complaint. Before the next scheduled appearance in court, the Northern Pacific paid a negotiated tax of $1,172.25. [15]

Corbin and Hauser spent the summer months of 1888 in New

York, conferring with officials of the Northern Pacific. Relations had deteriorated. There was a good measure of dispute over rate protection, for lower rates were a foregone result of two overland railways to the mining district. Everyone expected that Corbin would sell, and to consolidate his system before selling Corbin bought Glidden's Canyon Creek Railroad from Burke for $41,620.18 on August 29, 1888.[16]

Inevitably, Corbin leased the Coeur d'Alene Railway and Navigation Company to the Northern Pacific for 999 years on October 1, 1888. The road had assets in line and equipment valued at $987,000, a surplus in its treasury, and had paid its bond holders an eight per cent interest regularly. During the first year of its lease, the Northern Pacific spent $21,400 renovating the track from Old Mission to Wallace, an amount roughly half the original cost of grading and tracklaying. After a series of washouts in 1890, the NP abandoned Corbin's south fork route and served the mines with its new road from Missoula. The last spike on this portion of the trackage had been driven December 23, 1890, by Miss Garrett Glidden, the ten-year-old daughter of S. S. Glidden, back in the railway's favor. The entire Coeur d'Alene Railway and Navigation Company was sold by court order in 1897 to satisfy two mortgages, dated September 1, 1886, and September 1, 1888, amounting to $1,238,000, held by the Central Trust Company of New York City. The Northern Pacific repurchased the road on June 11, 1897, for $220,000, so that bond holders at that time realized approximately fifteen cents on the dollar.

Two months after Corbin leased the Coeur d'Alene Railway and Navigation Company to the Northern Pacific, the Washington and Idaho entered Wallace with its standard-gauge track, and reached Mullan in March, 1889. The anticipated rate reduction occurred on January 1, 1890, when the NP issued its Tariff Number 944, prompting a citizen who signed himself "Justus" to write the *Review*:

The Coeur d'Alene branch of the Northern Pacific has been run for all there was to get from its patrons, and rates have been charged in the past three years that would make a mule-puncher ashamed of himself.[17]

"Justus" patently lacked an appreciation of the economics of railroading, but he spoke for most of the line's patrons. Nevertheless, the mine owners shipped their ores and concentrates to smelters at a profit, and made money simply because Dan Corbin had the vision and determination to build them a railway.

What the Northern Pacific acquired from Corbin by its lease in October, 1888, must surely be one of the more fanciful rail systems devised by man. The Coeur d'Alene Railway and Navigation Company's track wound around trees, crossed and recrossed the south fork a score of times, and its single track climbed so continuously that engines headed for Old Mission merely braked the cars going downhill. The Canyon Creek branch rose an average of three per cent, and a favorite pastime of editors was speculating on what might happen to a car turned loose at Burke: "If it could be kept on the track, [it] would make the whole thirty-four miles of road without any motive power but its own impetus." [18] When a light snow blew, railway employees swept the track with brooms so the engines would not stall on slick rails. One rider recalled:

> A light fall of snow would block the trains.... It was a common occurrence for the passengers for the Canyon Creek towns and mines to abandon the train and walk to their destinations or back to their homes. On the least indication that the train would not be able to get through, [the conductor] would hurry through the cars and collect the fares before the passengers realized that they would have to walk.[19]

Moreover, said a newspaper, Corbin's was "probably the only railroad in the United States run independent of telegraphic communication." Engineers leaving one end of the line watched warily for a train coming the opposite direction on the single track, and if one were due to pass, pulled onto a spur to wait for it. Sometimes one train would be delayed. Then both outgoing and incoming engineers dawdled on spurs, each waiting for the other. Generally a small boy could be found to run to one of the engineers with a message to resume service. Seven months after the Northern Pacific took its lease, the *Review* said the Coeur d'Alene Railway and Navigation Company "cannot make a rapid run as the roadbed is rather shaky and they carry their passengers in a caboose."

With the completion of overland railways to the district the Coeur d'Alene Railway and Navigation Company's raucous heyday fell silent. By 1890 its steamers lay idle, except for occasional pleasure trips, and eventually the *Kootenai* was dismantled for her machinery. Shaky and arrogant it had been, but Daniel Corbin's ten-mile-an-hour, graceless little railroad had opened the mineral storehouse of northern Idaho. In 1887, its first year of operation, the railway was responsible for carrying the ten thousand tons of concentrates shipped by the Bunker Hill and the Sullivan; one year later, seven mines consigned nearly three times as much mineral freight. In the year ending July 31, 1889, the Corbin road hauled 18,000 tons of freight for the district's consumption, and took out 80,000 tons of Idaho products, chiefly ores and concentrates, the highest tonnage of any railroad in the territory. Shoshone County produced mineral valued at $3,471,788 in the twelve months between November, 1887, and November, 1888. Within fifteen years the impetus provided by its first rail transportation would push the region into yielding nearly one-third of the domestic lead consumed in the United States. This outpouring rushed quickly beyond the poor capacity of mule teams and wagon roads.

Corbin had recognized the problems of building a railway to the mines and had overcome them. In his 1890 report on territorial affairs, Idaho's Governor George L. Shoup eulogized the Coeur d'Alene Railway and Navigation Company as "the entering wedge which opened the marvellous treasure of the Coeur d'Alene to the world." [20]

CHAPTER FIVE

TWO WEEKS TO START
A RAILROAD

ABOUT SIX MONTHS BEFORE D. C. CORBIN SOLD THE COEUR D'ALENE Railway and Navigation Company to the Northern Pacific, he had fallen in with a scheme hatched by James Monaghan to build a railroad northward from Spokane Falls through the Colville country, a fertile valley in northeastern Washington, to a connection with the Canadian Pacific Railway. Although Monaghan accorded his railway promotion a good deal of time, it was only one of a number of enterprises: He had sold out his interest in the Coeur d'Alene City townsite, and had become president of the American District Telegraph Company in Spokane Falls, the Cariboo Mining, Milling and Smelting Company, the Spokane Falls Cab Company, and much else that promised to make money.

The men behind Monaghan's railway, the Spokane Falls and Northern, were substantial Spokane Falls businessmen, most with mining or banking connections or both, and several had been associated with the Northern Pacific. "My friends, James Monaghan, James Glover, A. A. Newbery, Frank Moore, and some others..." solicited him to build the Spokane Falls and Northern, Corbin said later, recalling the names of the men who were the railway's principal early supporters. Corbin's alliance with Sam Hauser was virtually severed, and he had intended to go East after selling his Coeur d'Alene road, but he stopped off in Spokane Falls for a few days in October, 1888, to scrutinize Monaghan's project. He found the town grown to seven thousand citizens, thriving with its capture of the Spokane County seat in 1886 and the flow of wealth from the Coeur d'Alene mines over the railroads he had built.

On every hand, Corbin saw prosperity. At the end of 1888, Spokane Falls' banks would report a sixty-one per cent increase in capital stock in twelve months, deposits eighty-six per cent higher, and loans up sixty-one per cent, "which just about tallies with the general increase in all values and business in Spokane Falls for the same time," observed the *Review*. The Spokane Mill Company had doubled its lumber output in the past year by working night and day for one period of seven months, and the Spokane Manufacturing and Lumber Company had erected a new mill twice as big as its old one, to utilize Idaho timber delivered by rail. The town boasted brick, lime, and granite industries; its flour mills ground three hundred barrels a day. Echo Mills sold flour to dealers in midwestern cities, as well as to the mining towns of Idaho and Montana, and the farming communities of the Palouse whence the wheat came.

Of the nearby mines, the *Spokane Falls Review* commented:

> As most of the owners of the best Coeur d'Alene mines are residents of Spokane Falls, and as the business of running and managing them is conducted mainly from this point, the Coeur d'Alene mining district would alone make of Spokane Falls a city of importance. The development of this district has already contributed largely to our city's growth.[1]

The newspaper pointed out that three smelting companies maintained Spokane Falls representatives: the Montana Smelting of Great Falls, the Omaha and Grant, and the Helena Works of Denver. During 1888, thirty-one plats had been filed for additions to Spokane Falls, and eleven companies that inquired for water power had to be turned down, prompting several Spokane Falls men to organize a water power company with the intention of parceling the riverbank among desirable applicants. The *Review* estimated that "fully five thousand people reached Spokane Falls by the various [railroad] lines every month" during 1887 and 1888, although many were simply bound somewhere else, and in every direction from the business district, clustering along Howard Street on the south side of the river, hastily erected whitewashed houses glimmered among the scrub pines.

Most of the stores were frame with false fronts but a few had been constructed of native-clay brick embellished with local granite. Among the new industries were an oatmeal factory, a foundry, and an electric generator. J. J. Browne and Anthony Cannon had run street railway tracks down the middle of Riverside Avenue, leading to Browne's and Cannon's additions, and because Riverside was not paved, in wet weather men had to pole a raft across the slough at Riverside and Howard. Indeed, none of the streets was paved, and many were no more than trails flattered with names. Laden teams clopped through the dirt thoroughfares, sometimes as many as twelve mules pulling three wagons in tandem. A truss-and-plank wooden bridge sprang across the river from basalt island to island. The business district ended at the Northern Pacific tracks a half mile south of the river.

By 1888, railroads extended east, west, and south from Spokane Falls, and Monaghan and his colleagues organized the Spokane Falls and Northern to serve the town from the north. Incorporated in Washington on April 14, 1888, the company's directorate included Monaghan, King, Newbery, Browne, and nine others: Tom E. Jefferson, insurance broker and mine owner; Glover, president of the First National Bank of Spokane; Moore, banker, and president of a water power and a transit company; W. H. Taylor, banker and president of the Board of Trade; the county auditor, Byron C. Van Houten; James Z. Moore, who a short time later was to be first temporary chairman for the first day of the first state constitutional convention; E. J. Brickell, hardware merchant, miller, and banker; Warren Hussey, banker and mine promoter; and Daniel C. Corbin, capitalist, who gave his home address as New York City. Corbin appears to have taken no active part in organizing the railroad company and probably lent his name out of friendship for Monaghan and King. Corbin was the only director who had built a railway, although Browne had planned two of them, Monaghan and King had operated steamers and stagecoaches, and Newbery had been a partner with Felix Warren from 1881–83 in a stage service out of Lewiston, Idaho. This was the sum of transportation experience among the incorporators of the Spokane Falls and Northern, but none of them considered inexperience of moment, for the West bustled with men who were successful doing what they had never done before.

On paper the Spokane Falls and Northern was a corporation typically ambitious: it projected a route north to an unspecified landing on the Columbia River, a fleet of steamboats to connect by river with the Canadian Pacific at Revelstoke, British Columbia, possible branches in territories other than Washington, and telegraph and telephone lines along its right of way. The company was capitalized for $2,500,000, a reasonable estimate of the cost of reaching the river.[2] To the company's own statement of its objectives, the *Spokane Falls Review* added an amplification:

> The object of this enterprise is to open up the Colville agricultural and mining country to the trade of Spokane, and to place at rest the question of a reduction works in this city. One who has not investigated the enormous resources which this new road will develop can form no conception of what it means. It means smelters, a union depot, an extensive wholesale trade, and a splendid business in outfitting the miner and agriculturist for the development of his new home.[3]

On the last day of April, 1888, the company had elected Newbery its president, Taylor, vice president, Jefferson, secretary, and the town's acknowledged first citizen, Glover, treasurer.

Spokane Falls burned with railroading fever just then. *Railway Age* listed no fewer than thirty-seven companies planning railroads in Washington Territory. Seven days after organization of the Spokane Falls and Northern, businessmen of Spokane Falls subscribed $175,000 for the Seattle, Lake Shore and Eastern, so it would not pass too far from the town on its way east from Puget Sound. The Seattle, Lake Shore and Eastern professed also to be interested in the Colville region, Newbery objected in letters to the newspapers, and the *Stevens County Miner,* published at Colville, took note of the two proposals with the observation, "It don't make much odds to the people of Stevens County who builds the line of road, but we think the Spokane and Northern should have the preference provided it is not backed by Canadian Pacific cash." Moreover, it was rumored that the Great Northern, building westward through Montana, would extend a branch into British Columbia, or the Canadian Pacific would drive southward as far as Spokane Falls, or that Victoria, British Columbia, financiers would construct a narrow-gauge line from the Little Dalles of the Columbia River fifty-three miles south through Colville to the settlement of Chewelah.

These tidings of likely competition for Colville's trade urged haste upon the organizers of the Spokane Falls and Northern, but they had done nothing other than sign documents and hold meetings with a certain prideful satisfaction. They enjoyed the distinction of being the men who were going to build the railroad, but excepting two sketchy surveys, the railway was no nearer construction than it had been four years earlier when Monaghan first contemplated a company.

Monaghan, himself, had run one survey from Little Dalles down the east bank of the Columbia to Kettle Falls, and thence overland to Spokane Falls. He knew the region well because he homesteaded the site of Chewelah in 1871 when it was called Fools' Prairie, and had traveled it as military wagon master and school superintendent. The second survey, directed in 1887 by F. E. Habersham, chief engineer of the proposed Spokane Falls and Northern, had covered much of the same ground. Habersham's study had cost $2,000, half provided by the men who were to incorporate the railway, and half by the Spokane Falls contractor, Cyrus Burns, but the *Stevens County Miner* scolded:

> The surveyors sent out to locate a line for the railway have done their work entirely on theory, and without much regard as to benefitting the country. They have traversed a serpentine course through the county and escaped the chief productive portion thereof.

Colville might well look to the Canadian Pacific for its railroad, after all, the *Miner* concluded.

With the railway at a standstill, Monaghan and King rode their horses wistfully through the Colville country. King estimated eighty thousand tons of timothy could be harvested annually, but eschewed any suggestion that future crops might be shipped over the Spokane Falls and Northern, and the *Miner* asserted that tons of hay stood uncut in the fields because there was no transportation to market. The company's activity consisted almost wholly of issuing letters denying that the railway was to be a subsidiary either of the Northern Pacific or of the Canadian Pacific—to no avail, for the rumors that the Spokane Falls and Northern was tied to a transcontinental route never died. And so, when Dan Corbin sold his Coeur d'Alene Railway and Navigation Company, appearing to free himself from any immediate obligation, Monaghan, Newbery, King, Moore, and the others could hardly reach him fast enough to ask Corbin to take their railway in hand. Corbin arrived in Spokane Falls on October 18, 1888, to investigate Monaghan's railroad plan, doubtless recording pertinent observations in a vest-pocket notebook, as was his custom, and after a few days, went to New York without committing himself. As president of the Spokane Falls and Northern, Newbery entreated Corbin by letter.

Newbery could not truthfully aver that the country through which the railway would run to the Columbia offered an immediate, sizeable commerce. This part of northeastern Washington was known, geographically, as the Okanogan Highlands, much of it covered with forests of fir, tamarack, pine, larch, and cedar, with even its scattered, fertile valleys timbered heavily enough to retard agricultural development. Sections near the line between Stevens and Spokane counties had been logged off and few trees grew in the gravelled river banks, so that a prospective railway might follow streams through hilly country. The one established farming district was the Colville Valley, supporting a line of settlements for twenty-eight miles on loamy bottomland left by glaciers, and relatively treeless. Nearly all the valley's residents raised hay, oats, wheat, potatoes, and other truck, as well as cattle, sheep, and pigs. Cattle from the valley would infrequently be driven to Montana over the decayed Mullan Road but losses in animals generally were high on such trips. Some settlers were former employees of the Hudson's Bay Company, or their sons and daughters, who turned to farming when the company withdrew; most others had come prospecting for mineral and stayed to farm.

Colville, itself, was simply an unincorporated country town, a handful of frame buildings and houses along rutted dirt streets. The Silver Crown, "a bar that had a hotel," had erected a balcony over Main Street so its patrons who had removed their boots might walk out to observe clamors without muddying their feet. The area was regarded as a promising mineral region, and prospectors crossed it constantly. The first discovery had been a lead and silver claim at Embry Camp in 1883, two miles east of Chewelah, and the most important, the Old Dominion mine, staked near Colville in 1885 by E. E. Alexander, William Kearney, and A. E. Benoist. As a result, a maladroit smelter, the Mutual Smelting and Mining Company, had been assembled on a granite bluff behind the town in 1887 by Major B. P. Moore, who knew little about smelting but liked the looks of the district. The plant had cost $25,000, coke had to be hauled by wagon from Spokane Falls, there were no fluxes nearby, and ore was hard to obtain, but forty or fifty men worked in the smelter whenever ore could be bought.[4]

There had been a Fort Colville once, a pinpoint of civilization in the western wilderness, and another hamlet named Colville, but all that remained of them in 1888 was a few piles of mortar. The citizens of old Colville had scavenged most of the brick and iron from the fort to build their own town, then abandoned the ground when its title seemed disputable, and carted off the materials to build another Colville. The territorial legislature designated Colville the seat of Stevens County in 1883 but its jail and records remained at Pinckney City because there was no legal plat of a place called Colville on file. After the plat had been recorded, the county government moved, but in March, 1888, it had still been conducting its business from various private homes. By the end of the year, however, the government had leased a building to be used as a courthouse. James R. MacDonald, president of the Seattle, Lake Shore and Eastern, dismissed the area with the remark that a railway had no hope "for years, at least, of realizing any direct benefit from local traffic between Spokane Falls and Colville." [5]

The practiced eye of Daniel Corbin saw the region north of Spokane Falls with optimism as "a vast, undeveloped country. Its possibilities lie in the future, not the least of these possibilities being the connection with the navigable waters of the Columbia." [6]

Obviously a railway and steamer connection from Spokane Falls to Revelstoke would open Spokane Falls to the traffic of the Canadian Pacific as well as the Northern Pacific, provide a feeder between these two transcontinental routes, and perhaps enable a judicious shipper to take advantage of lower rates. Until 1888, the Canadian Pacific had been prohibited by charter from building southward from its main line. Moreover, Corbin's good sense told him that transportation could develop northeastern Washington as it had southeastern, where Walla Walla and Palouse farms prospered, and that a railroad could create a market for the flour, lumber, hardware, and other goods manufactured or distributed from Spokane Falls. Enough was known of Stevens County to recognize that its timber, marble, granite, clays, and water power offered profitable opportunity beyond its farms and mines. Of seven mining districts tributary to Spokane Falls, a railway north would approach four: the Kootenay in southeastern British Columbia, the Metaline, the Colville, and the Okanogan.[7] Corbin frequently grubstaked prospectors so he would have friends in new country.

D. C. Corbin was not alone in his favorable estimate: citizens of Goldendale, Washington, were organizing a $10,000,000 railroad to intercept the Northern Pacific near Pasco and continue north to Colville, and actually were to incorporate as the Klickitat and Colville in March, 1889, but their line was not to be built. The Northern Pacific studied a proposed branch to Bonners Ferry in northern Idaho where it could connect with steamers running down the Kootenai River into Kootenay Lake, and thence to the British Columbia mining camps. The Canadian Pacific proposed to reach these camps by steamers south from Revelstoke on Arrow Lakes and the

Columbia River, connecting with Kootenay Lake via a twenty-eight mile railway. Geographically the Kootenay lay tributary to Spokane Falls and a brisk trade had grown up between the two, secured, as well, by the fact that most of the prospectors in southeastern British Columbia were Americans. Spokane Falls wanted to concenter the commerce of all the tributary mining districts, as the *Review* advocated:

> Already Portland capitalists and papers are talking about a smelter at that city and Tacoma is actually erecting one. We must see to it that nothing is left undone to control the entire Coeur d'Alene business and center it here. If such a thing is possible, we must smelt the ores of the Coeur d'Alenes at Spokane Falls....
>
> The country north of our city is not less important to us than the Coeur d'Alene country.... The Spokane and Northern [*sic*] must be built at once. It is not too much to say that when built, it establishes our career as a great and prosperous city, beyond the possibility of successful rivalry.[8]

After three months in New York, Corbin returned to investigate the railway route in person, and one must conclude that his time in the East had been spent promoting the scheme among men who might invest in it. In February, 1889, Corbin, Arthur Newbery, and Jim Monaghan sleighed a two-hundred mile course through Stevens County, ostensibly "looking over some mines." Two days after their return, Corbin announced that he had examined the proposed route and that he would build the railroad, if the citizens of Spokane Falls contributed $100,000 toward it. The *Review* applauded:

> His proposition to build the road if the citizens of Spokane Falls will guarantee subscriptions to the stock to the amount of $100,000 is regarded as fair and liberal, and there can be no doubt that it will be promptly accepted.[9]

The Spokane Falls and Northern would be independent, the *Review* quoted the railway's officers as insisting again, with "an attitude of friendly independence in relations with all lines leading out of the city."

By the time the general populace learned of Corbin's terms, the Board of Trade had met in answer to Taylor's circular headed "Urgent and Important," and had endorsed the proposition. Taylor had reviewed the company's trials for Board members, recalling that he and Cyrus Burns had gone East the previous summer to solicit funds, and had procured a freight arrangement, but no money, from the Canadian Pacific. Other railroads, including the Northern Pacific, had offered financial assistance but Taylor and Burns had turned them down to preserve the company's independence. Now the officers of the Spokane Falls and Northern agreed that "Mr. Corbin was the man for their work." Taylor had explained Corbin's overture: the company must permit him complete charge, and Spokane Falls must subscribe $100,000 to the railroad's stock, half to be paid when the tracks passed Chewelah, a fourth additional on reaching Colville, and the final fourth when the line was completed to the navigable waters of the Columbia River. For his part, Corbin pledged to build as far as Colville by the end of the year, 1889.

After several speeches favoring Corbin's plan, Fred Furth had moved that a committee of seven draw a contract with Corbin and raise the $100,000, and his motion had passed by acclamation. Furth, himself, was appointed chairman of the seven. The others were Brickell, Frank Moore, Burns, Mason Smith, D. B. Fotheringham, and Herbert Bolster. They had discussed a detailed agreement with Corbin that same evening.

A full account of the Board of Trade meeting appeared in the *Spokane Falls Review* the following morning, February 9, 1889, the first public announcement of Corbin's union with the Spokane Falls and Northern. The issue sold out, and citizens who came to the newspaper office seeking copies had to be turned away. The *Review* waxed effusive, devoting sixteen editorial paragraphs, separated by asterisks, to exalting the railway:

The construction of the Spokane and Northern Railroad will cheapen fuel in the city 25 to 50 per cent.

* * *

A smelter in Spokane Falls will be one of the immediate results
of the construction of the Spokane and Northern Railroad.

* * *

New flouring mills will be required in Spokane Falls to supply
the rapidly developing country north of this city upon the completion
of the Spokane and Northern Railroad.

* * *

The Spokane and Northern railway company will disburse three
million dollars in this city during the next twelve months if the
people promptly subscribe the required $100,000.

In a report of an interview at his rooms in the Grand Hotel,
Corbin repeated that he was "here without any alliance and no
interested associates save my own friends in New York," and that
none of them had interests in other railroads. He pointed out that
his friends would have invested a million dollars in the railroad
before it reached Chewelah, when the first half of Spokane Falls'
subsidy would fall due, and emphasized that without the $100,000
from Spokane Falls, he would abandon the project and "Spokane
may wait years for its railroad." He promised that the new railroad
would favor Spokane Falls bidders for contracts whenever practical.

At three o'clock on the afternoon of February 11, the subscription committee started work, and raised $40,000 the first day. But
in the next two days, the members produced little more, and talked
behind closed doors of giving up, while Corbin declared he would
leave Spokane Falls "in a day or so, should the committee meet with
no better success than they have met with so far." [10] By the fourth
day the contributions totaled $60,000 and the *Review* called it "an-
other day of doubt and uncertainty." The solicitors met several times
each day to compare results, finding many who had been expected
to take good shares of stock had refused them or purchased only
token allotments. All the city's affluent men had been canvassed, so
the committee visited scores of smaller prospective buyers, turning
up only two contributions greater than $500 on the fifth day, and
finding "the city has been pretty thoroughly overhauled." The committee urged Corbin to stay just two more days, and he agreed. At
the end of the sixth day, Arthur Newbery happily disclosed that the

$100,000 had been pledged, although Corbin, himself, had authorized one contribution that stipulated that the railway must be operating to the Little Spokane by June 20.

The *Review* published a list of subscribers totaling 224 individuals and companies, showing that eighty-four put in $100 each, forty-two promised $200, and the other ninety-eight, varying larger amounts. Glover, Frank Moore, Browne, and Brickell's Spokane Falls Milling Company subscribed $5,000 apiece; Monaghan and King, and Taylor and Jefferson, $2,000 per man; Burns and his contracting partner, John W. Chapman, $3,500 together; A. A. Newbery and Company, $1,500; and one other, $1,500. These larger amounts totaled $34,500, probably accounting for most of the $40,000 raised the first day. As a matter of fact, the $100,000 subscription was a small part of the estimated cost of the railroad, but promoters commonly called on towns along the route of a new line to buy stock to assure their jealous interest in its success.

The Spokane Falls and Northern Railway Company concluded a formal contract with Corbin dated February 16, 1889, which required him to construct, equip, and furnish the rolling stock for a standard-gauge railroad to the Columbia, and bound the company to pay him $40,000 for each mile of completed road in equal shares of capital stock and first mortgage bonds. Now, Newbery declared, "We intend to put a corps of engineers on the line of the proposed route next week, and as soon as they make their reports, a [construction] contract will be let."

Corbin turned promptly to James M. Buckley, who had resigned from the Northern Pacific a month previously, and who joined the Spokane Falls and Northern as superintendent of construction. From Buckley, Corbin received a list of engineers to consider for chief of the new railroad. Back in Spokane Falls, he was besieged by newspaper reporters, to whom he dismissed the route inside the city as a "detail," although two days after this interview, engineers were surveying east of Spokane Falls, and on March sixth the city council passed an ordinance establishing a right of way on Pearl, Mallon, and Joset [Cataldo] streets. Perhaps it was a hopeful omen of maturity that Washington became a state on February 22. Late in the month,

Corbin inserted an advertisement that ran for several days in the
Review:

> Notice is hereby given to all parties intending to bid for the
> construction work on the first eighty miles of the road—clearing,
> grubbing, grading, timber structures, and ties—that specifications
> with forms of proposals and contract will be furnished upon applica-
> tion to either A. A. Newbery, vice president, or myself. Bids will be
> received on Saturday evening, March 2, and successful bidders must
> be prepared to enter into contract and furnish bonds, if required, on
> March 4.[11]

The construction work advertised would take the railway to
Colville, and thus D. C. Corbin, in two weeks, had set in motion
the Spokane Falls and Northern. Jim Monaghan had not been able
to do that in four years of striving, and his company of April, 1888,
had not made so much progress in nine months. The call for bids
was, incidentally, the first public mention that Newbery was no
longer president, but now vice president, of the company.

On March fourth, when Corbin opened the tenders in Newbery's offices, he was good to his word that Spokane Falls contractors
would be favored, observing, "I made no effort to secure outside
bids." The contract for grading, clearing, and grubbing was awarded
to Burns and Chapman, and for ties and timbers to Monaghan and
King.

Not only was Burns and Chapman a local company, but it was
well qualified, for the men had been partners in construction since
1882, and had built sections of the Oregon Short Line in Idaho, the
Oregon Railway and Navigation Company, the Seattle, Lake Shore
and Eastern, and the renowned Cascade switchback, supervised by
James Buckley, for the Northern Pacific which had used it to cross
the mountains for a year preceding July, 1888.

Although he had organized his engineering staff by the time
he opened the bids, nobody knew it until Corbin remarked, in an
offhand manner, that he had hired a chief engineer, a slim, spunky
man named Edward J. Roberts, whose dedication matched that of
Corbin himself. Roberts had visited Spokane Falls in the summer of

1888, working under Paul Mohr in charge of surveying crews of the Seattle, Lake Shore and Eastern west from Cheney. He had begun railroading as an axman for the Chicago, St. Paul, Minneapolis and Omaha in 1881 after his graduation from Ripon College, and the next year, hired as a leveler for the Northern Pacific under Buckley, had been promoted to assistant engineer. Next Roberts had joined the Canadian Pacific, participating in locating and constructing the arduous link through the mountains of British Columbia, and watching on November 7, 1885, when the last spike had been driven at Craigellachie in Eagle Pass. Early in 1888, Roberts had been chief engineer for construction of Jim Hill's St. Paul, Minneapolis and Manitoba Railway from Minot, Dakota Territory, to Great Falls, Montana Territory, and under his energetic direction, the crews laid an average of three and a quarter miles of track each day, hammering down 643 continuous miles in seven and a half months, a speed record unequaled at the time for men working from one end of a line.

Roberts was widely recognized as a comer, therefore, when he received a telegram from a man he had never met, D. C. Corbin, containing one sentence: "Will you be chief engineer of a railroad north of Spokane?" Roberts was visiting his family in St. Paul at the time; he was thirty-one years old, temporarily unemployed, and he returned West to see what Corbin's telegram was all about. A man of Welsh descent, Roberts radiated a sturdy confidence in himself and he was hired, little realizing that he had signed on for life with D. C. Corbin.

CHAPTER SIX

CONSTRUCTION TO COLVILLE

WHILE CONSTRUCTION OF THE SPOKANE FALLS AND NORTHERN was to pour payroll money into Spokane Falls, the financial control of the railroad, once Daniel Corbin assumed its management, rested in New York City where it remained for ten years. Except for the stock subscriptions by Spokane Falls residents, some of them later defaulted, the railroad was financed by Corbin's friends in New York or its stock was sold to buyers who would not threaten its independence. Corbin's contract with the railroad company provided that he be paid $40,000 in stocks and bonds for each mile, so that when he had completed the eighty miles to Colville he would have received $3,200,000 in securities. It is hardly necessary to observe that Corbin expected to build the line for a good deal less than three million dollars, so that if the securities could be sold for their par value, he and the other shareholders could expect a generous profit.

On the probability of gain, a subsidy had been quickly arranged, and the men who were to pay for the road, or sell its paper, displaced Spokane Falls men as the company's officers. With one exception, they earlier had put money into the Coeur d'Alene Railway and Navigation Company, and were associated in some way with Austin Corbin.

D. C. Corbin's disclosure in his advertisement for bids that Arthur Newbery no longer was president of the railroad marked this change in the company's command. It also demonstrated the man's method, for Corbin kept his affairs to himself. Newbery, Monaghan, and the other animated Spokane Falls businessmen liked to talk about themselves; Newbery and Monaghan, said E. J. Roberts, "supplied the talk, and Corbin supplied the money" for the Spokane Falls and Northern.

The new president of the company was Horace K. Thurber, a respected New York wholesale grocer, who was also vice president of the Texas and Pacific Coal Company and a substantial investor in Latin American steamship lines and Idaho ranch land. Thurber was the exception; he does not appear to have been close to Daniel or Austin Corbin before joining the Spokane Falls and Northern. His association with Austin would have been noteworthy, had it existed; and doubtless such a relationship would have provoked comment in newspapers of the time, for Austin was by now widely known in the East, not only as operator of the Manhattan Beach Railway but as the head of his own Corbin Bank which dealt in farm loans, and as reorganizer of the Philadelphia and Reading Railroad, at the time in receivership. Austin had also gained notoriety for advocating underground railways for New York City, as owner of a fabulous private game preserve and zoological garden in Sullivan County, New Hampshire, and late in 1890 was to achieve his cherished control of the Long Island Railway.

Thurber probably was selected deliberately by the other men simply because he was, until then, an outsider with interests in western lands and an honorable reputation. These others, who subsidized the Spokane Falls and Northern, as they had the Coeur d'Alene Railway and Navigation Company, were intimates of Daniel Corbin, so that he was not to them merely Austin's younger brother who had popped into New York from the far west.

One was James K. Ogden Sherwood, Dan's erstwhile partner in Helena, who most probably met Austin through Daniel, and now served as a director of the Long Island and several Austin Corbin railroads. Another was Alfred C. Chapin who maintained his legal offices in Austin Corbin's bank building, 192 Broadway. Daniel Corbin also kept his New York offices there, listing himself in the *New York City Directory* in 1889–90 as a banker and in 1890–91 as a real estate broker. The third, Chester W. Chapin, managed piers in partnership with Alfred and rented his office space in the same building as Austin Corbin, One Broadway. In 1885 Sherwood and the two Chapins had organized the Land and Security Investment Company as a Connecticut corporation to deal in real estate and securities, and in 1890 they formed The Securities Corporation under Connecticut laws. Both firms were managed from New York offices in the Corbin bank building.[1] Financial control of the Spokane Falls and Northern reposed in these offices at 192 Broadway as long as D. C. Corbin managed the railroad.

Both Chapins came from families whose backgrounds lay in transportation. Chester's father had served as president of the Boston and Albany Railroad after establishing his fortune as a stagecoach proprietor and mail carrier in Massachusetts. The son, in addition to his interests in D. C. Corbin's railways, managed two East River piers, was president of the New York and New Haven Steamship Company, and had been an organizer of the Central New England Railway.

Chester's cousin, Alfred Clark Chapin, was a son of the superintendent of the Cheshire Railway of New Hampshire. Alfred had been successful in politics, serving in the New York State Assembly and in Congress, as well as winning election as Mayor of Brooklyn and appointment as New York State Railroad Commissioner.

Thurber became president of the Spokane Falls and Northern in February, 1889, when the originators of the company turned it over to Corbin. Newbery was vice president; Alfred Chapin, then mayor of Brooklyn, secretary-treasurer; Chester Chapin and Sherwood, directors; Corbin's son, Austin Corbin II, assistant treasurer and purchasing agent; and Daniel, himself, general manager. Corbin also brought Harry J. Skinner to Spokane Falls from Brooklyn as supervisor of bridges and structures and hired O. D. Mott from the Manhattan Beach company to perform the duties, if not hold the title, of purchasing agent.[2]

Thurber's role in promoting the Spokane Falls and Northern required him to peddle roughly one and one-half million dollars worth of stock in a railroad that not one New Yorker in a thousand

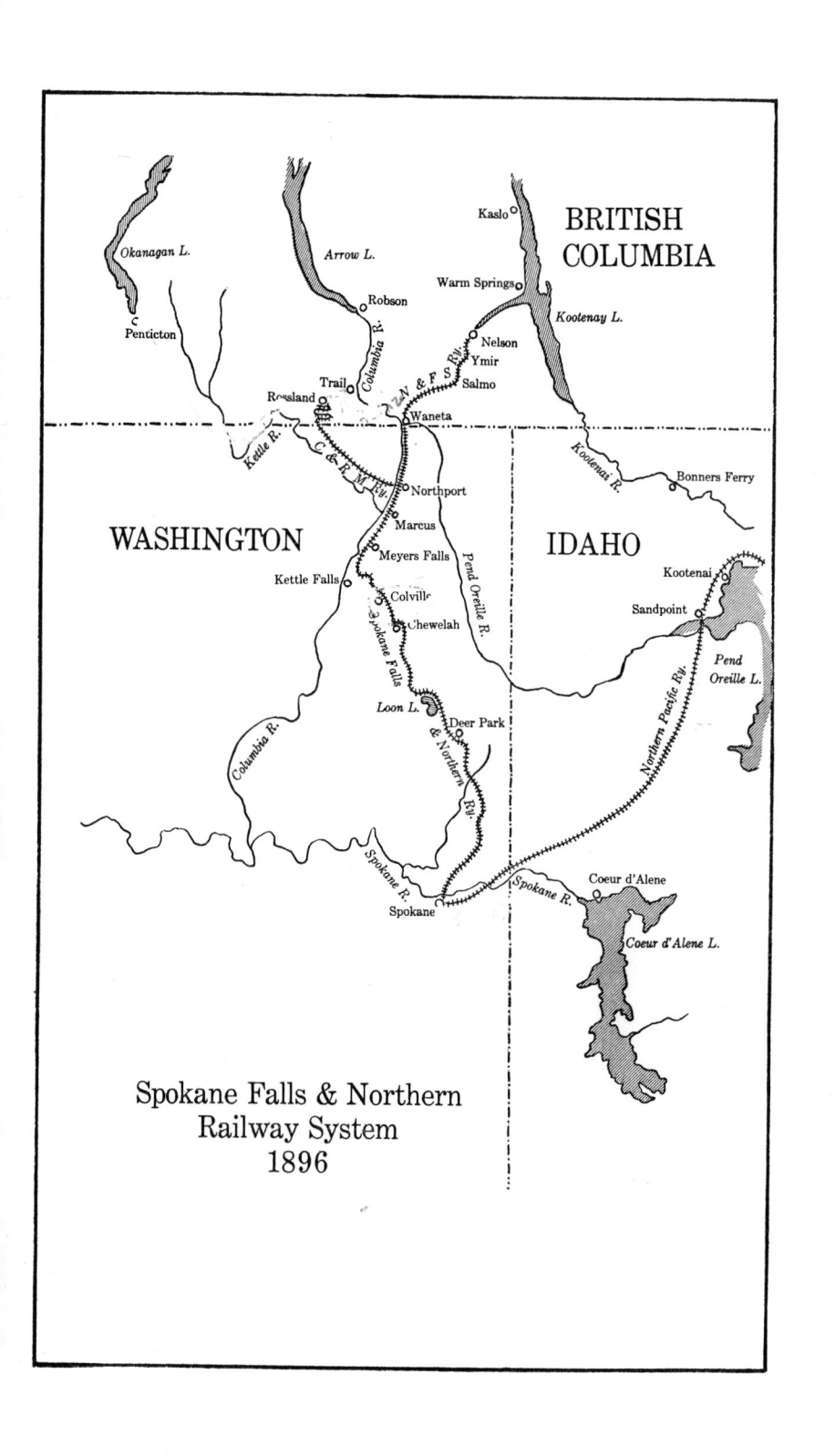

Okanagan L.

Arrow L.

Kaslo

BRITISH
COLUMBIA

Warm Springs

Robson

Kootenay L.

Penticton

Nelson

Ymir

Trail

Salmo

Rossland

Waneta

Northport

Bonners Ferry

Marcus

WASHINGTON

Meyers Falls

IDAHO

Kettle Falls

Colville

Kootenai

Chewelah

Sandpoint

Pend
Oreille L.

Loon L.

Deer Park

Columbia R.

Coeur d'Alene

Spokane R.

Spokane

Coeur d'Alene L.

Spokane Falls & Northern
Railway System
1896

could have discovered on a map. He apparently sold the stock easily, for there were many investors willing to put their money into ventures patronized by prominent men. According to the *New York Herald,* Thurber and the other directors invested a million dollars themselves, as the newspaper explained:

> The development of the northwestern corner of the country is being rapidly brought about by railroad extensions. The Northern Pacific and its auxiliary lines have gone into various portions of that section, and now another line is to be constructed that will connect directly with the Northern Pacific, and by means of water communication with the Canadian Pacific, although it is absolutely independent of either of these two transcontinental lines. D. C. Corbin, Austin Corbin's brother, has taken hold of the proposed road, which is known as the Spokane Falls & Northern, and has interested a number of New Yorkers in it....
>
> Alfred C. Chapin, mayor of Brooklyn, is treasurer of the company, and with Chester W. Chapin, Horace K. Thurber, J. K. O. Sherwood and two or three others, has subscribed $1,000,000 of the bonds of the company. According to Mr. Corbin's estimates, $2,500,000 will be needed to construct this road. It is expected that $500,000 more will be subscribed at once by those parties whose interest has been aroused by the bright prospects of that part of the northwest section through which the road will run. This will leave only $1,000,000 of the bonds to be taken by general subscription. The subscription paper will be in charge of Mr. Thurber.[3]

While Thurber sold the railroad's paper, Corbin set about building the Spokane Falls and Northern, opening temporary offices in the Eagle Block, and leasing permanent space in the new Washington building being erected by John D. Sherwood, although it was to burn before completion. More important was the new survey: under Buckley and Roberts, crews entered the field by March ninth to locate the route of the railway, running a line east of the right of way approved by the General Land Office for the company in 1888.[4] From an elevation of 1,900 feet above sea level at Spokane Falls, where one surveying party ran a course four and one-half blocks from the river to the city limits, the railway would climb to 2,432 feet at Summit, a station near Loon Lake, and then descend through a country of trees, hills, and scabland to Colville at 1,590 feet. The one major barrier to the Columbia would be the Huckleberry Mountains, between Colville and the river, but except for passage through the mountains, the rail would be all downhill from Colville to the Columbia. As mapped, the railroad would run 88.1 miles from Spokane Falls to Colville. Roberts believed that tracklaying could begin about the middle of March.

The country between Spokane Falls and the Columbia buzzed with anticipation, the forests teeming with home hunters, eager to homestead a little land and sell it at an inflated price. When James Monaghan tramped through the Colville Valley cajoling free right of way from his former neighbors, bands of enthusiastic citizens trooped with him, badgering their friends to give the railway access, and the *Stevens County Miner* joined in urging farmers to cooperate with the railroad. This was a money-saving junket because, under Washington's law, the railroad had the power to condemn when its whole capital stock had been subscribed. Monaghan, at Corbin's bidding, told Colville residents that the Spokane Falls and Northern expected them to furnish the right of way without charge and to donate forty acres to the railroad, setting an example by handing over a parcel of land from his own holdings near the town. The *Colville Miner* styled Monaghan's demand "the most reasonable of any we ever knew a railroad to make to any town," perhaps revealing unintentionally the town's general relief that the railway wanted only land, for land abounded.

In six days, a three-man committee—Gilbert B. Ide, John Rickey, and John H. Young—collected all but $145 of the $2,000 they needed to buy the forty acres the railroad had chosen from a Colville pioneer, John U. Hofstetter, and shortly after, the entire amount subscribed, the land was taken. Surveying the forty acres accurately proved perplexing, however, because Louther W. Meyers, who in 1883 had owned much of the area that later became Colville, had reserved a buffer strip all around the perimeter of his property so that if later surveys showed his plat in error, he would have enough extra land to adjust any difficulty. There was nothing to do but honor Meyers' bulge, and it continued to confound surveyors until well after 1900.

The railway bought additional property from Samuel Hanauer for $5,000 for station grounds. The *Miner* printed a letter asserting that Corbin's contract required him to grade to Colville by September first, and lay the track soon after.

The once quiet countryside stirred: an Indian interpreter, Robert Flett, reported that Chewelah lots worth ten to fifteen dollars in January had risen to fifty dollars in March because the railroad was coming. James Buckley purchased eighty acres northeast of Colville's limits to lay out as town lots, sold one-fifth of his enterprise to E. J. Roberts, and put $5,000 into lots in Meyers' Addition to Colville. Advertisements in the Spokane Falls newspapers clarioned Colville's awakening, one claiming that the Spokane Addition, between the town and the railway depot site, commanded $300 for a lot, and in the center of the town, commercial lots brought $500 to $2,500, prices that compared with those paid for Spokane Falls property. Another advertisement whooped that Colville was growing twenty per cent each month and now held eight hundred residents. So rapidly was it sprouting that Colville established the Stevens County Immigration Bureau, with offices in Victor Dessert's three-story Pacific Hotel in Spokane Falls, to reply to questions about the area and direct settlers headed there. In Colville, itself, a $30,000 hotel was rising; the school board authorized construction of a new building. The town's one sawmill had been mortgaged to Jim Monaghan some time before but now it was so busy that "people can't build a hen house for want of material." [5]

Within eighteen days after Corbin had opened the construction bids in Newbery's office, Buckley announced that the railroad line "was practically located from the city to Little Spokane with but one per cent grade," a distance of seventeen miles. Then locating stalled while the engineers sought a useable crossing of the Little Spokane River, trying first near Dart's mill, then at Peavine Charlie's where the old Cottonwood stage had forded, and finally concluded to build a bridge fifteen miles upstream from the confluence of the Spokane and Little Spokane rivers. By mid-April, the *Stevens County Miner* reported twenty-five grading outfits at work on the railway, some as near as thirty-five miles from Colville.

With construction thus begun, Corbin prepared to go to New York to purchase rails, four locomotives, and passenger and freight cars. But first he studied a report prepared by Roberts and Buckley which described commercial opportunities in the new region, and he instructed Roberts on his wishes. Corbin was emphatic, Roberts recalled later, in wanting the Spokane Falls and Northern built as inexpensively as possible because the country would have to be settled before it produced revenue, and therefore, he observed, there would be no need to run the trains fast so the engineer could curve the tracks to avoid costly construction. He wanted Roberts to build around even big trees, rather than spending the money to cut them, blast out the stumps, and fill the holes, and Roberts guessed that he saved $1,000 a mile by simply going around the largest trees, those three feet in diameter or more. According to Roberts, their conversation ended with his own remark to Corbin: "I'll build it cheap, and you run it cheap!"

Roberts, who was paid $300 a month, adhered to Corbin's directions carefully, as his accounts would prove. The final route of the Spokane Falls and Northern generally followed the old Colville military trail that had meandered northward through eastern Washington; it was serpentine at best, as the *Stevens County Miner* had complained of the proposed paths, and once the tracks were down, the men who ran the trains nicknamed their railway, "The Snake." As a result of changing the line to avoid costly natural obstacles, the Spokane Falls and Northern deviated slightly from its approved survey, so that a later land office inquiry showed that "in some places the line as constructed does not appear to be on the exact line located.... However, the line as constructed, as near as we can say, falls substantially on the location shown in ... maps." [6]

Corbin, himself, offered one further explanation for the comparatively low construction cost of the Spokane Falls and Northern, remarking in a newspaper interview, "I believe in pushing an enterprise of this kind. It works things up to a high pressure and is, in the end, the cheapest." On this, he and Roberts agreed wholeheartedly. Both men set a brisk pace, were impatient with delays of any kind, and seemed tireless.

Roberts, using crews directed by six assistant engineers, rushed construction of the railway, and John R. Reavis, secretary of the Board of Trade, described the work for the *Spokane Falls Review:*

> Following the surveyors, who locate the line, there is a small army of woodchoppers who cut the space for the road through the forest. Then come the graders who are stationed at various points and who gradually fill up the vacant spaces between them. Most of the work is on an easy grade....
>
> Then come the tie-cutters who are working all along the line getting out and piling up the ties ready to be put down when track-laying begins. Sawmills are also busy at various points cutting timbers for bridges.... The white tents grouped along at various camping places reminds me of an army in the field. Indeed it is an army, for there are about 1,000 men employed in the grading alone.[7]

By modern standards, the tools that built the Spokane Falls and Northern were primitive: horse-drawn plows, handscrapers which resembled large garden hoes, wheelbarrows, shovels, and boards, all used in grading, and space bars and sledge hammers added to this small selection for tracklaying. The surveyors were equipped with such instruments as transits, levels, an aneroid barometer for judging heights, a clinometer to measure slopes and angles, a pocket compass, a steel tape, and one-hundred-foot chains. In 1890 a track-laying machine was to be tested, and Roberts was to decide that hand labor was faster and set the machine aside in favor of horses and hands.

Corbin had returned from New York by the middle of April and within five weeks the first shipment of rails reached Spokane Falls via the Northern Pacific. Locomotives numbered 310 and 311 for the SF&N had rolled into Spokane Falls on May 23, pulled tandem over the NP from the Baldwin Locomotive Works in Pennsylvania where they were manufactured, and had been sidetracked in the Northern Pacific freight yard. Spokane Falls citizens flocked to inspect the engines, painted olive green, on which the name of the railway had been misspelled "Spokehane" so that the lettering had to be repainted before the locomotives were put into service. Quite a number of hoboes had nested in the tank of one engine which had to be cleaned of discarded boards and clothing. The two locomotives were wood-burning moguls, the most popular heavy-duty design of its day, with iron boilers capable of 130 pounds of working steam pressure to drive pistons which were cast-iron rings sprung into solid heads. Each locomotive weighed 90,090 pounds, and had a wheelbase of twenty-two feet, eight inches, with the wheels arranged to provide six driving wheels and a front truck. Although the frontier had marveled at the fabled "iron horse," much of the cab was actually constructed from ash lumber; the bumpers, from oak; and the tender framed in oak.[8]

With rails at hand and equipment arriving, Corbin determined to commence tracklaying northward from Spokane Falls, hoping to begin quietly on the afternoon of May 30, 1889, with only a few officers of the railway present. The nosey citizens got wind of the furtive ceremony, however, perhaps when a number of cars were loaded with rails, and approximately two hundred persons watched as an annoyed Daniel Corbin hammered home the first spike.

Once started, tracklaying went fast under Roberts' urging. Within ten days the track glistened to Dragoon Creek, twenty-one miles north of Spokane Falls, and by August fourth, extended to the north shores of Loon Lake, forty miles from the city. As the track was spiked down, a construction train ran over it and would pick up freight for delivery along the line. When the *Review* reported that four new Troy passenger cars had arrived for the railroad, it also announced that the line would terminate at a union depot on the north side of the river to be shared by the Seattle, Lake Shore and Eastern—now familiarly the "Seattle and Elsewhere," the Oregon Railway and Navigation Company, and the Spokane Falls and Northern. The red brick depot, built by the SF&N, was two stories high and stood on the river bank on the east side of Division Street.[9] The site was covered with rocky hillocks, and crews working day and night shifts shook the city awake at two o'clock each morning blasting to level the area. The rock debris was dumped into ponds and used to extend the property toward the river by filling, an operation that cost approximately $100,000.

August 4, 1889, was to be an historic day for Spokane Falls.

The Spokane Falls and Northern was ribboning northward from Loon Lake, men and horses toiled within shouting distance of Colville on the last section of grading, businessmen often hitched rides on the dusty construction trains rather than waiting for the slow stagecoach. Sunday, August fourth, was a hot, motionless day when the countryside seemed a giant tableau. Smoke from fires in northern Idaho's forests had drifted over the city and hung a gray canopy before the sun. In a row of frame buildings near Railroad Avenue and Post Street, opposite the Northern Pacific depot, an orphan wisp of smoke rose straight up. A handful of idlers spotted the little fire, anticipating the moment when the volunteer fire fighters would come clanging through the streets. The firemen arrived on the run, hitched their hoses to hydrants—and nothing happened. No water came. The picture scene was suddenly shattered with shouting and running, men spinning hydrant handles while others dumbly held empty nozzles. The fire grew insolently, its finger of smoke broadening. The great Spokane Falls fire had begun. When Monday dawned thirty-two city blocks lay scorched.

Early in the spread of the fire, Corbin was warned at the Grand Hotel, so he hurried to the five rooms in the Eagle Block that served as temporary offices for the Spokane Falls and Northern, Roberts at his heels. Each man scooped up what he considered most valuable, Corbin dumping vouchers, ledgers, contracts, and other papers into boxes and dragging them into the street, and Roberts collecting his field notes, maps, and construction data. These were hauled by wagon across the river. Buckley arrived in time to see the office furniture kindle.

New company offices were established in two combination cars near the union depot site. Corbin expected the structure to be completed by the end of the year, when he could move his offices into it, on the upper story of the building that was to serve as depot, roundhouse, machine shop, and freight warehouse.

When news of the city's fire reached them, many workmen left the railway camps to rush to Spokane Falls but as the burned city pitched tents and took up normal commerce, railroad construction also regained its pace. In the nineteen days that followed the fire, the Northern Pacific delivered fifty-six carloads of rail and iron for the Spokane Falls and Northern, and Roberts' tracklayers spiked it down at the rate of 6,000 to 8,000 feet a day.

By August 21, grading had been finished to Colville and tracks reached Squire's Ranch, forty-eight miles north of Spokane Falls. C. O. Squire had homesteaded the area when it was known as Walker's Prairie, platting a town he called Squire's City, but the railroad called its station Springdale instead of Squire's and the post office took the railroad's name. Now trains ran daily schedules between Spokane Falls and Loon Lake, leaving Spokane Falls at 4:30 P.M. and returning the next morning. On September 2, the Colville stage began accepting freight and passengers from the railroad at Springdale, where the tracks crossed the wagon road. The tracks were laid, by then, nine miles farther north. The Spokane Falls and Northern published its first timetable on Sunday, September 1, 1889, and the event was memorialized by a praiseful editorial in the *Review*.

SPOKANE FALLS & NORTHERN RAILWAY

Time Table

To Take Effect Monday, September 2, '89

Leaves		*Arrives*
7:05 A.M.	Spokane Falls	5:50 P.M.
7:50	Peone	5:05
8:45	Crescent	4:15
9:05	Buckeye	3:50
9:25	Deer Park	3:30
10:00	Summit	2:55
10:25	Loon Lake	2:30
11:05	Springdale	1:55

The names on the timetable listed stations, not towns, for there were communities only at Spokane Falls and Deer Park. Towns did root at points along the railway line, such as Springdale, and Valley and Northport, established by Corbin as the Spokane Falls and Northern pushed northward, but these came later. The timetable indicates that the trains traveled approximately sixteen miles an hour with ten-minute stops at each station.

As the railway advanced, the countryside bustled with increased activity, and to assure its continuation, Corbin hired Randall H. Kemp, a one-eyed geologist who frequently contributed to the newspapers, to "write up the mines for the mining and news journals," and to remind the public frequently of the attractions of the Colville district. Kemp's articles were uniformly appreciative, duly recording the expansion of the railroad's country. In one article, Kemp noted that a number of sawmills had sprung up between Spokane Falls and Loon Lake and "pine timber is being shipped by daily trainloads into Spokane." He wrote:

> Colville . . . deserves more than a passing notice. The Indian and halfbreed method of doing business has become a thing of the past. New blood is being infused. . . . It is expected a few of the principal streets will be graded this fall. A two-story brick bank and a brick school house is in course of construction.[10]

Kemp had no need to exaggerate, for the district was fully roused. Prospectors tramped the brush, locating what seemed the most promising claims near Chewelah, and eight miles northwest of that hamlet James Buckley bought a group of free-milling silver prospects, the Finley, Silver King, May Tompkins, Mary Anderson, Granite State, and others. With E. J. Roberts and three others, Buckley organized the Columbia River Marble Company. Aaron Chandler, a promoter from Gardner, North Dakota, who exploited railway construction in western states by buying townsites and business property, began designing the Hotel Colville on six town lots purchased from John Hofstetter, modeling the structure after the admired Grand Hotel in Spokane Falls, and relocating only the entrance in his copy for Colville.

The railway gained some revenue from fashionable parties that rode the Spokane Falls and Northern to Loon Lake for outings where Corbin was developing a park. The roundtrip fare was two dollars, and the railroad ran a regular Sunday special for the sportive, leaving Spokane Falls at 8:30 in the morning and returning at six in the evening for a dollar and a half. Moreover, when the track passed Chewelah on October first, the company published a new timetable extending its service to the stations of Valley and Chewelah. Trains that left Spokane at seven in the morning arrived in Chewelah at half past noon. Breakfast in Spokane Falls and lunch sixty-five miles to the north seemed fast, indeed, to men accustomed to travel by horse, for the stagecoaches left Spokane Falls at 6:00 A.M. on Monday, Wednesday, and Friday, and reached Colville at noon the next day. The train pulled out of Chewelah at 1:30 P.M. and deposited its passengers back in Spokane Falls at 7:10 P.M.

By the first week in October, the tracks lay within twelve miles of Colville, and by the middle of the month, were only three miles away. The town was in an uproar of anticipation, and the passengers on the Colville stage pushed toward the windows to watch the construction crews at work, shooing aside chickens in the farmyards the railroad was passing through. In Colville, Main Street was graded, a new board sidewalk hammered down, the $4,500 bank and $3,800 schoolhouse rising, the only buildings of brick in the town, harbingers of prosperity that would come with the railroad. Corbin, with Buckley, Monaghan, and Newbery, hustled into Colville to see that all was prepared for the first train, and then Corbin dashed again to New York, his departure noted passingly by the newspapers which were preoccupied with the imminent completion of the Spokane Falls and Northern to Colville, and the entry into Spokane Falls of the first Union Pacific train, a special, that arrived at 2:20 P.M. on October 7, 1889, to be followed by a regular passenger train at 10:10 P.M.

Colville's great day arrived on Saturday, October 18, when the tracks were laid to the frame depot about noon, and a construction train puffed to the end of the rails. Hearing that the road was completed as far as Colville, a trainload of Spokane Falls citizens rode to Chewelah in passenger cars and then hopped a construction train to finish their journey into Colville, arriving at dusk. Colville celebrated the arrival of the Spokane Falls and Northern with a forty-two gun salute from farmers' rifles and pistols, punctuated by cries of "Let 'er go, Gallagher!" It was the popular phrase of the time.

After cheering the train's crew and the Spokane Falls visitors, the joyful populace of Colville elbowed into Meyers' Opera House to hear speeches. Jacob Stitz, who presided, maintained order enough to appoint a five-man committee to plan a later formal celebration "in a becoming manner." [11] While the celebrants were congratulating themselves, Sheriff Gilbert B. Ide walked quietly 'round to the station house to sign a contract to deliver freight from the railway to merchants of the community, and thus probably became the first tangible beneficiary of the Spokane Falls and Northern at its newest station.

E. J. Roberts' construction records indicate that the Spokane Falls and Northern laid 88.1 miles of track to reach Colville, which would mean that Corbin, at $40,000 in stock and bonds for each mile, collected $3,524,000 in securities at par of the railroad under his contract with the company. Roberts' figures also show that the total cost of the railroad to Colville had been $1,297,842, including construction, stations, rights of way, and equipment. He had followed to the letter Corbin's instructions to build economically, for the cost of preparing the roadbed, laying track, grading station grounds, and erecting buildings averaged $8,604.50 a mile. At the time, $10,000 a mile was considered cheap, and typical roads in the Pacific Northwest averaged $23,000 for each mile of standard gauge construction.

Roberts listed the cost of locomotives at $40,421; of coaches, $17,834; boxcars, $27,000; flatcars, $38,490; and right of way, $15,-000. Some indication of the relative importance of stations was evident in the cost of buildings, for the Colville freight and passenger depot cost $1,525; that at Chewelah, $1,400; Springdale, $1,200; and Crescent, $1,122, all patterned to a uniform design by Harry Skinner. The headquarters building and depot at Spokane Falls had cost $7,200, and was unique in that it did not consist simply of a long, one-story building with a wide platform beside the tracks, while the freight house attached to the depot in Spokane Falls cost $2,700, and the roundhouse and shops, $5,500. [12]

The furiously busy summer of construction suggests that Corbin and the others associated in fashioning the Spokane Falls and Northern had little time for other ventures, but during that same period, Corbin, Monaghan, and King cooperated to install a water and electrical system for Coeur d'Alene City. Monaghan, King, Buckley, and W. S. Norman organized the Spokane Savings Bank. Norman and Frank R. Moore promoted the Washington Water Power Company, listing as a reference in their prospectus one D. C. Corbin of New York City. Monaghan, King, Newbery, Moore, and B. M. Whiting projected a $100,000 rapid transit line along north Monroe Street in Spokane Falls. The contractor, Cyrus Burns, campaigned for mayor, although he was to lose in the fall election. The summer of 1889 had been a busy one, therefore, for everyone concerned with the Spokane Falls and Northern.

In retrospect, it is hard to realize the fervor of Colville's welcome for the railroad, until one reflects that every town believed that a railway would bring it prosperity, growth, stability, and, if anyone had time for it, culture flowing from the outside world. Isolation would be at an end, and the people of Colville spent a good deal of time arguing, as the railway came toward them, what kind of specimens of produce they should send to the various expositions that would be opened to them. Some of the benefits were immediate in terms of commerce: four of Spokane Falls' lumber mills began using timber from the Spokane Falls and Northern line, and three brick companies set up kilns adjacent to the right of way. Telegraph service came with the railroad, A. J. Hammond and Company secured a franchise to install an electric light and telephone system, and James Buckley took the contract to establish a $50,000 water system for Colville, all before 1889 had ended.

And yet, mere commerce and growth did not express fully the sentiments of people in a lonesome land, now suddenly linked to the vast fellowship that lay beyond their valley. For a week as the Spokane Falls and Northern approached, Colville had been reading the morning *Review* on the evening of its publication in Spokane Falls, and when the railroad arrived, a correspondent marveled, "Surely civilization is dawning upon us."

CHAPTER SEVEN

EYES ON CANADA

Daniel Corbin's contract with the Spokane Falls and Northern covered its construction only to the Columbia River, but Corbin had conceived a far more extensive rail system: he intended to penetrate British Columbia with his railway and proposed to extend it to the Pacific Coast by a route that lay substantially through southern British Columbia. The southern area of the province was promising and undeveloped, the trade organizations of Victoria and Vancouver clamorous for a connection with the interior, but few Canadians honestly wanted a railroad controlled in the United States, and Corbin encountered stern, unmitigating opposition to his plans to cross the international border.

He found support generally among Canadians who felt that, by encouraging Corbin, they would compel the Canadian Pacific to build through southern British Columbia, and among the thousands of American citizens who had invaded British Columbia pursuing their fortunes in the mines. Before he completed the Spokane Falls and Northern as far as Colville and undertook its promised extension to the river, Corbin actively sought entry into Canada. Canadian attitudes, consequently, are relevant to the activities of Daniel Corbin from this moment. The immediate effect of his Spokane Falls and Northern Railway on Spokane Falls also is salient, for Spokane Falls' expanding influence in British Columbia mines frightened many Canadians who foresaw that their wealth, and perhaps even the land itself, might slip away from them.

Both of Corbin's railways—one to Colville, and the other to the Coeur d'Alenes—had funneled profitable traffic to Spokane Falls, and after its great fire of August, 1889, the city embarked on a building spree. If all the buildings erected in the six months after the fire could have been marshalled on a single street, they would have stretched more than two miles, said the *Spokane Falls Review,* and their total value was more than five million dollars. On Riverside Avenue alone more than $2,697,000 worth of new construction rose, making Riverside, rather than Howard, the central business street. With the perfection of elevator systems, two Spokane Falls buildings, the Frankfurt and Daniels blocks, were seven stories tall, and eleven others rose six stories. Between December 1, 1888, and the same date, 1889, sales of property in Spokane Falls amounted to $18,756,323, and the valuation of the city's real estate rose 125 per cent between 1886 and 1889.

Moreover, new timber industries bloomed alongside the Spokane Falls and Northern tracks, tapping the forests of Stevens County, so that by the end of 1889 there were seven lumber manufacturers in Spokane Falls doing an aggregate yearly business of $2,230,000. From a population of seven thousand in 1887, the city grew to twenty-two thousand by June, 1889. The names of scores of new companies to exploit the mines, forests, quarries, and farms of the region tributary to Spokane Falls puffed the city directories. Colville's unwieldy smelter managed to run a few months, encouraged by cheap transportation, and fifty tons of Colville ore went daily by rail to the Tacoma smelter. Soon Spokane Falls was to organize a mining exchange, opening it July 10, 1890.

Spokane Falls' surge was not lost on its Canadian neighbors, who realized all too plainly that the long narrow valleys of the Kootenay district, where British Columbia's principal mines lay, ran north and south across the international border while high mountains and swift rivers separated their area from the rest of Canada. The Kootenay was geographically a vast triangle, two hundred miles deep, with its base on the border and its apex near the spot where the Columbia begins its sweep southward. These deep valleys and strong rivers impeded Canadian attempts to organize effective transportation east and west, while they formed a continuation of the topography that centered on Spokane Falls. The Kootenay was naturally, if not politically, tributary to Spokane Falls. British Columbia attempted to combat this natural convenience during the gold rush of the sixties by hacking the Dewdney Trail eastward across the province to compete with American trails, but it was little used and existed chiefly, observed one Canadian, as "a monument to the good intentions of the British Columbia government."

Canada's historic concern that the United States would monopolize her commerce had prompted the assistant surveyor general of British Columbia, Walter Moberly, to spend four years in the United States studying railroad projects. He "wished to ascertain the probable effect... [the Northern Pacific] railway would have in drawing Canadian trade into American channels," so that his proposed railroad might compete using branch lines.[1] The Northern Pacific had been chartered only three years when Moberly looked over its prospectus, and the country it proposed to serve teemed with Indians and buffalo. Moberly's consuming dream was of an east-west railway across British Columbia; toward this he helped build the Dewdney Trail, located some suitable mountain passages including Eagle Pass, and advocated a route utilizing the Fraser River valley.

Obviously apprehension of American railway domination was as old as transportation in Canada. For twenty years, the Dominion, by its contract with the Canadian Pacific, could not authorize a railway south of the CPR main line, and the CPR could not undertake such a route, but this contractural monopoly had expired in 1888, and from that time, the Canadian Pacific was to maintain a virtual monopoly by aggressive tactics. Daniel Corbin took into account Canada's licit capability to grant him a charter in competition with the Canadian Pacific when he contracted to build the Spokane Falls and Northern. For a few months in 1888, British Columbia seemed more friendly toward American railway enterprises, but in 1889 John Robson became the province's premier. A striking figure, always immaculately dressed, his white mustache well brushed, Robson's policy was founded on his abiding fear of annexation to the United States. No attempt was seriously made toward political annexation, but the Americans, if not their government, showed every evidence of a commercial annexation by making the trade of southern British Columbia their own. Robson bent his government to favor Canadian industry and the Canadian Pacific Railway. During his first year in office, his administration reluctantly approved subsidies to four local projects, evoking a scolding from the opposition that increased Robson's traditional caution and persuaded him to work personally toward reforming the British Columbia land and mineral statutes that permitted subsidies.

Regardless of the competitive and political hazards, Corbin discerned that he must lay track to the Kootenay district mining camps for two reasons: first, his experiences in Idaho had taught him that a route partly by rail and partly by water would neither handle a large tonnage of freight nor resist a rival who might build overland, and second, only rails offered transportation during the winter months when the rivers froze with ice too thick for steamers to crash through. Between September 7 and December 17, 1889, Corbin's surveyors, therefore, located a route to the international border, 140.6 miles from Spokane Falls.[2] Corbin also had men in the field under Roberts seeking passage in other directions, and the Spokane Falls Board of Trade suggested an expansive system in its annual report for 1889:

> Mr. Corbin has already taken steps to make extensions of his system which will ultimately end in giving Spokane Falls direct railroad communication with the Canadian Pacific, and in opening up the immense mining regions which lie to the east, north and west.[3]

Approximately forty miles east of the Spokane Falls and Northern route to the border lay the Metaline district, where low-grade lead and zinc had been discovered, although zinc was considered useless and smelters imposed a penalty for ore containing it. Roberts sent the capable young engineer John F. Stevens to survey a route to this corner of Washington. (By 1892, Stevens had helped to locate the Great Northern's route to Puget Sound and had discovered the Cascade mountain pass that bears his name.) [4] West of the Spokane Falls and Northern, in north central Washington, was the Okanogan where, in 1887, silver had been located on the Salmon River. Cyrus Burns had organized the Okanogan Mining and Railroad Company to build a railway that he proposed to connect with the Spokane Falls and Northern. Sam Hauser had an interest in the Fourth of July mine in the Okanogan, sending small shipments of ore to his East Helena smelter.

Both the Okanogan and the Metaline remained to be proved as mining camps, however, a railway to the Coast must wait for future years, and Corbin's immediate objective was the Kootenay district of southeastern British Columbia. Since this area was to occupy Corbin for ten years and was to be the scene of a bitter strug- gle between Canadian and American mining interests for mastery, its circumstances in 1889 warrant examination.

There had been a gold rush into the Kootenays in the sixties, almost wholly American, which subsided within three years but prospectors continued to poke through the region. In the fall of 1886 two brothers, Oscar and William Hall, found silver and lead deposits about four thousand feet up squat Toad Mountain, some five miles west of the arm of Kootenay Lake. The Halls started from Colville with twenty-one horses, each carrying two-hundred pounds of gear, planning a long inspection. A half-breed, Billy White, actu- ally found the first mineral. Because there was no other prospecting party near them, the Halls searched at their leisure until snow drove them out, then returned the following spring, and in July, 1887, recorded the Silver King, Kootenay Bonanza, and American Flag claims. One twenty-two ton shipment to Butte was reputed to have netted the brothers $7,000, and when a rumor spread that Silver King assays ran as high as 1,600 ounces of silver and averaged $800 a ton, prospectors raced across the border from the states over the elementary boat service and hard trails to Kootenay Lake.

The Halls erected a frame house on Toad Mountain and started digging ore, intending to pack it to Kootenay Lake, ship it by steamer up the Kootenai River to Bonners Ferry, Idaho, then by wagon to Kootenai, a flag stop on the Northern Pacific. As a result of the mining boom, and the proposal for a railway between the Columbia River and Kootenay Lake projected by George Ainsworth and Gustavus B. Wright to connect by steamers with the Canadian Pacific, the provincial gold commissioner, Gilbert Malcolm Sproat, came to the district to select a place for the metropolis of the Kootenays. He chose a camp already begun at the head of navigation twenty-two miles west of the main body of the lake on its west arm, explaining:

> I chose this site because it is close to promising mining camps. It is at the meeting of two valleys along which land traffic from the south and west will have to come. . . . My dream was that . . . could we but keep out newspapers and lawyers, [it would become] the town of all towns for civilized habitation.[5]

His town, which Sproat saw in 1888, was first called Salisbury, next Stanley, and finally Nelson, honoring Hugh Nelson, then lieutenant governor of British Columbia. Some years before, fire had skimmed off the timber of the hills nearest Nelson, so the town was at first a haphazard collection of tents and huts with sod roofs. After Sproat's endorsement, a postmaster was appointed and Nelson surveyed in the expectation that the Canadian Pacific would run a branch to it. A Victoria company erected a hotel and laid a wharf; a railroad, the Kootenay and Athabaska, was chartered to build south from Revelstoke through Nelson to the international border. Nelson abounded in railroad rumors: Corbin would build north, the Canadian Pacific would build south, Victoria men would build east, the Galt line would build west from Alberta, and these half-truths and fantasies aggravated Nelson's itch for year-round transportation to the world outside, for like other raw towns, Nelson believed that rails assured prosperity. North on the lake at Ainsworth, or Warm Springs, clotted a group of mining claims, principally the Little Donald, Number One, Gallagher, Krao, Spokane, Skyline, Neosha, and the historic Blue Bell, most of them controlled by Americans. This camp, too, required only transportation to make it famous, and the Vancouver *Telegram* expressed what everyone in the Kootenays thought:

> There is a concurrence of reliable testimony ... that the Kootenay country, comprising the two camps of Hot Springs [*sic*] and Nelson —will make another Leadville or Butte. The reason the country has not before this come to the front is traceable to the almost total absence of transportation facilities.[6]

Transport to the Kootenays was, indeed, difficult, no matter which of the three favored routes a prospector chose. He could ride the Canadian Pacific to Revelstoke, then boat south on Arrow Lakes into the Columbia River, and at some point due west of Nelson be put ashore to find his way through the deep forest; he might ride the Spokane Falls and Northern to Colville, then strike out afoot to the Columbia and boat upstream or follow the dim trails overland; or he might ride the Northern Pacific to Kootenai, walk or ride a stage to Bonners Ferry, and take a steamer 140 miles down the Kootenai to Nelson. The bulk of the prospectors were Americans—one Canadian newspaper guessed five-sixths of the Kootenays' population was Americans—so the Columbia and Kootenai routes carried the heaviest traffic, and both were wicked. One traveler who went by the Northern Pacific wrote about it:

> The trip from Spokane Falls to the Kootenai mining district is at once a misery and a delight. The man looking for discomfort will be fully accommodated. He will have his first night broken into by being compelled to leave Spokane on the midnight train over the Northern Pacific....
> At Kootenai, seventy-four miles from Spokane, he will be dumped into the chill grey of the morning in as desolate a spot as there is in all of Idaho.... A few hours later the kicked takes his own life in his hands...and boards the stagecoach for Bonners Ferry. He will do this just once. The next time he will walk.
> The distance is only thirty-four miles but it takes six hours and an ocean of blasphemy to traverse it....[7]

Those who chose to go north via the Columbia River fared worse, according to another report:

You cross the Columbia River at Marcus Ferry. Here you are put in charge of two "Klutchmen" who paddle you across in their birchbark canoe to the opposite shore where an old Indian trail is pointed out to you and at once plunge into the deep forest, following the Kettle River 125 miles, when the trail turns and leads up Rock Creek a distance of twenty miles.[8]

Such hardships for individual travelers posed the question: how could anyone get ore out? The answer could only be commercial transportation, and since most of the miners were Americans, they demanded transit to the United States. Spokane Falls naturally rallied behind Corbin. If he could extend his railroad as far as Nelson, the ore that might otherwise be shipped by steamer and wagon to the Northern Pacific for smelters in Montana could ride instead directly by rail to Spokane Falls and, with the ores already available in the Coeur d'Alenes, establish Spokane Falls as a smelting center.

British Columbia recognized, on the other hand, that smelters would be required in the province to prevent the flow of ore to the United States which, in 1888, had lifted its tariff on lead imports. The provincial legislature in 1886 had voted a bonus of $7,000 to any works erected in the province after it treated a thousand tons of ore, an act intended to encourage local smelting, and a London financier, Lionel H. C. Boyle, with the Home and Colonial Debenture Corporation, organized the Kootenay Trading and Smelting Syndicate on February 21, 1889, to erect the first interior smelter in British Columbia on the Canadian Pacific at Revelstoke. Completed late in 1889, the Revelstoke smelter's chief benefit was symbolic, a sentinel guarding Canada's interest in her own mineral wealth, for the works were a failure. The syndicate had hired a competent manager from Denver named John Campbell, but the sixty-ton plant was faulty in conception, litigation arose over the land it occupied, and freighting from the Kootenays and other interior mining districts proved laborious and expensive. The Kootenay syndicate had expected to buy its own mines but found none worth the prices asked. By 1892 the Revelstoke smelter would be closed, although its owners wielded political force for some years after, and in 1897, its machinery and buildings would be ordered sold.

Revelstoke's link with the Kootenay mines was tenuous at best and while Nelson's Canadian citizens demanded a wagon road be built between the Columbia River and Kootenay Lake to give them access to steamers from Revelstoke, Corbin strove to advance his own interest. He began to be mentioned frequently at Victoria, usually cited as a menace to holding the Kootenays' trade. Corbin appeared to have a head start to the mining camps of Toad Mountain and Ainsworth despite the overt opposition of the Robson administration, the Canadian Pacific, and of various British and Canadian investors who would spend money, as they had at Revelstoke, to trammel his railway. John A. Mara, who represented British Columbia at Ottawa, put the Canadian view in these words:

> The cost of transporting ore from Toad Mountain to Helena, Montana, is at present $33.00 per ton. With a good road to Sproat's Landing and large steamers on the Columbia River, ore can be transported to Revelstoke for one-half that figure, leaving a good margin in favor of the mine owner. Mr. Corbin, president of the Spokane and Northern R. R. Co., has engineers exploring for a route from the Columbia to Kootenay lake, via Salmon River and Cottonwood Creek, with every prospect of securing a good line. Their line will be completed to the Dalles by next spring and unless an effort is made by the provincial government and the C. P. R. Co., the holders of the present charter, the trade of the district will surely drift to Spokane Falls.[9]

Speaking at Kamloops in November, 1889, Premier Robson warned his audience, "We have felt that it has almost come to be a race between us and our American neighbors for the trade of that great and promising district [the Kootenays]." His government, Robson explained, had deferred its proposed wagon road between the Columbia and Nelson because "we had the earnest assurance" of the Canadian Pacific that a railway would be built as fast as the province could hope to complete its road. Moreover, the need for communication in all areas of British Columbia was so acute that half the government's total budget was allocated to road construction. The Americans kept the pot boiling. A man named George Herb wrote the editor of the *Spokane Falls Review:*

I have just received a private letter from the Warm Springs...
district, stating that the miners are circulating petitions which are
being unanimously signed, requesting the British Columbia parliament to grant a charter to the Spokane Falls & Northern, or any
other American lines which will open up the great Kootenay region
from the south.[10]

Corbin's men in the field did nothing to discourage the peti-
tioners. Roberts, himself, scouted a way to Nelson and sent John
Stevens over the ground to confirm his observations, while Corbin
engaged Charles Wilson, a one-time prospector who had risen to
prominence among Victoria attorneys, to write his application for a
charter and guide it through the assembly. British Columbia's legislature, convening in January, 1890, was engrossed by transportation
to the Kootenays from its first day when the chief justice, Sir
Matthew Baillie Begbie, speaking on behalf of the lieutenant governor, told the members:

The discovery of rich and extensive ledges in Kootenay is at-
tracting the attention of miners and capitalists, and there is every
reason for anticipating the early commencement of quartz mining on
an extensive scale. It will be for you to consider whether that desirable result shall be accelerated by improved means of communication.[11]

Certain representatives of the government had been negotiating
with the Spokane Falls and Northern for some weeks before the assembly gathered, and had encouraged an alliance with an old soldier,
Colonel James Baker, the member for Kootenay. Baker was also
promoting his own railroad, west from the Alberta border to
Kootenay Lake and Nelson, to exploit his coal fields in the Crow's
Nest region, and his application for a land grant and extension of
his charter was to come before the 1890 legislature.

The colonel's railway had been chartered in 1888, authorized to
distribute $4,000,000 worth of stock, but had undertaken no con-
struction. A small amount of the stock had been given to engineers
and surveyors rather than paychecks. The land grant Baker anticipated would include thousands of acres of coal, which he had lo-

cated during eight years of prospecting with William Fernie and
Arthur Fenwicke of Fort Steele. The *Inland Sentinel* of Kamloops,
B.C., called the Baker holdings "equal, if not superior, to any known
coal fields in the entire world," which proved an exaggerated estimate
although the coal was extensive, in seams six to forty feet wide,
capable of speedy and inexpensive development. As a correlation to
his projected railway, in 1886 Baker had purchased the 18,000 acres
on Joseph's Prairie owned by John Galbraith, named this estate
Cranbrook for his family's home in Kent, and secured British financing amounting to $325,000 for a townsite company, although the
company was not to function.[12]

At Cranbrook, Baker operated a prosperous store stocked with
imported wares, established a stock ranch, ran one of the few horse-
drawn threshers in the interior, and became politically influential.
Born and educated in England, Baker had served in the Crimea,
then raised and commanded the Cambridge University volunteers
in 1859, retired in 1875 with a permanent rank of lieutenant colonel,
published a book of his observations entitled *Turkey and Europe,*
and in search of fortune, had migrated to Victoria bearing the attractive reputation of soldier and author. A tall, brisk man with full
mustache and pointed beard both quite gray, Baker was elected to the
legislature the year he bought Cranbrook and was returned in 1890.
He was considered an able legislator and eventually rose to important cabinet appointments, but Baker also tenaciously pursued his
personal affairs and devoted himself to bagging transportation for
his coal fields with the bold intention of competing with the western
coal barons, the Dunsmuirs.

Baker had not enough money to build his railway, he had not
been able to cajole the Canadian Pacific to cross his realm, he had little hope that the Alberta Railway and Coal Company—the Galt line
—would construct the line surveyed in 1888 between Lethbridge,
Alberta, and Sandpoint, Idaho, and consequently the colonel was
heedful when Daniel Corbin disclosed in December, 1889, that he
would petition British Columbia for two railway charters, one for a
route north from the confluence of the Pend Oreille and Columbia

rivers to Nelson, and the second westward from the Kettle River valley to the mouth of the Fraser near Vancouver. Charles Wilson, the attorney, explained the reason for this second route to Premier Robson:

> The construction of these lines would form one continuous line of railway from the south end of Kootenay Lake to the Coast, with a short detour in American territory, rendered necessary by the difficulty of penetrating the chain of mountains on the west bank of the Columbia River.[13]

Such a railroad, connecting Kootenay Lake with the British Columbia seacoast, would not only put the mining camps in direct communication with New Westminster and Vancouver, but in Colonel Baker's quick mind, provide most of the rails he needed to carry his coal to market. As a result, when members of the administration conferred on Corbin's petition with his representatives, Arthur Newbery and the Spokane Falls attorney, Albert Allen, the conversation turned inevitably to the possibility of combining the Baker and Corbin charters to provide a rail line across the entire southern part of British Columbia. The legislative executive council advised an amalgamation, as Wilson noted:

> It may not be out of place to explain that our original idea was to build a line of railway from Nelson to the seaboard of British Columbia. It was only after taking the preliminary steps...that it was suggested to us that we acquire the Crow's Nest Coal and Kootenay Railway Company's charter...controlled by the Crow's Nest Coal and Mineral Company.[14]

While Wilson, Newbery, and Allen bargained with Baker, they reported by cable to Corbin who had gone to London to see his wife and daughters. Corbin replied with various offers of concession: he would, if the government wished, construct the proposed railway between Nelson and the Columbia River which had been allowed by the province some years earlier, blocked by Ottawa, and was now again to be chartered for the Canadian Pacific. Corbin's agents were

still contending with Baker when the colonel introduced Corbin's
petitions for charters on February 18, listing three proposed railways,
the Nelson and Kootenay Lake, the West Kootenay, and the South
Kootenay, one of them to run from Nelson to the southern end of
Kootenay Lake. Corbin had organized a Canadian-American company that included himself, Newbery, Allen, Wilson, and two
Victoria men, Joshua Davies and Thomas B. Hall. As a subsidy,
the railways asked for 17,500 acres of provincial land for each mile
completed, to be selected in alternate twenty-mile blocks on both
sides of the right of way.

The charters were tabled; the discussions continued with James
Baker who, by coincidence, was chairman of the standing committee
on railways. Finally, a kind of agreement was reached, not a merger
but a connection of the Baker and Corbin routes, requiring Corbin
to construct both. Baker introduced a new motion for a charter on
February 27, explaining that the railway now was to be called the
British Columbia Southern, and that it would

> make a through line of railway from the Crow's Nest Pass to the
> Coast of the Province ... and would, by reason of the great navigable
> waterways which intersect the said line of railway at right angles
> at four different points, be the means of developing the vast natural
> resources of the whole southern portion of the Province.[15]

Certain restrictions had been inserted in the draft charter, however, which doomed the railway because Corbin would not accept
them. The restrictive provisions required that Corbin must begin
work on both sections of the line "this year," 1890, and he must
complete the western portion to the Crow's Nest in four years and
the section to the Coast in six years from the granting of the charters, "and that, in default of these terms ... both charters, together
with the rights appertaining thereto, shall be forfeited." Fortunately
for Colonel Baker, the terms of the British Columbia Southern charter fit neatly with his own; his charter for a railway between the
Crow's Nest and Kootenay Lake would expire in five years if no
line were built, but Corbin would be bound to construct this section of his cross-province line in four. Baker had spent thousands

of dollars traveling to Europe trying to attract capital to his coal fields and his railroad without success; now the fruition of his scheme seemed at hand, and shares of the coal company, sold originally for their two-dollar par value, began a rise that would advance their market price beyond one hundred dollars, bringing small fortunes to early purchasers.[16]

Time limits inserted in the provincial charter for the British Columbia Southern were not solely for Baker's personal motives, however, for many members of the assembly, including the premier, considered them prudent guarantees that British Columbia would actually get the railway it had wanted for so long. There were a significant number of charters on the books for railway companies that had not built the line projected, and the Canadians intended that Daniel Corbin should actually run his tracks to the Coast, not simply promise such a route in order to coax a charter that would allow him to connect the Spokane Falls and Northern with Nelson and siphon the commerce of the interior mines to Spokane Falls. For their part, American newspaper editors called the terms of the British Columbia charter "practical confiscation."

British Columbia approved the charter of the British Columbia Southern and sent it on to Ottawa, where the railway committee had set aside consideration to await a recommendation from Victoria. Corbin had returned from England to be on hand when Parliament deliberated his charter. John Robson had telegraphed the federal premier, Sir John A. Macdonald, who also served as minister of railways, the views of British Columbia:

> The provincial government are strongly in favor of and desire your assistance in the granting by the Dominion of the railway charters applied for by the Spokane Falls & Northern Railway, provided that the line from Pen d'Oreille to Nelson be extended by the Dominion charter to the western terminus of the Crow's Nest and Kootenay Lake Railway, and also that work on the lines granted by the two charters be carried on simultaneously, and that both charters be forfeited if both lines are not completed in the time specified in the charters.
>
> s/ John Robson
>
> Victoria, B.C., 24th February 1890 [17]

To John A. Mara, who represented British Columbia in Parliament, Robson sent a similar telegram, adding the statement in his reference to the requirements for completion of the two segments of railway, "Without these provisions, the enterprise will not be acceptable." In Victoria there had been sentiment to waive the restrictions, to let Corbin build as he pleased simply to provide the cross-province southern route. Corbin's spokesmen had denounced the confiscatory clauses, pointing out that much as Corbin wanted to build his railways, he would not proceed on the terms laid down by British Columbia. With or without Robson's telegrams, Corbin had little honest hope that Ottawa would charter his British Columbia Southern over the energetic opposition of the Canadian Pacific. In earlier years, Macdonald's government had supported the Canadian Pacific as a patriotic project, regarding the transcontinental railway as an instrument of national unity, tying together isolated areas of Canada of which the Kootenays were an example. The premier was not likely to change his views for an American railway builder. Moreover Canadian Pacific engineers were surveying south from Revelstoke toward Spokane Falls with the intention, thought the *Spokane Falls Review,* of "heading off the Spokane Falls & Northern."

On March 4, 1890, the house railway committee opened its consideration of the Corbin charters, hearing first from Mara, who bore the political sobriquet, "the strong man of Sicamous." [18] Mara described the proposed railway and read his telegram from Robson. A member remarked that the Corbin lines "would transfer the whole traffic from the rich Kootenay district to the United States, whereas the object of Parliament should be to build up cities in British Columbia," and others agreed. Charles Wilson spoke next before the committee, making plain Corbin's rejection of the conditions put on construction and length of time. Sir John Macdonald reported receiving a telegram from Robson similar to the one read by Mara, and a letter from William C. Van Horne, president of the Canadian Pacific, stating that his company would build the railway between the Columbia River and Nelson which would open

the Kootenay district via the river, Arrow Lakes, and Revelstoke.
As Wilson would not accept the province's terms, Sir John observed,
he supposed that ended the matter. When the vote was taken, only
three committee members balloted to charter the British Columbia
Southern, and more than fifty voted against it. Corbin's application,
in the words of Kamloops' *Inland Sentinel,* had been "ignomin-
iously kicked out."

Ironically, two months later, the United States Congress approved a bill granting the Spokane Falls and Northern a right of
way across the Colville Indian Reservation, which would have provided the first leg of the Corbin railway to the Coast. The act required completion of the railway within three years and stipulated
that the line was to be constructed with "due regard for the rights
of the Indians, and especially so as not to interfere with their irrigating ditches."[19] Without a Canadian charter, the right of way
was of no practical value to Daniel Corbin.

A good many Canadians were disappointed by Corbin's failure
to obtain a charter for the British Columbia Southern, and understanding provincial politics, concluded that there must have been a
plot against the Corbin project from the first. The *Victoria Truth*
asserted that the legislature must have insisted on its restrictions
"with the intention of burking the scheme of the Spokane & Northern Railway," and the Revelstoke *Kootenay Star* commented:

> It is now seen there was from the first no prospect of obtaining it.
> The resolution sent from Victoria to Ottawa...effectually killed it,
> and if this had not been done other equally efficient means would
> have been found to defeat it. Can any man be called an intelligent
> friend of the scheme who saddled it with such conditions of forfeiture
> that no capitalist in his senses could take the risk of investing his
> money in it?[20]

In the opinion of the *Victoria Colonist,* the charters were defeated by British Columbia men "because it will interfere with
little schemes of their own." Charles Wilson listed four reasons for
Corbin's failure at Ottawa: the opposition of the Canadian Pacific,

"apathy" by British Columbia members of Parliament, obstruction-ism by the Revelstoke smelter company, and "that resolution of the legislative assembly of the province of British Columbia."

So ran the explanation and recrimination, but all the talk de-livered no charters, and Canada continued to control the Kootenays even though the district was flooded with Americans who ordered their supplies from towns in the United States, and had these goods hauled over the rude trails or consigned to steamboats that anchored 325 feet offshore when water was low at Nelson. So much for Colonel Baker's expectations, for the time being. Three years later he dallied with Montreal and Toronto investors who took one-third of his coal fields and attempted to build the British Columbia Southern, but gave up after four months. In 1896, Baker appealed to the Canadian Pacific, arranged a government subsidy of $11,000 a mile for the British Columbia Southern route, and contrived that the railroad finally constructed should overlook the most direct route and curve, instead, toward Cranbrook which became a Canadian Pacific divisional point in return for awarding the CPR a generous portion of the townsite.[21]

Daniel Corbin's defeat at Ottawa amounted to a defensive maneuver. Most Canadians hoped for some positive move to provide transportation for the Kootenays, and continued to warn that, unless Canada somehow provided railways for the district, the region would fall under American domain. George C. Tunstall, Kamloops district gold commissioner, wrote in his annual report for 1890:

> The businessmen of the State of Washington have not been slow in detecting the advantages offered.... Nearly all the supplies needed have been...procured from Spokane Falls, notwithstanding the duties imposed, as being the most accessible point.[22]

The rejection of his charters at Ottawa had been a lesson in Canadian attitudes to Daniel Corbin who concluded that his down-fall had resulted from opposition "from the Canadian Pacific Rail-way and also from a majority of the British Columbia members of the dominion Parliament—and I confess it was much of a surprise." He was not convinced that he would be kept out of Canada forever, and had abandoned neither his plan to build to the Coast nor his plan to reach the Kootenays. While he had been busy with applications, Corbin's construction crews had gone into winter camps, but good weather would soon return. "I do not intend to give up the idea of getting into British Columbia," Corbin declared. "We will build this spring to the Little Dalles which will bring us within fifteen miles of the boundary."

CHAPTER EIGHT

RAILS REACH THE COLUMBIA

CORBIN'S CONTRACT WITH THE SPOKANE FALLS AND NORTHERN company specified that he complete the railway to the navigable waters of the Columbia River where steamers could connect the line with the Canadian Pacific. This meant extending the track approximately thirty miles beyond Colville to a rippling, rocky stretch of the river known as the Little Dalles. In low water, even the shallow steamers designed to run close to lake shores could not always slip through the Little Dalles and although both the Canadian and United States governments were urged to clear away the obstructions, neither did anything about them. The route as surveyed would carry the Spokane Falls and Northern to Marcus, on the Columbia, and then northward on the east bank of the river. Grading had been completed on half of the fourteen miles between Colville and Marcus before winter drove the crews to their tents in the last days of 1889 to wait for better weather. "I have two gangs of men, numbering one hundred and fifty all told, lying in camp to resume operations," Cyrus Burns told the *Spokane Falls Review*. "We will have seven miles of grading to complete and then Marcus will be reached."

Construction to the Little Dalles would also carry the railway nearer the international border, for Corbin did not intend to abandon his plan to lay rail into Canada. After his defeat at Ottawa in March, 1890, he had a better understanding of what he must do to realize this purpose. Moreover, once he had effected the water connection with the Canadian Pacific, his Spokane Falls and Northern would have the same entry to the Kootenays as did the Canadian road. Consequently Corbin continued to build toward the border.

On the Colville River, on a route requiring only a slight deviation from the most direct course from Colville to the Columbia, lay Meyers Falls, regarded as the best natural source of water power in eastern Washington next to Spokane Falls. Here the river tumbled 135 feet over a series of rocky shelves in a distance of three-eighths of a mile and was estimated capable of producing three thousand kilowatts of electric energy; its thrust had been used to drive the wheel of a Hudson's Bay grist mill early in the nineteenth century; and after the area was adjudged American soil an industrious Canadian, Louther W. Meyers, homesteaded the land in October, 1862, giving his name to what had been known before as Mill Creek. Meyers' land, a good portion of it in his wife's name, afforded a suitable townsite beside the falls, and he was the heaviest single contributor to the Colville collection for the Spokane Falls and Northern, pledging $500, so he expected that the railroad would bend a little to put Meyers Falls on its line. Moreover, bulging the route toward Meyers Falls would permit the Spokane Falls and Northern to follow the Colville River toward the Columbia through the Huckleberry Mountains with an average grade of approximately six-tenths of one per cent. The more direct way to Marcus through the mountains required grades of two and one-half per cent. The elevation fell from 1,590 feet above sea level at Colville to 1,274 feet at Marcus.

As Meyers anticipated, the railroad was surveyed to take in his waterfall, and the round, balding Meyers hastened to offer the Spokane Falls and Northern free land for its station and a town that might be established beside the Columbia. This was not enough. Meyers stubbornly refused to cede an interest in the falls itself, protecting his resource with the frugality that had prompted him to build a mill using timbers from the old structure, and so the railroad passed him by. Corbin's surveyors moved the line four miles northeast of Meyers Falls, and as they resurveyed a little town started up. The first buildings were to rise in 1890 on the third, and final, site that was to be known as Meyers Falls, and like the others, located on land owned by Louther Meyers to whom Corbin paid a dollar for station grounds.[1] The first two attempts to establish a town of Meyers Falls failed because both sites were too far from the railroad.

A second hamlet that anticipated railway service from the Spokane Falls and Northern was Kettle Falls, on the Columbia, named for the peculiar rock formation in the river nearby. This hamlet had not the power potential of Meyers Falls but occasionally when the water was high, small steamers navigated downriver as far as the kettle-shaped rocks, and Kettle Falls also represented an easier grade than a route directly through the mountains from Colville to Marcus. Three possible lines had been surveyed to Kettle Falls during July and August, 1889, one an alternate of the Spokane Falls and Northern main road, a second a 2.8-mile spur southward from it, and a third an 11.2-mile branch north from it. None of the three was built and Kettle Falls' residents never ceased to wonder why the railroad forgot their town.

Corbin did not explain bypassing Kettle Falls but his reasons seem evident. A group of Rochester, New York, men had already begun primping Kettle Falls as a resort, and had maintained a project manager, H. D. Bushnell, on the ground for two years to plan an extensive town and to negotiate a railway directly to Wallula Junction, Washington, where it could meet the Northern Pacific and the Union Pacific. In 1890 they were to erect "the handsomest and best hotel west of Helena," the $18,000 Rochester, at Kettle Falls.[2] Moreover, A. M. Cannon and other Spokane Falls men were promoting a railway from Kettle Falls up the Columbia and Kettle rivers to the Canadian Pacific, intending to connect with the Spokane Falls and Northern, but after Corbin's subversion at Ottawa this project withered. Because the Rochester group loomed as rivals, Corbin doubtless shrugged off Kettle Falls as offering more trouble than trade.

Finally Corbin concluded that he would build the Spokane Falls and Northern over the most direct route to Marcus on the Columbia, curving his track to avoid natural obstacles. At Marcus the railroad would cross a narrow plateau about forty feet above the river near the grave of the lone British subject who had died during the residence there of the North American Boundary Commission 1860–62. On flat land ten feet lower than the depot stood a neat quadrangle of log houses left by the commission where a trader, Marcus Oppenheimer, had opened his store shortly after the commission moved out, and was reputed turning merchandise worth a thousand dollars a month. His goods had to be hauled by mule and wagon from Walla Walla at four cents a pound. William V. Brown opened a second store but travelers continued to call the settlement Marcus, after Oppenheimer, the last American supply point for those heading upriver to Canada. By 1889, when the railway approached, the old handmade brick chimneys and low long houses were still usable, a weathered nucleus for a new town on the Spokane Falls and Northern.

Had Canada chartered the British Columbia Southern, Corbin had planned to cross the river at Marcus; and even after his failure at Ottawa, Corbin believed this route might soon be open to him. Consequently he again applied for a right of way across the Colville Indian lands for a railroad that would run 75.3 miles in United States territory, coursing generally west toward Ruby City and the other rousing mining camps of the Salmon River country in what today is Okanogan County, then veering north along the Okanogan and Similkameen rivers into the agricultural areas of south-central British Columbia.[3] Corbin's petition was to be approved by the General Land Office in 1891, and had he been able to wangle a charter from Canada, this would have been the first segment of a 320-mile line partly in the United States and partly in Canada between Marcus and the coast which Corbin expected would require three years to build.

In the early months of 1890, however, both the Indian reservation and Canada were closed to Corbin's railways, so he continued construction in the direction remaining to him, northward along the Columbia River. Buckley told the *Review,* "We will build at least to the Canadian line which is forty-two miles from Marcus," a statement issued, incidentally, a few days before Buckley resigned from the railroad company. Corbin explained that he had ordered more rails and other material than he needed merely to reach the Little Dalles.

Meanwhile, Corbin faced the need to attract settlers to the Colville area to provide commercial freight for the Spokane Falls and Northern. He spent $2,500 to print fifty thousand booklets praising the region, written by Randall Kemp and A. D. Burnett, and circulated thousands of these in eastern states. This thirty-page pamphlet, *An Open Door to a Magnificent Country,* contained a map showing trails and wagon roads leading in all directions from Colville and in particularly heavy lines traced the projected railway across the international border. It was illustrated with idyllic pencil sketches and contained advice to "good" farmers, urging them to settle in the ninety-thousand-acre Colville Valley where hay "seldom" brought less than eighteen dollars a ton.[4] Despite these blandishments, few homesteaders came after they learned that eighty per cent of the area had not been surveyed by the federal government. Even in surveyed areas continual bickering arose over land ownership, owing in part to a curious habit of the Stevens County recorder who wore his rubber overcoat summer and winter, stuffing its pockets with papers, including deeds, that were forgotten and unrecorded.

Winter broke in March, 1890, and construction resumed to Marcus. The graders reached the town May 15 with tracklayers only steps behind them and the first Spokane Falls and Northern train entered Marcus on May 20, puffing to the depot and roundhouse on the flat land Corbin purchased from Jim Monaghan for one dollar. Corbin had let contracts at Colville on April tenth for extending the railway to the Little Dalles, dividing the work among nine contractors, the most prominent of them J. W. Hendricks of Salt Lake City who used teams from his own Utah ranch for grading. By the time the railroad established service to Marcus, consequently, the road was well underway upriver with five hundred men working on the line. On May third, the *Spokane Falls Review* reported:

> The contractors for the Spokane Falls & Northern extension to the Little Dalles have nearly completed their work. The grading is largely finished, the trestles built, and as the track-laying is done by the recently invented machine, it is thought trains will be running through to the Little Dalles by June 15.[5]

Newspaper opinion notwithstanding, the tracklaying machine hindered rather than speeded construction, in E. J. Roberts' opinion, and he soon relegated it to crossing trestles and marshland or to those occasions when important spectators might be impressed with the machine as a testimonial to the company's progressive management. Roberts preferred his system: his men pushed a flatcar along the tracks as they were laid, the car stacked with rails and ties in such a manner that the rails spilled off one side and the ties off the other. As one gang hurled ties into position, two men checked the gauge with a spacebar and a second gang spiked the rails. This had been Roberts' method on the Manitoba when his crews set a speed record and on the Canadian Pacific; he claimed he could finish eight thousand feet a day.

As the Spokane Falls and Northern left Marcus driving northward on the Columbia's east bank, the hills grew steeper and granite cliffs, furrowed by ravines, crowded against the river. An editor who rode the train over this section later described it.

> After leaving Marcus...the train wound its way along a path that had been hewn for it along the sides of gigantic mountains or built over deep ravines that make the beholder shudder. When it comes to wonders being accomplished in the way of difficult railway construction, the Spokane & Northern can well rank with the railroads which...form one of the seven wonders of the world.[6]

While the railway was creeping toward the Little Dalles, it inaugurated a series of special excursions. On July 4, 1890, the Spokane Falls and Northern sponsored its first holiday round trip from

Spokane Falls to Colville at a rate of four dollars per person. At Colville, the Honorable S. C. Hyde addressed the tourists, Colville's residents fed them a free meal, after which they were treated to horse racing. Next the railway organized a businessmen's excursion at $3.50 per head to Marcus where Corbin was erecting a new frame hotel overlooking the Columbia. Two hundred men went in four passenger coaches. Corbin accompanied the tour, behaving with rare exuberance. At Loon Lake he held a thermometer in the water to show that it registered seventy degrees and told his listeners, "I will build a $30,000 hotel here before next summer and will also erect a number of cottages." He took in the wooded shoreline with a gesture. "I mean to have roads all around here. . . . I will have a number of ponies and light buckboards for traveling over these roads and I think the lake will soon become popular as a summer resort." [7] A few weeks later Corbin had the lake stocked with eastern black bass, despite criticism from sportsmen, and fenced the outlet to prevent the fish from escaping.[8]

As the businessmen's special twisted northward from Colville it crossed a high trestle near St. Ignatius Mission where Corbin ordered his engineer, P. A. Van Houten, to pause for several minutes so his passengers could view the Columbia sparkling in the distance. At Marcus, when the train stopped so the tourists could lunch, Corbin slipped away to inspect the roadbed leading toward the Little Dalles. In addition to Fourth of July and merchant excursions, the Spokane Falls and Northern attracted charter parties of the best society who rode to Loon Lake for dancing in a pavilion hung with Japanese lanterns while other lights twinkled along paths leading to the boathouse.

Although the railway provided these diversions, its serious and immediate purpose was to connect with the Canadian Pacific by steamers between Little Dalles and Revelstoke, and late in July, 1890, Corbin visited Victoria to conclude arrangements with a new steamship company. When he returned to Spokane Falls, the newspapers accorded him the title "honorable" as if he were a judge or senator. Corbin announced that service to the Canadian Pacific would begin on August 12, when the railway would be completed as far as Little Dalles, and the Columbia and Kootenay Steam Navigation Company's new sternwheeler, the *Lytton,* would be prepared to run twice each week. When enough business developed, daily steamer service would be provided.

The steamship company had been organized by Canadians to serve the traffic to the Kootenay district mines and, although it contracted to meet Corbin's railroad, the company's management was dedicated to maintaining Canadian control of the area. The driving force behind the Columbia and Kootenay Steam Navigation Company was the same John Mara who represented British Columbia at Ottawa, one of those Corbin described as apathetic in support of his application for a charter for the British Columbia Southern. Mara was the son-in-law of the late Frank J. Barnard, founder of the British Columbia Express Company, and had owned wholesale and retail stores at Kamloops and Sicamous until January, 1890, when he sold them to devote his time to organizing the steamboat line. The older Columbia River Steam Navigation Company had approached Mara, who had operated steamers on Kamloops Lake, to form a new company with enough money to build the new boats that the increasing lake and river traffic required but which the old company could not afford. The Columbia and Kootenay Steam Navigation Company was incorporated in February, 1890, by Mara, J. F. Hume, William Cowan, John Irving, Robert Sanderson, and Frank S. Barnard, Mara's brother-in-law, to operate boats both on the Columbia and Kootenay Lake. All the directors were widely known in British Columbia: Barnard also represented the province at Ottawa and operated the express company founded by his father; Irving and Sanderson were veteran interior steamer captains. The new company, capitalized for $100,000, opened offices at Revelstoke and set about building and buying steamers for freight, passengers, and barge towing.

To direct its operations, the Columbia and Kootenay lured Captain James Troup, already famous on the lower Columbia, and hired Alexander Watson, a noted Victoria ship builder, to construct a deluxe sternwheeler, the *Lytton,* for $40,000 at Revelstoke beginning in December, 1889. The *Lytton,* the queen of the fleet, was 131 feet long, capable of carrying 125 tons of freight, and approximately two hundred passengers in its cabins. Tested for two weeks on the river after launching on April 29, 1890, she ran twelve and a half miles an hour and was pronounced "fast and capable of handling a big business." On the *Lytton's* maiden commercial voyage in July, Canadian Pacific President Van Horne was a passenger.

From the old company, the Columbia and Kootenay had acquired two small vessels, the *Marion* and the twin-hulled *Despatch.* The thirty-seven ton *Despatch,* a wood-burning sternwheeler, struggled to handle the Columbia River freight; she was only 54 feet long, had been built at Revelstoke in 1888, and was never strong enough for the demands of the traffic although she drew little water and was considered valuable as a river carrier particularly during low water. The *Marion,* also a wood-burning sternwheeler, was only seven feet longer than the *Despatch,* and had been built by Watson for Captain Sanderson at Golden, in 1888, using equipment from the homemade steamer *Duchess;* she soon was to be relegated to shuttling freight and passengers up the Columbia to Revelstoke from Arrow Lakes when the river was too low for larger steamers to navigate. Like the *Despatch,* the *Marion* had seen heavy service on interior streams during the early rush to Nelson.

While the *Lytton* had been under construction, the Columbia and Kootenay Steam Navigation Company—popularly known only by its initials as the "C.K.S.N."—had purchased the old *Kootenai,* another wood-burning sternwheeler that had been lying idle at the Little Dalles since 1887. It was said the company got her for nothing more than $10,000 in promissory notes. The boat had been built near Little Dalles in 1885, using machinery and materials salvaged from the *Katie Hallett* which had run on Pend Oreille Lake in northern Idaho during construction of the Northern Pacific along the lake's north shore. The *Kootenai* hauled supplies for the Canadian Pacific construction crews and had been tied up after the railway was completed in November, 1885, to await better times. Although she was nine feet longer than the *Lytton,* the *Kootenai* was a lighter and less powerful boat.

These four steamers, one new and three renovated, had been

running between Revelstoke and the shadowed landings in the timber where trails ran from the Columbia toward Nelson, and were the boats the Columbia and Kootenay intended to put into service for its traffic with the Spokane Falls and Northern. In 1891, the company was to add the $75,000 *Columbia,* the largest of its fleet, which would be built near Little Dalles by Watson. Although Daniel Corbin had named August 12 as the target for inaugurating rail and steamer service between Spokane Falls and Revelstoke, during a meeting in Spokane Falls among Robert Kerr, CPR general freight and passenger agent, John Campbell, manager of the Revelstoke smelter, Corbin, Cyrus Burns, and W. S. Norman, the date was adjusted to August 15, 1890. The timetable issued after this conference indicated that boats would leave Revelstoke on Mondays and Thursdays to arrive at Little Dalles on Tuesdays and Fridays. One-way fare from Spokane Falls to Revelstoke was $13.50.

The connection with the Canadian Pacific generated a large measure of enthusiasm in Spokane Falls, so the special train Corbin ordered to meet the *Lytton* for the first time was crowded with merchants and railroad officers. They arrived at the Little Dalles an excited throng, expecting to see the steamer within an hour. Their anticipation scarcely waned as the hour passed, followed by a second, with no sign of the boat. The group at Little Dalles had no way of knowing the *Lytton* had been delayed by a series of mishaps and a crowd of prospectors rushing to a new mining discovery along Trail Creek which flowed into the Columbia. Moreover, as the *Lytton* had come down Upper Arrow Lake, low-hanging branches damaged its stack, slowing her so the vessel reached Sproat's Landing ten hours late. After several hours the men at Little Dalles grew apprehensive; D. C. Corbin finally sent the train back toward Spokane Falls and called for another engine and cars to stand by. The waiting had been systematized as the day drew on: some passengers passed the time by watching crews grade a roadbed and lay track to the water's edge, and Corbin treated them all, in shifts, to free meals in the engineers' tent.

The *Lytton* had tarried at Sproat's Landing to unload a large cargo for the mining camps, finally pulling away at two o'clock in the afternoon, and stopped again at Trail Creek to land her frantic troupe of miners hurrying to stake claims. Finally the weary watchers at the end of the Spokane Falls and Northern tracks sighted the steamer four miles upstream rounding a bend of the river. They had come in the morning; now it was 5:30 P.M. The railroad engineer sounded his whistle; echoes answered from the granite cliffs and the *Lytton's* captain gallantly responded. The salutes continued alternately as the steamer pulled toward a quiet pool near shore. The crowd pressed forward to meet Mara, among the sixty-four passengers, while the steamer took aboard men and baggage for the return to Revelstoke and after a few minutes, started back upriver. One observer thought the *Lytton* looked "like a bird on the bosom of the majestic Columbia."

Thus Spokane Falls gained its connection with the Canadian Pacific, and as direct a route as then existed to the British Columbia mines. Daniel Corbin achieved heroic stature in the eyes of the city's residents, who agreed with the *Helena Independent* that "the story of the Spokane Falls & Northern reads like magic." Corbin's railway seemed but one of Spokane Falls' good fortunes, for the *Review* cited the town's growing fame, saying that in the national capital, stores displayed Spokane hats, Spokane ties, and Spokane cigarettes, and "the name Spokane is as familiar throughout the east as is Chicago." A group of real estate promoters circularized a fictitious town, Columbia, claiming that it was the foot of navigation on the river, and Corbin bought newspaper space to deny the railway's connection with the canard, advertising "that said proposed town ... is not and never will be the terminus of the Spokane Falls & Northern Railway." In building his railway to the Columbia, commented the Board of Trade, Daniel Corbin had given Spokane Falls one of its two largest projects, the other being construction of the Oregon Railway and Navigation Company line into the town. The Spokane Falls and Northern had completed 110.7 miles of track to the Columbia, according to E. J. Roberts, so that under its contract to pay him $40,000 in securities per mile, the railroad company had issued Corbin slightly more than $4,400,000 worth of its paper.

Although there was no town of Columbia, Daniel Corbin had

in mind another town not then on any map which would furnish
a railhead for his various extensions and provide superior anchorage
for river steamers. Moreover this town would all be his, and he
chose two grassy benches overlooking the Columbia approximately
seven miles upriver from the Little Dalles, not more than half a
mile from the mouths of Sheep and Deep creeks, two streams that
would provide a comparatively easy water grade that could be followed by a railway into British Columbia. Throughout 1890 and
1891, Corbin contented himself with surveys, politics, and financing,
without constructing additional track, but in 1892 the Spokane Falls
and Northern resumed laying rail toward the border and Corbin's
new town which he called Northport.

One of Corbin's agents, Frederick Farquhar, had bought the
townsite of 158.75 acres for $198.44 from the federal government;
and, the day after receiving his deed, had transferred the entire area
to Corbin for $250 and a small share of the stock of a townsite com-
pany to be organized.[9] Late in 1890 Edward Roberts had begun
quietly laying out the site as a village five avenues deep from the
riverfront and nine streets long. On May 24, 1892, Corbin signed a
warranty deed for the land to the Northport Townsite Company,
and four days later the company filed with the county its plat of
the town, listing Roberts as president, and another Corbin aide,
T. A. Herrick, as secretary.

Early in 1892 a veteran newspaperman, William P. Hughes,
had come over the trail to the prettily wooded flats called Northport
with a team of oxen straining at the wagon that carried his printing
equipment, urged on by Hughes and his brother-in-law and com-
positor, Charles F. Murphy. Now thirty-five years old, Hughes had
been a journeyman printer since the age of fifteen, carried card number six in the New York printers' union as a trophy, and had edited
newspapers in New York State, Illinois, Colorado, Wyoming, and
California. When he reached Spokane—the town discarded "Falls"
from its name in 1891—Billy Hughes signed a contract with D. C.
Corbin to establish a newspaper, and hopefully a town, at Northport.
Hughes found the place colored with wild roses and flowers. Three
homesteaders' cabins graced the slopes and there was a store run

by T. L. Savage who had moved from Kettle Falls onto the route of the Spokane Falls and Northern. His shack was the first building on the lower bench intended as a commercial district; a homesteader's cabin, that of Frank George, construction superintendent of the railroad, stood on the upper bench reserved for residences.

Hughes erected a rude shanty, Northport's second business structure, and on July 4, 1892, published the first issue of the *Northport News*. Its front page contained only one story, a wordy boost for Northport. "Doubtless the most interesting item of news in the paper," remarked a fellow editor, "was the one giving currency to the report that there was, actually, a town of Northport."

That first issue of the *News* and subsequent issues displayed the identical front page story for several months and championed Corbin's railway as if rails already glistened alongside the Columbia. It also printed its ration of chatter about travelers who looked over the town for themselves, noting that among the early residents was Mrs. Margaret "Gertie" Egan, who opened an inn where tourists might bed and eat, unless Gertie, brandishing her skillet, took a notion to run this or that one out of town. Tall Billy Hughes fancied himself a frontiersman, claimed to have been a Texas Ranger, always wore boots and asserted he would die with them on. As he aged, his boots were to become an obsession so that he often slept wearing them and in his old age, it is said, he was found dead alone in his cabin, boots laced on tight.[10]

Corbin by the middle of 1892 had assurances that he could enter Canada, and consequently on June 24, 1892, Roberts let a contract to J. R. Marks and Company of Spokane to extend the Spokane Falls and Northern to Northport by July fourth. Various delays moved back the date for completion of the line to September 15, and the railroad crept over the seven miles between Marcus and Northport with grading crews blowing out twelve to fifteen stumps on a single blast. At the very edge of Northport an iron railcar broke down, halting construction after Roberts' crews had laid the track in seven days. By now, a lumber mill had been established at Northport and several families lived in tents billowing on the upper terrace. Roberts ordered the railcar fixed as quickly as possible, and when his mechanics reported the repairs done on Sunday morning, September 18, Roberts forthwith routed his crews and finished spiking track to the depot site. Billy Hughes was impressed:

> The sight of E. J. Roberts, the energetic chief engineer of the Spokane Falls & Northern Railroad, clothed in a long duster and a regulation broad-brimmed hat, walking with slow majestic tread and commanding mien, giving his orders in a clear and forcible voice to a large crowd of men who were following him, putting ties in their proper places and laying rails, with the construction train slowly moving behind the whole, was a pleasing and astonishing sight, and one that will never be forgotten by the pioneers of Northport, the future mining, milling, smelting and agricultural city of northeastern Washington.[11]

When the tracks reached the place where the station house was to be, the construction engine nudged a boxcar to the end of the rails to serve as a temporary depot. After a desultory cheer, the workmen straggled off, many to prospect for the rest of the day, encouraged by miniscule ore strikes during construction. One Sunday three weeks later, two workmen did find a gold vein as they walked through the hills, swinging an ax at likely rocks.

The day after Roberts laid the tracks, the first passenger train arrived in Northport. The next day, a Tuesday, the railway pulled into town Cy Townsend's post office and saloon, a small building that had been hoisted onto a flatcar. For more than a year, Townsend had been postmaster at the Little Dalles, and as the tracks were extended, he had his cabin put on a car and accompanied the railway crews. Northport's citizens lifted Townsend's post office to the ground and set it by the steamer landing, but a few days later, picked it up and moved it to Columbia Avenue, the main street. So far as the United States postal service knew, the office was located at Little Dalles all this time. Townsend's custom was to spread the letters across his bar with a generous gesture and bellow, "Step up and select your mail!" A postal inspector, shocked at this cavalier treatment of federal mails, objected but nothing was done because there was no other post office to be found.

When Townsend's little building reached Northport, the town's citizens celebrated the arrival of the railroad in a suitable manner, and the post office tinkled with glasses and merry voices far into the night on the shadowed flats overlooking the moon-streaked Columbia.

CHAPTER NINE

BACKWARD TO NELSON

For two years after the Spokane Falls and Northern had been completed to the Little Dalles and there connected with steamers plying the Columbia in Canada, D. C. Corbin essayed no railway construction. The steamer service had begun in August, 1890, and not until September, 1892, was the railway stretched the seven additional miles to Northport. Corbin passed the two intervening years in surveying proposed routes, in making a second fruitless attempt to win a Canadian charter, and in forming a Canadian company which, by selling Corbin its charter, provided his means of entry to Canada. The character of the Kootenays changed dramatically between 1890 and 1892 because, after 1890 when two prospectors struck rich ore on Trail Creek west of the Columbia, the center of Kootenay mining shifted from Nelson to Trail Creek. Although evolution of the region affected Corbin's plans, he clung to his early purpose to build a railway into Nelson.

The railway that was to open Canada for Corbin was organized late in 1890 by five British Columbians to run between Fort Sheppard, where the international border met the Columbia, and Nelson, and was named appropriately the Nelson and Fort Sheppard. The old fort had been established by the Hudson's Bay Company in 1857, then abandoned three years later for lack of arable land and pasture, reopened 1866–69, and closed permanently in 1870 with its single dwelling and three storehouses put in care of an

Indian.[1] In 1890 charred remains of the fort, which had burned in
1872, lay in the sand of the west bank of the Columbia, overlooking
a great bar on the east side of the river where vestiges of sluices and
flumes, discarded twenty-five years earlier by gold prospectors, were
visible. Except for the fort and bar, the Columbia was timbered to
the water's edge, its banks uninhabited, and the only purpose of a
railway to this ghostly spot could be a connection with the Spokane
Falls and Northern. One of the railway's promoters, Gustavus Blinn
Wright, visited Spokane Falls in August, 1890, to discuss it with
Corbin.

The incorporators of the Nelson and Fort Sheppard were respected British Columbia businessmen who had united to exploit
the Kootenay area and believed a railroad necessary to their success.
Foremost among them was Wright, one of the founders of Ainsworth on Kootenay Lake, a trustee of the first West Kootenay mining company, promoter of the railway between Nelson and the
Columbia, merchant, and miner. The other four were Charles
Thomas Dupont, Peter Curran Dunlevy, Charles George Major,
and inevitably, an attorney, Henry Slye Mason.[2] Dunlevy had hunted
gold all over British Columbia as a young man; he now owned
stores and planted a thousand acres near Soda Creek, and was one
of the eight promoters of a silver-copper company on Toad Mountain near Nelson. In this company and also the Nelson City Land
and Improvement Company was Dupont, a native of Quebec, who
had come to Victoria in 1872 as a member of a commission studying
western resources and remained to be acclaimed for his interest in
the militia and sports, and as an organizer of the Victoria street
railway. Major, who reached British Columbia from Ontario in
1859, claimed to have been the first man to drive a stagecoach over
the old Cariboo highway, and with young John Robson in the early
days, he had cleared a large part of New Westminster townsite.
The barrister, Mason, owned a handsome home on Bird Cage Walk
in Victoria, where the provincial museum stands today, and with
Thomas Alsop held real estate interests throughout the province as
a result of their partnership which, formed in 1878, had grown into

the British Columbia Land Investment Company. The names of these five Canadians silvered the lining of a cloud of American control that hung over the Nelson and Fort Sheppard.

Incorporated February 4, 1891, the Nelson and Fort Sheppard was chartered without a subsidy by the British Columbia legislature of that year.[3] After this, Corbin appeared more confident of his eventual penetration of Canada, and one wonders if he did not find ironic satisfaction in the fact that the initials of the Nelson and Fort Sheppard were an exact reversal of those of the Spokane Falls and Northern—N&FS and SF&N. Was it Corbin's little joke, signifying that because he could not seem to reach Canada head first, he would back across the border? The railway's intended terminus, Nelson, now bragged it was the sixth largest city in British Columbia with a half-dozen streets and six new hotels, telephone connection with Ainsworth and telegraph lines to the Little Dalles joining the Spokane Falls and Northern wires to Spokane, a newspaper, the *Nelson Miner,* established in 1890 by John Houston (later accused of biting Richard Marpole, the CPR superintendent, during a political argument), and a standing offer of $100,000 in property and cash to anyone who would erect and operate a smelter at Nelson.

Although the Nelson and Fort Sheppard had been chartered without subsidy and its incorporators were Canadians of good repute, a number of British Columbians voiced their open criticism of the project. Its opponents pointed out that no bond had been posted to assure its construction, called it a shameless gambit to promote Nelson and Kootenay Lake, an accusation emphasized by Gustavus Wright's sale of the Ainsworth townsite to directors of the Nelson and Fort Sheppard, or asserted, as did the *Inland Sentinel,* "that this particular charter is on the market for $100,000." Victoria businessmen generally supported the Nelson and Fort Sheppard, nevertheless, as the most direct route to the Kootenays. John Robson was saying, at the time, that two proposed roads, the Shuswap and Okanagan and the Okanagan and Kootenay, might join to provide a connection between the Canadian Pacific and the mines. Interior editors found this impractical: Robson's winding route would be three hundred miles long while a direct connection between Nelson and Revelstoke would run no more than one hundred.[4]

Nelson, too, supported the Nelson and Fort Sheppard, although its connection had been improved in 1890 with the completion of the Columbia and Kootenay, a twenty-eight mile railway from Robson [Sproat's Landing] on the Columbia to Nelson, by the Canadian Pacific. This had been a bitter task, interrupted by disputes with workmen over wages, wholesale decampings by employees to prospect when the grade uncovered a tiny vein of ore, and was frankly regarded by CPR President Van Horne as "a railroad from nowhere to nowhere."[5] The Columbia and Kootenay was intended to keep the district from becoming wholly Americanized and the Canadian Pacific hinted that it might "eventually form a portion of a line running through Crow's Nest Pass." Nelson's support of the Nelson and Fort Sheppard, consequently, was designed to flaunt the threat of a connection with Corbin to force the Canadian Pacific to build a southern leg of its main line, and in this the town succeeded, for in 1891 the CPR announced that it would apply for a charter from the next provincial legislature for a railway from the Crow's Nest to the coast, saying,

> The growing trade with China and Japan, and the desire to reach the rich mining region in south British Columbia ... necessitated this alternative route.[6]

Indicating Nelson's true attitude, the *Nelson Miner* suggested that both Colonel Baker and the owners of the Nelson and Fort Sheppard peddle their charters to the Canadian Pacific.

The Nelson and Fort Sheppard company did nothing toward building its railway except to urge that Corbin take its charter. His only public reply was his recommendation that the railway petition for a provincial land grant because land could be used as collateral to enhance the bonds that would have to be sold to pay for the construction. Consequently in 1892 the Nelson and Fort Sheppard applied for and was granted a subsidy of 10,240 acres of public land for each mile of railway completed, a grant that eventually delivered

Daniel Corbin between 580,000 and 614,000 acres.[7] The land was exempted from taxation for ten years, the road's rolling stock for five, and the members of the assemby at Victoria agreed that this was a good bargain, for the land between Nelson and the boundary was next to worthless. "They openly declared not one acre in ten thousand fit for agriculture," recalled a legislator later when the subsidy became a political issue. They understood that the grant might help finance the railway, however, and therefore allowed the Nelson and Fort Sheppard to select some land not adjacent to its right of way.

While the Victoria legislature approved the land grant that Corbin recommended for the Nelson and Fort Sheppard, it rejected Corbin's own petition for a route up the Kettle River without subsidy which would enable him to reach the American Okanogan district by the easiest course. He had needed only twelve miles of trackage in British Columbia. Part of the reason for this refusal lay in British Columbia's understandable preference for Canadian lines, and part in the provincial government's increasing caution about chartering or subsidizing railroads. In 1890, British Columbia had discontinued cash bonuses although it maintained its policy of granting 10,240 acres for each mile of completed line. The federal government usually subsidized railways at $3,200 per mile, an amount representing the cost of steel in 1882 when the grants were established, and left bonuses of land to the discretion of individual provinces.

Once the Nelson and Fort Sheppard had been chartered with its land subsidy at Victoria, the railroad required authorization from Ottawa. The Canadian Pacific formally leased the Columbia and Kootenay between the Columbia River and Nelson in April, 1892, in time for its interest in the mining region to attract the attention of the House railway committee which commenced its hearing on the Nelson and Fort Sheppard charter on June seventh.[8] The minister of justice, Sir John S. D. Thompson, opened the deliberation with his flat assertion that "Parliament should not give American connections with our own country before Canadian connections were obtained." The Nelson and Fort Sheppard's principal advocate be-

fore the committee was John Mara, who contended the route would
allow Victoria businessmen to ship by rail to the Kootenays, and
reminisced about his own arrival at Nelson in 1889 when he found
the camp dominated by American trade. "There was a rough trail
built by the provincial government," Mara recalled, "over which
freight costing ten cents a pound was carried, but owing to these
exorbitant rates there was little traffic done." By his recollections,
Mara hoped to demonstrate the Kootenays' need for transportation;
he argued that the Canadian Pacific could not push its alternative
route through the region in less than two years and the Kootenays
required a railway sooner than that.

In Mara's opinion, the Nelson and Fort Sheppard would not
present "the slightest danger of Canada losing the trade of the
Kootenay country." A committee member who failed to accept this
as hyperbole asked where Mara thought the Kootenay trade would
go if the Nelson and Fort Sheppard were allowed to connect its
line with the Spokane Falls and Northern, and Mara rejoined some-
what lamely that his constituents wanted the railway, twenty Nelson businessmen had telegraphed him their support of it, and he
merely reflected their views. At this point, Sir John Thompson proposed that the Nelson and Fort Sheppard charter be "postponed
for another year with a view of securing, if possible, that the
Kootenay country should be reached and supplied by Canadian
sources and connected with Canadian lines." That was what the
committee voted to do: postpone a federal charter for the Nelson and
Fort Sheppard for one year.

With Ottawa's assurance that it would charter the Nelson and
Fort Sheppard after twelve months had passed, D. C. Corbin revealed in Spokane on April 14, 1892, that he had "closed the deal
ten days ago" to construct the railroad. Doubtless he had ordered
the Spokane Falls and Northern extended to Northport as soon
as he perceived that the railway committee would not reject the
Nelson and Fort Sheppard charter outright. Mara and Frank Barnard both worked for Corbin's charter, although they had been
listless in support of the British Columbia Southern, and despite
the threat of the Nelson and Fort Sheppard to their steamboat line.

In the light of subsequent events, Corbin's agreement with the Nelson and Fort Sheppard appears similar to his contract with the Spokane Falls and Northern, stipulating that he receive all assets of the line including its land grant, that he construct and equip the railway at his expense, and that he be paid $25,000 a mile in securities of the company. Selling the securities and financing the Nelson and Fort Sheppard reverted to the Chapin cousins, Sherwood, and William Duryea of New York, who discovered that peddling railway stock was harder in 1892 than it had been in 1889 because the nation had been shaken by bank closures in 1890 and was sliding toward the Panic of 1893.[9] Corbin deposited $25,000 with the provincial secretary at Victoria as his bond against actual construction of the Nelson and Fort Sheppard and set about completing surveys of the most practical route in the year of waiting that lay before him.

Two surveying parties had studied alternative routes, one along the east bank of the Columbia to Robson and then eastward to Nelson on a track parallel to that of the Canadian Pacific's Columbia and Kootenay, the other leaving the Columbia north of the international boundary and following eastward generally the course of Beaver Creek to Cottonwood-Smith Creek, around Toad Mountain and down its slopes to Nelson. John Stevens, working under Roberts for $150 a month, laid out a sixty-five-mile route through stands of white and sugar pine, cedar, and hemlock, following streams over the tumbling country between Northport and Nelson. The surveyors climbed from 1,345 feet above sea level at Northport to 3,060 at the Salmon River summit twelve miles from Nelson, and then descended to 2,365 feet at Five Mile Point [Troup Junction].[10] Five Mile Point hung 620 feet on the hillside above the town of Nelson. After Stevens had surveyed this course, Corbin and Roberts traveled it together to satisfy themselves that none better could be located.

Corbin showed his interest in all the mining camps on both sides of the border. He sent Roberts on a two-week swing in June, 1892, through the Slocan, north of Nelson, seeking a passage that the Nelson and Fort Sheppard might use later. Jim Wardner was in the Slocan at the time, buying two-column advertisements to promote the district in the Spokane *Review*. Roberts was quoted as saying he had accurate figures on distances in the Slocan for the first time but Randall Kemp, who tried to interview him, found Roberts "uncommunicative as a church oyster." In July, Roberts drove a buckboard loaded with mining gear over a rutted trail from Marcus to Oro, in the Okanogan, in twenty-two hours and concluded the trail could be improved for a wagon road cheaply if towns along the route would contribute. Next Roberts tried to promote a wagon road from Northport to Trail Creek as a community effort financed by warrants to be issued by the Northport Townsite Company. And he set about extending the Spokane Falls and Northern, in August and September, 1892, to Northport.

If Corbin seriously considered the proposed route up the Columbia with track parallel to that of the Columbia and Kootenay, he soon discarded it in favor of Stevens' more direct line. The Nelson and Fort Sheppard had to be completed in the shortest time practical because its charter provided that the road must reach Nelson by the end of 1893 to qualify for its subsidy. Moreover, its New York promoters were scratching for money to construct it, got some by borrowing from their Land and Security Investment Company, and more from a series of securities: first mortgage bonds valued at $25,000 a mile, a land-grant stock issue at $25,000 a mile, and a capital stock issue in the same amount. Even E. J. Roberts chipped in some money, and the contractors were to pay their own men during the line's construction. Fortunately, British Columbia's new government led by Premier Theodore Davie who had succeeded on Robson's death in London, was more sympathetic toward railway projects of all kinds, and adopted a policy of chartering railways so that the companies and the enterprises they attracted could be placed on the provincial taxrolls.

Goaded by the specter of speed, graders began work between Northport and the border in the fourth week of November, 1892, under supervision of engineer W. C. Mitchell, prompting the Spokane *Review* to comment, "Undertaking the project in the middle of winter shows how anxious President Corbin is to connect Spokane with Nelson." Even though the railway was ostensibly under construction, Canadian criticism did not abate; strong rumors circulated that Corbin was building toward a junction with the southern extension of the Canadian Pacific under "some kind of agreement," and the *Inland Sentinel* declared the Nelson and Fort Sheppard "wrongfully subsidized," chiding Victoria's merchants for accepting Corbin's assurance that his road would benefit Victoria because goods would be handled fewer times between Nelson and the Tacoma waterfront. The newspaper warned that Corbin's "affable talk was for the purpose of securing a stronger hold . . . upon the mines and business of Kootenay Lake." Corbin's attention to British Columbia was not, however, confined to his railway; he and Roberts invested in mining property in Trail Creek, inspected coal deposits near Osooyos, and Corbin sank $12,000 into a quarter interest in the Bluebird claim in the Slocan on the advice of John M. Burke. Wardner, Burke—there were many familiar faces from the Coeur d'Alenes now in the Canadian camps.

Despite the urgency imposed by the Nelson and Fort Sheppard charter, little was done in the winter of 1892–93 toward building the line. When its year of waiting ended, however, the railway was chartered by the federal government "for the general advantage of Canada," the language prescribed by the railway act of 1883, and article six of the charter permitted the company to amalgamate with the Spokane Falls and Northern on approval of two-thirds of its stockholders and the governor-in-council.[11] The incorporators were committed to the merger, and promptly accomplished it, but there is no record that Corbin obtained the order in council.

As was his custom, Corbin had wintered in New York, returning to Spokane in February, 1893, with the remark that he was back to carry out his design of three years earlier to extend his railway "into all the region north that should be tributary to Spokane." The track was down by then almost to the border, and on April 11 Corbin awarded a construction contract to Peter Larson and Patrick Welch of Helena, Montana. Six had submitted bids, including Burns and Chapman of Spokane, ranging from $750,000 to $850,000, but an unwritten specification obliged the contractor to pay his own crews and the wealthy Larson qualified, on this score, without question. The contract required that the track be laid and ballasted to Nelson before the first snowfall, and in any case, not later than October first, excepting only the bridge that would span the Pend Oreille River near its junction with the Columbia. Larson had been a subcontractor on construction of the Northern Pacific's Cascade division and entered a partnership with Welch to bid on the Nelson and Fort Sheppard.

Now a familiar fabric of exploitation unfolded. Daniel Corbin joined four Victoria men to organize the West Kootenay Land Company to invest in real estate, insurance, and stocks. The other directors included: W. P. Sayward, a one-time Maine carpenter who now operated a sawmill at Pilot Bay on Kootenay Lake in partnership with Joshua Davies; Davies, himself, known throughout the province as auctioneer, appraiser, and commission merchant, who had succeeded to his father's business, the oldest of its kind in Victoria; Edgar Crow Baker, an organizer of the Victoria and Esquimalt telephone system, the man who in 1886 had introduced electric lights to Victoria, and now was prominent in business and government; and Thornton Fell, son of a Victoria mayor, a successful criminal defense attorney in his own right, and clerk of the provincial assembly beginning in 1879. Davies, Baker, and Joseph A. Sayward were also among the large shareholders in the Nelson City Land and Improvement Company, as was Charles Dupont, one of the incorporators of the Nelson and Fort Sheppard.

Managed by Davies, the West Kootenay Land Company preempted the townsite of Sayward on the Columbia at Beaver Creek, two miles north of the border where the Nelson and Fort Sheppard would leave the river and bear toward Nelson, and also secured waterfront property in Nelson as the terminal grounds for Corbin's railway, adjacent to the station of the Columbia and Kootenay. Davies set out to promote Sayward, a principal supply point for the Nelson and Fort Sheppard, as an up-and-coming metropolis, taking newspaper advertisements urging prospective landowners to buy at $100 to $150 a lot before prices inflated in the prosperity that, warned the ads, was sure to come.

Corbin also began selecting provincial land in the name of the Nelson and Fort Sheppard, land he would acquire when the line actually operated in British Columbia, choosing alternate blocks six by sixteen miles on either side of his proposed route. The assembly had graciously conceded that the blocks need not front on the track because there were to be so many curves in it, and accommodated Corbin by reserving his choices after August, 1892, although Ottawa was not to charter his railway for six months and the company filed no map of its route until March, 1893. Because the legislators agreed that the land was useless for agriculture, they consented to the Nelson and Fort Sheppard selecting part of its subsidy from lands not on the railway; and Corbin chose 4,600 acres already in litigation on a bench of Red Mountain, north of the original townsite of Rossland, the bull's-eye of the Trail Creek mining district.[12]

Although the contractors attempted to begin grading in May, landslides and mud delayed most of their work until warmer weather. To save freight costs, avoid duties, and perchance impress his Canadian friends, Corbin ordered food stuffs, hardware, boots, and harness from Winnipeg firms. Larson and Welch cleared south from Nelson while Roberts cleared north from the border. By the middle of June, Roberts had laid track from Northport across the boundary to the mouth of the Pend Oreille River, engines were hauling up steel to bridge the river, and on June 26 the Spokane Falls and Northern inaugurated daily-except-Sunday service between Spokane and the Canadian border. By this date eight hundred men worked on the railway construction and more were being hired daily. Roberts predicted that he would soon lay a mile of track a day and reach Nelson by October first. When he had a free moment, he spent it in arguing with the Canadian customs men who demanded that he pay duty on his steamshovel every time it crossed the boundary although he had paid the first time.

By midsummer the workmen were paid irregularly as a result of the sweeping Panic of 1893 that followed a market decline on May 5 and a crash on June 27, but construction of the Nelson and Fort Sheppard continued, the men trusting that Corbin eventually would make good his warrants. When the company did declare a pay day, Austin Corbin II rode the line in a special car handing out cash from its rear platform. Larson and Welch paid their men by check, requiring that the checks be cashed at their office in Sayward, thus saving some cash, for a number of workers held their checks until they happened to be near the town. Nelson's merchants objected that the contractors were boycotting them by this system, but Larson and Welch continued it.

Early during the winter of 1892–93 Roberts had called bids on the Pend Oreille River bridge, receiving seven, some with comments on his specifications like that of the Edgemoor Bridge Works, Chicago, regarding reamed steel: "We do not consider it necessary and most roads do not do it." [13] Hugh L. Cooper, the young engineer representing the Dominion Bridge Company, a subsidiary of the San Francisco Bridge Company, recommended reamed steel, however, and his company won the contract on its bid of $47,700 when he agreed that it would also build the substructure. [14] The bridge quickly became a local wonder, for Cooper's workmen had seated its concrete piers in freezing February on rock foundations that would be covered by the river as soon as warmer weather came.

Roberts took an immediate liking to Cooper, allowing him leeway in bridge design which resulted in a singular cantilever that Roberts called "Cooper's grasshopper." A provincial inspector who examined it thought the structure "apparently good for all time to come." The fascination of the steel span brought men from miles around to see it. Requiring the sharpest turn on the entire Nelson and Fort Sheppard route, a twelve-degree curve at its southern approach, the bridge consisted of a main span 250 feet long and two others, each 125 feet, at either end. Concrete abutments, set on solid rock and encased in riveted Belgian steel, lifted the roadbed thirty-five feet above anticipated high water. By the middle of July the wondrous steel bridge was almost done so that painters could start at its ends while Cooper's men completed the center.

By July, too, Larson and Welch broke their camps at Waneta, British Columbia, on the Columbia River at the boundary, and at notorious Boundary, Washington, which had lived six months as a town, boasted a population of twelve hundred, and had run wide open with saloons, dance halls, and gaming tables until the construction crews moved on. Then the pianos fell silent and the buildings were knocked down for their lumber.

Roberts started laying track on the Canadian side of the international line on July 16, using English rails shipped via San Francisco as ballast in wheat vessels to avoid duties, estimating they were five to six dollars a ton cheaper than importing steel from the United States. The tracklayers worked northward from the border, rather than beginning at both ends as the graders had, and within a month Roberts had them putting down his mile a day. By early September when the tracks still were twenty-five miles from Nelson, the citizens of the town were looking expectantly toward the hills to see the first engine poke its stack into view, and on September 14 Roberts summoned all idle men in the area to join him, declaring he would reach Nelson in a few weeks.

Five days later the Archduke Franz Ferdinand of Austria momentarily diverted public attention from the railway construction when he sailed down the lakes from Revelstoke on the steamer *Columbia* and boarded the Spokane Falls and Northern at Northport. Spectators lined the track when the duke's special train reached Spokane, and the city staged an afternoon military parade in honor of the man whose assassination twenty-one years later was to kindle a world war. Perhaps the martial music stirred Nelson W. Durham, editor of the *Spokesman-Review* (the *Spokesman* and *Review* had merged earlier in the year) to write:

> I desire to say that Spokane owes to Mr. D. C. Corbin an enduring obligation.... He is doing more today to develop the wilderness and strengthen Spokane than any other man.

By October twenty-first the tracks had been spiked down within twelve miles of Nelson. Snow was in the air, and Corbin could see that he might have to battle the weather to complete his line by the end of the year and thus qualify for his land grant. A rumor, soon dispelled, aroused Nelson; Roberts, said the gossips, was using a machine that laid two miles of track a day. Roberts had the machine on display again but he continued to lay rail by hand. Nelson citizens bundled against the chill to walk out to see the railroad coming, not a few inquiring whether the trains would operate in winter, and the engineers replied that the Nelson and Fort Sheppard was to be an all-weather line.

Corbin, himself, repeated this assurance when he visited Nelson near the end of October, announcing that he had purchased a $14,-000 rotary snowplow to clear the tracks during the winter. He had intended to spend several days in Nelson completing details for his waterfront depot near the Columbia and Kootenay, but now the Canadian Pacific produced a letter written by the late John Robson reserving the lakefront to the Canadian Pacific, alone. This document extinguished Corbin's plan to run the Nelson and Fort Sheppard to the water or to provide transfer facilities to the Columbia and Kootenay. He actually spent only one night at Nelson, for shortly after his arrival the busy Corbin received a telegram summoning him to Hall Creek where a locomotive waited to carry him over the newly completed track, and he hurried to ride it as the Nelson and Fort Sheppard's first passenger to Spokane on October 28, 1893.

The tracklayers hove in view of Nelson on November 18, and mindful of curiosity about it, Roberts used the machine. The *Nelson Miner* described the scene:

> The first locomotive with the tracklaying machine and sidecars came around the hill into view of Nelson Sunday. Every three or four minutes the engine whistle would toot and the train advance thirty-two feet, indicating another set of rails down.[15]

Time was growing dangerously short, however, to complete the railway to Nelson, to have it inspected by a provincial engineer, and on the basis of his report to receive authority to begin operation. All of this had to be accomplished before the end of December or forfeit the Nelson and Fort Sheppard's land grant. With cold weather closing in, E. J. Roberts resorted to laying his ties and spiking track along the construction wagon road to Five Mile Point, gentling an engine over this makeshift trackage, and demanding the inspection. The next spring he was to tear up his wagon-road rails and rebuild these last few miles in the substantial manner intended. By this time, the company's funds were so low that Peter Larson was paying the costs of construction.

With the railway ostensibly as near Nelson as the Canadian Pacific would allow, the provincial government assigned George A. Keefer, a civil engineer who also acted as the Davies-Sayward mill agent at Nelson, to inspect the line. Had Keefer discovered any shortcoming that would require extensive adjustment, he could conceivably have delayed legal completion of the railway beyond the end of 1893, but he received red-carpet treatment and reported that the Nelson and Fort Sheppard was admirably constructed. Only seventeen days before the end of 1893, on December 14, Keefer rode over the Nelson and Fort Sheppard in a special train, accompanied by E. J. Roberts and Austin Corbin II. He found that

> as the entire distance is absolutely wilderness, further than telegraph stations or ore shipments, there can be little demand for station accommodations for some time to come.[16]

Despite the snow that precluded a minute inspection of the roadbed, Keefer said, "I have no hesitation in pronouncing the road as a good, workable, well-built railway, with an exceptionally smooth track." He thought the Pend Oreille bridge would "stand for all time," and considering the nature of the mountainous country, the route's "percentage of curvature ... is less than the average on similar lines." At every curve of four degrees or more, Roberts had ordered steel braces spiked to the tamarack ties to reinforce the rails so they would not spread under the centrifugal thrust of the engine's wheels. Keefer counted eight 1,000-foot sidings, each holding twenty cars, at Waneta, Beaver, Meadows, Salmon, Hall, Summit, Kootenay, and Nelson. With the inspector's approval certain, Roberts announced that the temporary frame depot at Five Mile Point would be finished on December 19, and the Nelson and Fort Sheppard would open for freight that day.

On the appointed day for the first scheduled train, the citizens of Nelson marched up the hill and marched down again, as the *Miner* reported:

The first train over the Nelson & Fort Sheppard arrived in from Spokane on Tuesday evening. It was expected that D. C. Corbin would accompany the first batch of passengers, and arrangements were made...for a rousing reception at the depot. The band was induced to turn out, and half a dozen teams were waiting to take those averse to walking up the hillside to the depot. Before train time, nearly every man in town was at the station.[17]

The train arrived nearly an hour and a half late but the *Miner's* editor, Houston, pointed out that the cars had been behind schedule at Northport and apparently ran between Northport and Nelson without delay. Thus Daniel Corbin finally had his railroad into Canada. To be sure, wasteland lay between stations, the contractors had not been paid, and the track ended five miles out of town; but the Nelson and Fort Sheppard was operating, nevertheless, Corbin's tangible trophy. Without the railway, said the *Rossland Miner,* "southern Kootenay would be practically at a standstill for six months of the year." The winding road swooped and glided over the mountains along the various waterways John Stevens had chosen as the best route, climbing steadily from Nelson on the line's steepest ascent, a two-and-a-half per cent grade, to the Salmon divide. Here, said the *Spokesman-Review,* one saw "to all points of the compass...bold, rugged, majestic mountains." The Nelson and Fort Sheppard was fifty-five miles long; if extended to the Nelson waterfront, it would be sixty.

The railway promptly published rates. Ore valued at not more than one hundred dollars a ton in carloads of 20,000 pounds or more could be shipped by boat from Kaslo in the Slocan to Nelson, for example, and by rail from Nelson to Tacoma at nine dollars a ton. Trail Creek ores could be barged down the Columbia to Northport, so that the Nelson and Fort Sheppard could be said to serve both the principal mining camps of the Kootenays. Much of the ore hauled by the railway eventually went as far as the Selby smelter in San Francisco or via the Great Northern to the United Mining Works at Great Falls, Montana. The *Rossland Miner* regarded the railway's rates as "extremely fair," while complaining that because the company had not provided equipment for transferring freight at Waneta, the Nelson and Fort Sheppard had no means of delivering goods from Nelson directed to Trail Creek, other than hauling them across the border for consignment to a northbound steamer on the Columbia.

Much had not been done as planned, for despite Corbin's long fight to enter Canada, now that he had his railway it was not particularly successful. Snow or mud slides occasionally delayed trains or swept away sections of track. The wagon road between the end of the track and Nelson constantly hampered the railroad, as the *Nelson Miner* complained: "Nelson people have to rise at five, go a mile and a quarter to the Nelson & Fort Sheppard station on the hill and wait until eight or nine when the train pulls out." Moreover, Corbin discovered that, although his charter permitted him to erect and operate telegraph and telephone lines along the railway's right of way, his attorney had neglected to obtain permission to collect tolls for these services.

In its first full year of operation, 1894, the Nelson and Fort Sheppard was buffeted both by nature and by financial worries. Early in the year, Corbin bought two locomotives, and later was to add two passenger cars and a caboose, but although the railroad used twenty-one freight cars regularly, it never owned any, borrowing most of its rolling stock from the Spokane Falls and Northern. In June, floods on the Columbia and its tributaries cost Corbin nearly a quarter of a million dollars in repairs, money his railways could ill afford. A wall of muddy water sucked the earth from beneath the tracks at Five Mile Point, narrowly missing the depot. At Northport, rising water drove residents to higher ground, and some drilled holes through the outer walls of their houses to tie them with heavy ropes to their foundations. Water covered the rails near Colville deeply enough to put out a locomotive's boiler fire.[18]

Meanwhile, in February, Peter Larson had ridden a special train to Nelson to file a mechanics' lien of $328,044 against the Nelson and Fort Sheppard for work accomplished but not compensated. Andrew, John, and Richard Porter of Spokane, subcontractors who erected trestles, filed a second lien. Such a lien had long been recognized in many United States territories and states but, having been authorized by the provincial legislature in 1891, was neither tried in British Columbia nor recognized by the Dominion. The two liens broadcast Corbin's quest for more money, for he had been, as the *Nelson Miner* put it, "in the East for some time endeavoring to raise the wind." Both the land and physical assets of the Nelson and Fort Sheppard had been mortgaged to the Manhattan Trust Company, New York, and to compound its troubles, the railway's annual statement for June 30, 1895, was to show that it was operating $6,476 in the red. The *Rossland Miner* observed that

> the road was built, as everybody knows, under the most trying circumstances, it being utterly impossible to place any sort of railroad securities in New York or London. It was only by risking his own private fortune, and only because of the confidence that others had in the personal integrity of Mr. Corbin, that he was enabled to build the Nelson & Fort Sheppard road.

In May, 1894, the court at Nelson ruled that Larson and Welch's plaintiff's brief, showing that they ended their work on January 10, 1894, failed to contain a sufficient statement of time as required by the law, allowing an appeal to the British Columbia supreme court in order to test the 1891 statute. The higher bench dismissed the contractors' claims on January 12, 1896, ruling that the interest of bond holders superseded that of lien holders under the Railway Act of Canada, and observing that, if the mechanics' lien were applied, nobody would risk investing in a railway because workers might use the provincial law to acquire the line's assets.[19]

In later years, Corbin waxed poetic about this arduous struggle to pay for the Nelson and Fort Sheppard, saying, "After a long and anxious period I managed to sail my ship into calm waters and out of reach of receivers." It was, he added, "a time when a man either had to brace up and fight... or lay down and be wiped out."[20] The year 1894 proved the worst for the Nelson and Fort Sheppard, for despite repeal of the Sherman Silver Purchase Act in 1893, the mines of the Slocan continued to ship for a few years longer and most of their ore rode the Nelson and Fort Sheppard. British Columbia ore shipments through the United States customs at Northport were valued at $868,567 in 1895, and at more than $2,182,607 in 1896. Moreover, at the end of the fiscal year June 30, 1897, the Nelson and Fort Sheppard was to record a profit of $62,917, while W. C. Nolan, the customs officer at Nelson, reported that American goods shipped into Canada through his port amounted to more than thirty thousand dollars a month. New mining camps sprang up along the railway's route, notably at Erie, Ymir, and Sheep Creek, British Columbia, the last shipping from Salmo station, and although a number of claims proved shortlived, they provided a temporary profit for the Nelson and Fort Sheppard, the railway that allowed D. C. Corbin to back into Canada.

Corbin's final victory was denied him, however, for his railway never reached the waterfront. Nelson's citizens petitioned Victoria in October, 1894, to demand that the Nelson and Fort Sheppard complete a switchback into the town, and during the first months of 1895 various members of the provincial government attempted individually to persuade the Canadian Pacific to relent in its blockade, but even a conference called personally by Premier Davie failed to move the Canadian railroad. Finally in May, 1895, Colonel Baker, who had talked over the situation with CPR President Van Horne, said that the Canadian Pacific had consented to let Corbin pass, and that a letter had been written notifying Corbin of this decision. The letter, lost in transit for a month, turned out to be ambiguous, and although the Nelson and Fort Sheppard poked track tentatively nearer Nelson, its new depot lay one and three-tenths miles from town, so that the minister of public works reported that in 1896, the wagon road having been much out of repair, he had ordered it straightened and had put in three new bridges and culverts. And that was the end of the Nelson and Fort Sheppard. The trains now ran, reasoned the *Nelson Miner,* "to a spot which by a pleasing legal fiction may be regarded as at or near Nelson." [21]

CHAPTER TEN

RACE TO RED MOUNTAIN

L OOKING BACK, D. C. CORBIN'S THREE-YEAR STRUGGLE TO PENETRATE the Kootenay mining district with a railroad to Nelson delivered him a specious victory because, while he built eastward to Kootenay Lake, the axis of mining in British Columbia shifted westward to the Columbia River. Nelson strove to hold its mining commerce but nothing prevailed against the delirious tide sweeping over Trail Creek and the new camp at Rossland. Corbin, too, turned toward Trail Creek. Consequently, his contention with a flamboyant American promoter, F. Augustus Heinze, for the business of Trail Creek was to boom the camp. Its mines were barely uncovered in 1891 before prospectors were saying, as they had of Leadville, Butte, the Comstock, and would of the Yukon, that Trail Creek was the biggest bonanza of them all.

Nelson had just begun to brag that it was the province's sixth largest city when two grimy prospectors hove into town with a sack of ore samples that would puncture its pretentions. Repeal of the Sherman Silver Purchase Act by the United States shriveled the Slocan, Ainsworth's claims proved to be mostly low-grade, the Hall mines were sold to British investors, and the hub of the Kootenays flitted from Nelson to Rossland, seven miles up Trail Creek from the west bank of the Columbia. The Nelson and Fort Sheppard had been completed during economic panic, and for Spokane, 1893–94 had been hard years: the cereal crop failed in 1894, many mines in Idaho and British Columbia closed, and the heart of the city's business district was mortgaged to Dutch investors. But with general improvement in 1895, Spokane also perked up. Its first period of expansion had begun with arrival of the Northern Pacific in 1881 and ended in 1893. Now while Rossland bloomed in the competitive warmth of Corbin *versus* Heinze, Spokane basked in its second season of increase. To understand Corbin's part in developing Rossland and with it, Spokane, one must know something of Rossland; and to comprehend Corbin's contest for the Kootenays, one must know about the magnetic Fritz Heinze.

Rossland's story began when two prospectors working as partners, Joseph Bourgeois and Joe Moris, found ore on Red Mountain on July 2, 1890, near a claim called the Lily May, a gilded Lily lying about sixty-five miles west of Nelson on the hillside overlooking Trail Creek.[1] Bourgeois—the Americans called him "Bushway"—and Moris staked four claims, the Centre Star, War Eagle, Virginia, and Idaho, took some ore samples from each and walked to Nelson to have them assayed. Because the ore puzzled the assayer, he wrote a discouraging report and Bourgeois was ready to throw up the claims but Moris, as Moris later told his tale, urged that the partners at least record them and perhaps do a little more work. Bourgeois consented but would not pay the recording fees, although he was carrying seven hundred dollars, so the two prospectors offered the deputy recorder, Eugene Sayre Topping, an extension of the Centre Star if he would pay their fees and his own, totaling $12.50.[2] Topping asked to see the strikes first, walked back to Trail Creek with the two, decided that all five claims appeared worthwhile, sealed his bargain, named his extension the Le Roi, and realizing that these five claims would prompt a rush, pre-empted a townsite at the mouth of Trail Creek where it flows into the Columbia. The five locations lay on the eastern slope of Red Mountain, named for its reddish earth, in an area composed geologically of slates with a number of vertical basalt dykes. Investigations were to show that the important mineral bodies had collected where dykes intersected, a yellow, nonsulphide ore bearing copper, gold, and silver.

Thus were the great mines of Red Mountain found, as chance

would have it, by two prospectors whose earlier partners had quit them, and who bickered and argued as they searched, staking claims that returned disappointing assays so they would not even pay the recording fees.

Topping would have not become involved if he had not been down on his luck. A native of New York State, he had gone to sea in 1853 as a boy of eleven, given up sailing for scouting in Wyoming, Utah, and Montana in his twenties, and finally turned prospector. He hunted in the Yellowstone region without finding ore; he wrote a book, *Chronicles of Yellowstone,* which was briefly popular in 1883, and consequently tried newspaper work. Soon he returned to prospecting, first in the Black Hills, next for four unlucky years in the Coeur d'Alenes, and in 1888, the Kootenays. Topping had been injured so he could not poke through the hills and he temporarily secured an assortment of jobs: store manager for Lemon and Hume, real estate salesman, constable, and deputy recorder, and was performing them all in Nelson when Bourgeois and Moris asked him to pay their recording fees for a claim of his own. Fortunately, they found him just as Topping was enough recovered to walk to Trail Creek.[3]

Topping spread his report of the find quickly, starting a rush toward Trail Creek, the same stampede that had delayed the *Lytton* en route to its first meeting with the Spokane Falls and Northern, and by fall all the ground around Red Mountain had been staked, the notices fluttered on poles down the creek toward Topping's townsite, and still prospectors came. With them rose the familiar pleas for railroads, smelters, lower—or higher—tariffs, depending on the nationality of the speaker of the moment, and all the other tools of exploitation which prospectors demanded.

Topping did not have enough money to develop his Le Roi claim, but he sold it for $30,000 to George M. Forster and William Ridpath of Spokane, who formed a company and issued stock. In the spring of 1891, ten tons of picked ore from the bottom of a thirty-five foot shaft, smelted at the Colorado works in Butte, returned $84.40 a ton in silver, copper, and gold, which convinced the company that its property was worth working. Forster and Ridpath

DANIEL CHASE CORBIN
October 1, 1832—June 29, 1918

Taken from a program of the Northwest Mining Association, this portrait was captioned: "Spokane's Greatest Empire Builder."

The steamer Coeur d'Alene *beside the loading dock at Old Mission on the Coeur d'Alene River, and a CR&N engine on the spur that ran to the waterfront. This photo was taken about 1887.*

Wallace, Idaho, financial capital of the Coeur d'Alene district mines, in 1888. The Corbin railway depot stands at lower center, and the wooden sidewalks which Corbin cooperated in providing lead from the bridge across the south fork of the Coeur d'Alene River to the central business structures. (T. N. Barnard photo)

Glidden's Tiger Mine buildings, and the terminus of his Canyon Creek railway which connected with Corbin's line near Wallace. The Tiger buildings and others nearby became the town of Burke, Idaho. The Poorman Mine, left, and the Tiger, right center, eventually were consolidated.

The first OR&N train to pass through Harrison, Idaho, near the mouth of the Coeur d'Alene River on Coeur d'Alene Lake. The steamer Amelia Wheaton is tied at the Harrison dock. This was the rail line that built south of the lake to reach the Idaho mines.

The first Mrs. D. C. Corbin—Louisa. (Loaned by Mrs. Leo A. Doyle)

A portrait of D. C. Corbin donated to the Spokane Chamber of Commerce by its mining committee on the occasion of Corbin's election as the chamber's first honorary member.

From the Colville Indian Reservation, this photograph looks across the Columbia River to Northport, where the Lytton *is starting upstream and a SF&N train stands on the spur near water level behind the steamer. This picture was taken about 1897.*

Arrival of Spokane Falls and Northern No. 1 at the Northport depot on June 15, 1897. (E. J. Roberts glass plate)

The Le Roi smelter under construction at Northport in 1897.

Rossland, British Columbia, as it appeared in 1897.

Spokane International freight on the outskirts of Sandpoint, Idaho, about 1910. (Robert Pearson Collection)

D. C. Corbin home in Spokane in 1960. It has been used as an art center and park department headquarters, and its spacious grounds have been converted to Pioneer Park with those of the old F. R. Moore and George Turner home which was razed.

brought into the Le Roi company other Spokane men: Oliver Durant and his partner, Alex Tarbet, W. W. D. Turner, Harry Stimmel, and J. R. Taylor, and gradually sold its treasury stock to continue development. Informed mining men had long considered the ores of the region too low-grade for profitable treatment, however, and the stock moved slowly at twenty-five cents a share until Danville, Illinois, investors put in $25,000.

The depression in 1893 and momentary diversion of prospectors to the Slocan beginning in 1891 had slowed the germination of the Trail Creek camp, to which Ross Thompson had come on a prospecting trip from Bonners Ferry. He had the foresight to pre-empt 160 acres as a townsite on the flats below the Le Roi, and to form a townsite company which called the settlement Thompson and then Rossland. During 1893, Thompson was reduced to foraging supplies from the Centre Star simply to eat, but the Le Roi began shipments from its stockpile in 1893-94 by sleighing ore to the Columbia and barging it to the Spokane Falls and Northern, the War Eagle shipped small consignments, and both paid dividends: the Le Roi every month, the War Eagle quarterly. Rossland had puffed a little during a flurry of gold prospecting in 1893 but with two dividend-paying mines in camp, it experienced another stampede. By the end of 1895, 1,995 claims were recorded in the vicinity of Red Mountain, the town of Rossland would have grown to a rude collection of tents, huts, and frame stores (some built of lumber scavenged from defunct Boundary) with men gossiping about mines and whittling on street corners, and soon was to be described in a settlers' guide published in London as "cosmopolitan, with men of all nationalities" tramping its dirt streets, "a Chinese in white shoes, a Yankee spitting in season and out of season," an unpainted village surrounded by humpy peaks dominated by the fire-bald eminence of Red Mountain.[4] Ross Thompson became a civic leader and town councilman, typhoid was nearly as common as mineral fever, and Little Egypt came to shimmy. Three hundred feet up the hillside nestled the Le Roi at the end of a road that was everlastingly muddy with random planks strewn as duckboards.

Daniel Corbin was probably as aware of the area's potential as any man; in 1890 he had sent E. J. Roberts through the region scouting for coal deposits as far west as Osooyos, and in 1892 he had directed Frank George to ship two tons of selected Iron Mask ore to Anaconda for smelting with a return of gold and copper valued at $34.00 per ton. With Roberts, Corbin purchased the Yellowjacket and Standard claims, and his son, Austin, joined the War Eagle company, organized in December, 1894, with Roberts, I. N. Peyton, and Patrick Clark, who had pilfered ore in 1887 for Simeon Reed from the Bunker Hill and Sullivan.

Rossland was to pass through two periods of investment, the first spanning roughly the years 1895–97 when nearly all the money in camp was American, and the second 1898–1900, during which Canadian and British financiers bought out the Americans. Their investments would be profitable only when railroads and smelters stood readily at hand, for Red Mountain's transportation, like that of most mining camps, was primitive. Some ore had issued from the district in 1893, so Canadian customs stationed inspectors at Trail Creek and Waneta in that year,[5] but a good deal of the mines' production seems to have crossed the border without bother about tariffs, consigned by wagon to Northport over a rutted road that one driver said ran "four miles through a cedar swamp." No customs station was established on this route until 1895, when a Canadian officer was assigned to Sheep Creek, now Paterson.

Steamship operators successfully blocked provincial appropriations to improve sections of the road because ore that was not sent by wagon road was dragged or packed by mules, or carried by wagon, to the landing at Trail Creek and floated down the Columbia by steam barge. Palouse farmers often took their horses to Rossland to haul ore after the harvest, but Canadian tariff regulations, which allowed American horses into the country duty-free, would not let the same horses haul out ore without paying, so tariff-exempt Canadian teams pulled outbound wagons with American teams tied behind. Moreover, the United States waived its two-cents-a-pound tariff on Canadian ore when silver content exceeded the lead, but frequently suggested that bills of lading had been manipulated, for most ore seemed heavy with silver and light of lead.

Corbin estimated that $300,000 would be required to extend his Spokane Falls and Northern into Rossland. He took his first steps to reach Rossland by rail during 1894, after Roberts located a route that followed generally Sheep Creek across the Colville Indian Reservation, with an application to the General Land Office in July for a right of way across the Indian lands.[6] He and Roberts actively promoted a wagon road along the same route, and in November, 1894, Roberts escorted the Stevens County commissioners over the road and solicited their help in paying for it.

Corbin also applied for a Canadian charter for his railway, the Red Mountain, and was granted authority by British Columbia to build the line without subsidy and with the stipulations that he break ground before April 12, 1895, and complete the line in two years. Of twenty-one railways chartered to operate in the Kootenays between 1890-98, Corbin's was the only one to receive no government aid of any kind. The railway was to be seventeen miles long, running between Northport and Rossland. Corbin, his son Austin, Frank George, and the attorney, Albert Allen, incorporated the Columbia and Red Mountain on January 24, 1895.[7]

Thus as Rossland entered its first period of rapid expansion with American capital, Corbin was poised to build a railway, waiting only on approval of his right of way by the United States, and a federal charter from Canada. As usual, the Canadian Pacific overtly opposed him.

While Corbin waited, E. S. Topping busily promoted his townsite at the mouth of Trail Creek and the mines at Rossland, telling anyone who would listen his enthusiastic plans for his town, and keeping his eyes open for a man with money who would transform his talk into reality. As early as 1893, Topping had proposed Trail Creek as an advantageous smelter site, and later that same year, he and his erstwhile partner, a blacksmith from Nelson, Frank Hanna, had hacked the rude road between Trail Creek and Rossland. In 1894, Topping and Hanna erected a hotel, the Trail House, advertising it as a resort for those "satiated with the turmoil of Rossland city life. One of the proprietors will drink and the other will smoke with every guest."

By May, 1895, river barges could not handle all the ore piling up on mine stockpiles. The Le Roi, War Eagle, and Josie shipped a hundred tons a day by wagon to Trail Creek and steam barge down the Columbia to Northport. The camp was inspected by a number of Montana promoters; and among these, Topping found the man he wanted, a shrewd, bookish smelterman, James Breen, who worked for F. Augustus Heinze, the young owner of a copper smelter at Butte. Breen had scouted Nelson early in May, where the merchants had offered cash and land to anyone who put a smelter there, and then turned to Rossland where he paced through the claims, investigating each thoughtfully. Six weeks after Breen's first visit to Rossland, he returned with Heinze in tow.

Heinze was to compete with D. C. Corbin over command of the Kootenay for the next three years, for Corbin had acknowledged that his plans to enter Rossland included a smelter at Northport. This had roused Topping to seek a smelter builder for Trail Creek and to take a public stand against the Red Mountain Railway, with the old accusation that it would siphon Canadian commerce to the United States. The *Nelson Tribune,* commenting on a Topping letter to the newspapers attacking Corbin, supported the Red Mountain Railway with the equally musty opinion that it would hasten the Canadian Pacific's construction to the district. In the competition between Corbin and Heinze was to lie the genesis of the Rossland boom.

Heinze reached British Columbia in July, 1895, a few weeks after Albert E. Humphreys, a mining promoter from Duluth, Minnesota, had closed a deal with Topping for half the Trail Creek townsite and had set out, with Martin King, to raise a tramway from the Iron Horse mine through Rossland to the landing at Trail Creek. Soon Heinze was swooping about Rossland tossing off schemes that set the district buzzing, fancies plucked from the mountain air, laced with plausibility because Heinze had devised and owned a smelter in Montana. Breen had told the Canadians (at Nelson, as it happened) that if they demonstrated that ore could be smelted as cheaply in Canada as in the United States, they would have their smelter, and now he brought Heinze to squint at the hillside claims, turn ore in his fingers, and talk smelting with the mine managers.

In Heinze, Topping recognized experience and money, and like nearly everyone else, he was charmed by the glib, dashing youngster. Topping and Humphreys agreed to give Heinze one-third of the Trail Creek townsite plus twenty acres of his choosing as a smelter location. Legend has it that the three men drew for specific Trail Creek town lots and when one hundred and fifty remained, played poker for them. After being down to four chips, Heinze won them all. He was then twenty-six years old, athletic although a little pudgy, popular with men and women alike but partial to the company of rich men, a gambler, and a mining engineer. His parties rivaled anything seen in New York, his friends boasted, and Heinze and Breen both enrolled as charter members of the rollicking Rossland Banquet Club that included the town's influential men.

When he arrived in British Columbia, Heinze boasted a brief but spectacular career. Born Frederick Augustus Heinze on December 5, 1869, in Brooklyn, New York, he was the fifth of six children of a well-to-do importer, Otto C. Heinze. The father, strict in disciplining young Fritz and his two older brothers, Otto and Arthur, was also careful with their education, sending them to school in New York and Germany. Fritz took a degree from the Columbia University School of Mines in 1891, and then, against his father's wish, went to Butte, Montana, where with the help of Leonard Lewisohn he obtained a post as surveyor at five dollars a day with the Boston and Montana Company.

Heinze lived alone in Butte, a man about town, spent much of his time poring over surveyors' maps that showed in detail the arrangement of the Butte mines, and after a year, returned to New York with the intention of raising capital to build a smelter. His father refused to put money into a project he did not understand, however, and old Otto's friends proved similarly cautious. To maintain himself, Fritz joined the staff of *Engineering and Mining Journal,* "the only man who habitually came to the office wearing a top hat and a frock coat," observed his obituary in that magazine, and his coworkers noted that he avoided confining work and devoted much of his days to discussing his scheme for a smelter at Butte.[8]

Approximately a year after his return to New York, Fritz and his brothers came into their father's modest fortune, and with part of his fifty-thousand-dollar share, Fritz studied mining and metallurgical methods in Germany. In 1893 he went back to Butte with money from his brothers, former schoolmates, and his own resources, to build a custom smelter, ramshackle but operative. Fritz, who now was calling himself F. Augustus Heinze, held 51 per cent of the stock in his company, the Montana Ore Purchasing Company, incorporated March 1, 1893, in Montana. Brother Otto held 15 per cent; Arthur, 25; two friends, Stanley Gifford and John MacGinness, 7; and 2 per cent was retained. The smelter began treating ore in January, 1894, and made a profit so quickly that Arthur cast aside his legal practice and moved to Butte to administer the Heinze enterprises.

Fritz's earlier investigation of Butte tunnels convinced him the Rarus would pay, although it was generally considered worked out, and the Heinze brothers bought it for $30,000, all they could afford, guaranteeing to pay $270,000 more within twelve months. When Fritz dug the $270,000 out of the old mine before a year had passed, Butte was dazzled. Thus when Fritz Heinze appeared at Trail Creek, with Breen before him to tell what manner of man this was, and other Montanans to attest the truth of his tale, there is little wonder that Topping coveted Heinze as his partner in developing Trail Creek.

With his engineer's skill, Heinze chose his twenty-acre smelter site on a sandy, level plateau about two hundred feet above the Columbia River, where the height would allow him to operate trams and dumps by gravity, and talked boldly of establishing a refining plant at Spokane to treat the matte, the product of his proposed Trail Creek smelter. Heinze approached Corbin for a promise of reduced rates to carry the matte between Trail Creek and Spokane over the Spokane Falls and Northern, and also attempted to extract Corbin's pledge that the Columbia and Red Mountain would be completed promptly.[9] According to E. J. Roberts, Corbin rejected

an alliance with Heinze, athough the two were always outwardly
cordial. Corbin could not have promised anything with regard to
the Columbia and Red Mountain, at the moment, for he lacked
authority to cross the Colville Reservation, and understood he could
not hurry the national government.[10]

Breen propelled Heinze into action in British Columbia by ar-
ranging a contract with the Le Roi to process 70,000 tons of its ore,
using as his lever a struggle for control within the Le Roi company.
The Turner and Peyton factions had fallen out and it is said that
Heinze supplied George Turner $58,400 to buy 58,400 shares of
Le Roi stock, the balance of power, as an inducement for delivering
the contract. George Forster sold to Turner, remarking that he never
expected his stock to be worth one dollar a share. The agreement
provided that Heinze would buy 37,500 tons after sampling, would
deduct eleven dollars a ton for transportation and treatment, and
would purchase the second 37,500 tons at the lowest market price
at the time of delivery, minus eleven dollars a ton. Heinze also
stood to earn a half dollar a ton from the Canadian government, up
to a limit of $30,000, as a bonus for ore smelted in the Dominion.
Although the average cost of transporting and treating Trail Creek
ore was twenty-one dollars a ton, and Heinze's contract promised
to reduce this to eleven dollars, the provincial minister of mines
commented, in his report for 1897, "Mining experts felt Rossland ore
might be treated for seven dollars a ton f.o.b. profitably by the
smelter."

Heinze employed his Le Roi contract to induce the provincial
government, which now included helpful friends, to grant him two
square miles of timber for constructing and fueling his smelter.
British Columbia contained so much timber that the government
tended to regard trees as something of a nuisance, and two square
miles of trees seemed little enough for Heinze to ask.[11] Now that he
had a contract to carry and process ore, Heinze required some means
of transportation and a smelter. In September, 1895, he awarded
a contract to Thomas Olson of Spokane to excavate, ditch, cut wood,
and build the masonry sections of the smelter, and ordered surveys
of a tramway route that superseded Humphreys' between Trail Creek

and Rossland, intended to serve all the major mines rather than one. The survey proposed a number of switchbacks because Rossland lay 2,020 feet higher than Trail Creek and generally followed the winding course of Trail Creek as it tumbled the seven miles from Rossland to the Columbia River. Used rails for the tram were already on the ground. These had been reclaimed from portions of the Galt line that had been torn up in renovation of its Alberta track and ordered by Humphreys before Heinze bought him out.

Heinze met Corbin a second time, exacting a promise of reduced rates between Rossland and Spokane when Corbin's railway was completed, but when Corbin declined Heinze's demand for a written pledge that the Columbia and Red Mountain actually would be constructed, Heinze renounced his plan to erect a refinery at Spokane. He was not alone in wondering whether Corbin really meant to build the Columbia and Red Mountain, and when Senator John L. Wilson introduced a bill to allow Corbin's line to cross the reservation, the *Spokane Chronicle* was to print its text "for the benefit of skeptics who have been declaring that Corbin never meant to build to Trail Creek."

Soon Heinze was talking of a railway of his own, rather than a tramway, doubtless in the hope that a railway would deliver him a considerable subsidy from British Columbia and perhaps even from the federal government. Meanwhile, wagon loads of ore piled higher on the plateau where the smelter was being built of lumber, corrugated iron, and brick, and Heinze brought E. H. (Ned) Wedekind from Butte to supervise construction, and Herman C. Bellinger, his superintendent at the Montana Ore Purchasing Company, as his Trail Creek plant superintendent. Heinze also called on his brothers, Otto in New York and Arthur in Butte, to provide $300,000 for the smelter and railway to Rossland; in April, 1896, he was to transfer to Arthur all the Butte properties that stood in the name of F. Augustus Heinze to be used as collateral: the Liquidator concentrator, valued at $200,000, and Rarus, Johnstown, and Pennsylvania mines, worth $300,000. Fritz Heinze also negotiated to buy the Le Roi, but could not arrange what he considered a satisfactory price.

All the while the mining camp, despite its primitive transport, expanded: in 1894, Trail Creek had shipped ore valued at an estimated $100,000, and in 1895, the value was more than a million dollars.

With Corbin temporarily barred from Rossland, Heinze grasped his chance to monopolize both the smelting and transportation of the booming district. The shortest all-Canadian route to Rossland stretched approximately 560 miles from Vancouver to Revelstoke by rail and downriver by boat, while even the makeshift routes between Spokane and Nelson and Spokane and Rossland were less than half as long. Heinze conceived an all-rail connection between Vancouver and Rossland to be accomplished by extending his tramway, converted to a railroad, westward to Okanagan Lake, the terminus of the Shuswap and Okanagan that ran north to a junction with the Canadian Pacific. This plan was certain of enthusiastic support in Victoria; certain, too, of a liberal subsidy, and might forestall Corbin, or at the very least, coerce the Canadian Pacific into a generous settlement with the ambitious Heinze. So he awarded a contract in November, 1895, to Charles King and Nelson Bennett of Tacoma to construct his railway between Rossland and Trail Creek, stipulating that they complete a narrow-gauge line with fifty-pound reclaimed rail within one hundred days from November 18, inclining a maximum of three degrees, and a roadbed graded thirteen feet wide so that standard-gauge track might be laid later.

Heinze's secure position at the moment is evident in his statement to the newspapers that he would ignore location lines previously run by Corbin and by the Canadian Pacific in Rossland; his own route was to begin at the Le Roi, cross Rossland—where the citizens donated forty-eight town lots but complained that Heinze would not alter his survey ten feet even though it cut through a homesite—follow Trail Creek toward the Columbia, and terminate on smelter hill. Because the hills were steep, Heinze's surveyors laid out a thirteen-mile route of switchbacks to traverse the seven miles between Rossland and Trail Creek. Resourceful, frugal builders, King and Bennett had previously run 50.6 miles of their own Fair-haven and Southern Railway, designed to link Vancouver, British Columbia, with Vancouver, Washington, but had sold it in 1891 to the Great Northern.

Heinze's agent, Frederick E. Ward, published notice in January, 1896, that he would apply for a provincial charter to construct a railway from Trail Creek landing through Rossland, over the mountains to Midway, and on to Penticton on the southern tip of Okanagan Lake. To be called the Columbia and Western, the company was capitalized for a half-million dollars, and listed as directors Fritz Heinze, Ward, Arthur P. Heinze, and Chester A. Glass of Spokane, a director of the City Park Transit Company. Heinze went in person to Victoria to lobby for his charter. His manly charm proved as persuasive in the capital as in Butte and Trail Creek; his dinner parties at the six-story Driard Hotel, reported the *Nelson Tribune,* were the talk of the town:

> When debate on the [Columbia and Western] land subsidy bill was in progress, it was openly stated in the House that the change of heart on the part of some of the representatives...was distinctly traceable to a dinner given them in the Driard Hotel by Heinze.[12]

Among his supporters at Victoria Heinze numbered the lieutenant governor, Edgar Dewdney of the storied Dewdney Trail, now an old man with flowing white hair and beard, who became a director of the Columbia and Western, and the attorney general, D. M. Eberts. Eberts' law firm later represented Heinze against British Columbia when he contested a registration fee on the railway's first mortgage bonds. Heinze had asked a subsidy of 11,200 acres for each mile of narrow-gauge and 20,000 acres per mile of standard-gauge track completed, as well as authority in his charter to bond the land up to four million dollars.

With his roseate portrayal of a refining center at Vancouver that would use Slocan ores, matte from Trail Creek (where the smelter blew in in February), and cheap coal, Heinze convinced influential members of the government that his railroad would produce a new home industry. He alluded to the snail's progress of the Canadian Pacific and Daniel Corbin's onrush to the Kootenays. As if to emphasize his persuasion, while Heinze was in Victoria another smelter fired up on the Hall properties near Nelson. The Pilot Bay smelter on Kootenay Lake had inaugurated reduction the preceding March, shipping its matte to Aurora, Illinois; and two of its promoters were also organizers of the Nelson and Fort Sheppard, Edgar Crow Baker and Joshua Davies. Vancouver had been offering a cash bonus for a smelter since 1888. Heinze confidently asserted he would have rails laid to Penticton by November, 1896.[13]

Fritz Heinze's pretentious performance in Victoria produced two results: one, he received a charter with a land subsidy in March from British Columbia that was approved on April 17, 1896, without an additional land or cash grant by the federal government; and two, he openly challenged D. C. Corbin. Corbin reacted swiftly with an injunction from the provincial supreme court contending that Heinze's route near Red Mountain violated the Red Mountain Railway's right of way. This halted construction of the Heinze line which some citizens persisted in called a "tramway" although the Columbia and Western had absorbed the original Rossland and Trail Tramway Company. Forced to change his route by the court's direction, Heinze's compromise with Corbin included his agreement to connect his Columbia and Western with the Nelson and Fort Sheppard by construction of a three-rail line—to permit both narrow- and standard-gauge railcars—thirty miles long on the east bank of the Columbia to Sayward. He also guaranteed the Nelson and Fort Sheppard a share of the Trail Creek smelter's freight.

At the same time, Corbin threatened to disrupt shipments of United States coke bound for the smelter over the Spokane Falls and Northern, declaring that for two months several cars of bricks for Heinze had been sidetracked at Northport awaiting barge space up the Columbia, and he had to have those cars to continue coke deliveries. Heinze could do nothing but set aside other consignments to pick up his bricks.

Thus the contest that was to boom Rossland was fairly joined. Heinze had his smelter and his railroad charter, and within days, Corbin, too, was to have his last barrier to Rossland swept aside. The Le Roi and War Eagle mines were paying regular dividends and

Rossland contained, according to the provincial minister of mines, no less than sixteen promising prospects, chief among them the Iron Mask, Virginia, Poorman, Josie, and others. American money and American miners dominated Rossland, and American transportation was on the way to carry the camp's trade south to Spokane—or would it be west to Vancouver?

CHAPTER ELEVEN

TWO RAILROADS
TO ROSSLAND

D. C. CORBIN HAD COMPLETED THE NELSON AND FORT SHEPPARD Railway with the meagerest capital, and he seems to have undertaken the Columbia and Red Mountain with even slenderer resources. He could not choose a proper season for building; his provincial charter set certain limits on construction; and rivals reached to snare the commerce of the region tributary to Spokane, the trade of Rossland. Not only was the Canadian Pacific jealous of the Kootenays' trade but F. Augustus Heinze, posing as British Columbia's champion, threatened to monopolize the ores of Red Mountain and deliver its business to the coast. E. J. Roberts contended that Heinze had been in cahoots with the Canadian Pacific from the moment he stepped into Canada; much evidence supports this opinion, widely held during Heinze's years in the province, although at the time the Canadian Pacific manifestly resisted both Heinze and Corbin.

The race between Heinze and Corbin was to be to the adroit rather than the swift. Cornering the business of the mines required preoccupancy of transportation and smelters, and Heinze had preceded Corbin with his smelter. By the middle of February, 1896, it was clouding the sky with smoke and dust that were to blight the countryside as far south as Northport. Moreover, Heinze held a charter for a railway to connect with the Canadian Pacific, an errant route, it is true, but a way to Vancouver, nonetheless. While Heinze and Corbin were building during 1896–97, Rossland was to attain the fullness of its bloom. Its mines were soon sold to British and Canadian investors for prices that made Spokane men wealthy.

It is worth recalling that at the beginning of 1896, all the major claims of Rossland were owned by Americans, most of whom were from Spokane. According to the provincial mineralogist, the "chief mines...and principal prospects" included: the Le Roi, property of two intransigent factions of Spokane capitalists, the Turner and the Peyton groups; the Centre Star and Idaho, owned by Butte men; the Josie, Monte Cristo, St. Elmo, and Mayflower, by Frank C. Loring, Spokane; the War Eagle, Iron Mask, Virginia, and Poorman, by Patrick Clark, Austin Corbin II, I. N. Peyton, and Roberts; the Red Mountain, by F. Lewis Clark and Charles Sweeny, Spokane; the California, by Jay P. Graves, Spokane; and so on. Economically, Rossland was a satellite of Spokane. To D. C. Corbin it fell to provide the physical link between Rossland and Spokane despite Heinze's aggrandizement and the Canadian Pacific's pervading embrace.

The Red Mountain Railway had been incorporated in British Columbia in 1893 with the stipulations that the company commence construction within two years and complete its main line within four.[1] Corbin was engrossed with construction of the Nelson and Fort Sheppard in 1893, was building against time to qualify for its land grant, and had no money for additional construction. Moreover, the mines of Rossland shut down for much of the year after the stock market collapsed, with only a zephyr of gold fever to stir the camp. Consequently, Corbin did not apply for his right of way across the Colville Indian Reservation, to follow the route surveyed for the Columbia and Red Mountain, until July, 1894.[2] By this date, the Le Roi and War Eagle were shipping ore from Rossland and the Le Roi was paying dividends.

The route that Roberts had selected ran northwest from Northport, on the west bank of the Columbia in Indian territory, following Sheep Creek in a steady climb toward the international border, then swung northward with the creek's east fork across comparatively flat land, and finally left the waterway to ascend, by a series of loops, to the hogback of Red Mountain where Rossland was situated. The tumbling country spawned cascading mountain streams in deep

canyons, and Roberts proposed not only trestles over these but a
bridge across the broad Columbia. The bridge, like entry to reservation land, would require federal authorization. In all, the road would
be 17 miles long, 7.47 miles in the United States, 9.53 in Canada.
The Canadian section was chartered simply as the Red Mountain
Railway, the American segment incorporated as the Columbia and
Red Mountain in Washington State. To comply with the require-
ment of the provincial charter that construction commence within
two years of the company's incorporation, Roberts and a crew occupying only four tents broke some ground for the Red Mountain
in March, 1895, about three-quarters of a mile from Rossland. In the
summer months of 1895, Roberts directed a small force that graded
the line from Rossland to the international border.

The pace of organization and construction of the Columbia and
Red Mountain was funereal, for Corbin believed in pressure for
economy's sake and Roberts could lay more than a mile of rail a
day, but the year 1895 dwindled in correspondence with government
agencies both in the United States and Canada. Corbin applied for
an amended charter from British Columbia, asking for more time
to commence his railway, authority to construct a narrow- rather
than standard-gauge track, permission to operate boats, wharves and
docks, and telegraph lines in conjunction with the Red Mountain.
The provincial legislature received a flurry of unsolicited letters from
Canadians arguing that Corbin had received enough time, and in
the end, he was denied an extension, and denied, as well, permission
to build narrow-gauge trackage which would have been considerably
cheaper.[3]

Next, a special agent for the United States General Land Office
asserted that the Columbia and Red Mountain had changed its original map to encompass a useful waterfall not shown on the route
filed for approval. He wrote

> this right of way has been so amended that it will take in as part of
> the right of way said valuable water power. The map (intentionally
> it would seem) does not show the existence of the Falls.[4]

More letters, new maps, and that complaint was laid at rest.

Then some question arose over the suitability of Northport as a divisional point for Rossland, and the Columbia and Red Mountain asked the General Land Office to sanction a six-mile branch southward along the west bank of the Columbia to a spot opposite its landing at the Little Dalles, with a bridge at that point to connect with the Spokane Falls and Northern.[5] The land office rejected the proposed right of way, however, and shortly after the time for appeal had expired, Senator Wilson of Washington introduced a bill in Congress to convey right of way to the Columbia and Red Mountain through the Indian reservation. By law, Indians were considered wards of the President, who would have to satisfy himself that their interests would be safeguarded if he allowed certain of the lands to be turned over for public use. Maps sent the General Land Office were informational only.

Authority to build across the Colville Reservation was the last obstacle in Corbin's path to Rossland, for Canada granted him a federal charter in June, 1895, that provided, among other things:

> If the construction of the railway is not commenced and fifteen per cent of the amount of the capital stock is not expended thereon within two years of the passing of this Act, or if the railway is not finished and in operation within seven years from the passing of this Act, then the powers granted by this Act shall cease and be null and void as respects so much of the railway as then remains uncompleted.[6]

In Congress, the committee on Indian affairs approved a right of way across Colville country for the Columbia and Red Mountain on January 14, congressional authority was given March 6 with all the rights granted railways by the Act of March 3, 1875, and President Cleveland signed the bill on March 7, 1896.[7] The right of way was to be one hundred feet on each side of center of "the most feasible route" from the Little Dalles to the international border. The reference to the Little Dalles reflected Corbin's unsuccessful petition for a six-mile extension, because the Columbia and Red Mountain entered the reservation directly across the Columbia River from Northport.

The Act by Congress also allowed the Columbia and Red Mountain to use waters adjacent to its line for milling, for shops, and similar purposes, but specifically prohibited navigation. For some months afterward, Corbin exchanged correspondence with the General Land Office regarding the number of stations he would be allowed on his route, since the Act of 1875 permitted use of public lands for station grounds every twenty miles. As the Columbia and Red Mountain was considerably less than the twenty miles specified, Corbin urged that he be authorized a station, utilizing public lands, at either end of his line, but actually he built no stations on the reservation.

Once the President had approved the railway's right of way, Corbin wrote a contract with the Columbia and Red Mountain Company on July 20, 1896, under which he received $20,000 in stocks and bonds of the company for each mile built and equipped, and an additional $115,000 in securities for erecting a bridge across the Columbia.[8] Little stock in the Columbia and Red Mountain was offered for public purchase. Corbin, Sherwood, the two Chapins, and Duryea apparently advanced cash as it was needed for the railroad, taking securities at par in return, although some friends of the company became small stockholders, perhaps when it needed money quickly. Among these, E. J. Roberts held bonds valued at $34,400.

Like its financing, construction of the Columbia and Red Mountain was accomplished within the company, with the first camp established during May, 1896, according to the *Northport News:*

> The first camp for the construction of the Red Mountain Railroad...was instituted in Sheep Creek...about three miles from Northport last Saturday. The work is being done by the railroad company and the contractors who have been figuring on it the past two years of course are mourning. Only about twenty men were employed the first day but two hundred or three hundred will soon be put on.... Chief engineer Roberts will no doubt manage the entire construction, and Jack Tracy, Fred Farquhar, and others will have a hand in it.[9]

While Roberts' crews cleared the right of way and graded it toward the Canadian boundary, Captain P. D. Forbes directed construction of a ferry at Northport to carry locomotives, cars, and freight across the Columbia until the river might be bridged. Northport had now grown into a busy railway center, with a two-story passenger depot 180 feet long. John Reavis wrote in the *Spokesman-Review,* "I saw a large number of railroad cars loading, many four and six-horse teams; often the driver rides the rear wheel-horse using a jerk rein and hauls wagons in tandem." He also observed that the wagon road between Northport and Rossland was busy, hardly a moment passing "when you don't hear the jingling bells of the leader of a horse team."

Forbes's ferry was launched on September 3, 1896, with Corbin and Roberts looking on. In Reavis' eyes the ferry appeared "a frail, dizzy-looking affair," but it was deceptively sturdy, a boat driven by the river's current, running on a 1,500-foot cable one and one-half inches thick, fastened to two capstans anchored high on the rocky west bank and to a thirty-two-foot steel tower on the east bank of the Columbia. This was to be the railway's mode of crossing the swift river until a bridge could be completed—ten months after it opened for business. Again Corbin was working against time; by now Fritz Heinze had not only his smelter but his railway from Rossland to Trail Creek in operation.

Roberts reached Rossland with the Columbia and Red Mountain track in the first week of December, driving his crews through the cold mountain weather to complete the line, and on December 10, 1896, a provincial inspector, Henry B. Smith, walked the route with Roberts and E. G. Tabor. Smith pronounced the road satisfactory although he regarded its fifty-six-pound rail "light, considering the nature of the traffic and the weight of the engines." [10] More than half the Columbia and Red Mountain was a curve of some degree; Smith found 53.5 per cent of its seventeen miles given to curves, and he considered a good many of them severe for a standard-gauge railroad but not unusual in mountain construction.

Going from Northport to Rossland, the road was virtually all uphill, with a rise of 1,306 feet to conquer between the boundary and Rossland. Its average grade was 2.74 feet per hundred feet, and the steepest section consisted of three 2,500-foot loops with twenty-two degree curves. Five large trestles from two- to three-hundred feet long and fifty to seventy feet high crossed mountain streams. The Columbia and Red Mountain entered Canada almost due south of Rossland, ran generally north—excepting a westward jog to the Kingston mine—and terminated at a frame depot southwest of town near the Union Jack claim. Until the station could be erected, the road used a boxcar on the Centre Star flats as its ticket office. Rossland's was the only station on the line because homesteaders moved onto the intended depot grounds on the international boundary before a building had been put up.[11]

The railroad was equipped with two sixty-six ton Baldwin locomotives, a passenger car, and twenty freight cars from the Haskell and Barker Company, Michigan City, Indiana. Its other rolling stock belonged to the Spokane Falls and Northern.

Once the provincial inspector had approved the line, it opened for business on December 16, 1896, only weeks before the four-year deadline imposed by its provincial charter. The *Spokesman-Review* counted a hundred cars of freight consigned to Rossland waiting at Spokane on the first day of operation. Corbin scheduled one train daily, except Sunday, that connected at 12:57 P.M. with one arriving in Northport from Spokane. Passengers bound for Rossland stayed aboard as the cars were ferried across the river, and then submitted to a twisting roller-coaster ride through the mountains, scarcely daring to glance down as the train pitched on log trestles across deep chasms. Due to the curvature of the roadbed and lightness of the rail, the trains were restricted to speeds of fifteen to eighteen miles an hour. Ore from the Le Roi was delivered to the Columbia and Red Mountain by a gravity spur constructed by the railway between its grounds and the mine.

There remained the task of bridging the Columbia at Northport. To this end, E. J. Roberts had called for bids late in 1896, and Senator Wilson had a bill before Congress that was approved January 27, 1897, and promptly signed by the President.[12] Each of the bidders submitted his own design, based on specifications supplied by Roberts, and several offered alternatives that were adopted, as in the case of the Missouri Valley Bridge and Iron Works, Leavenworth, Kansas, which advised him

> We do not care to submit a plan for a bridge of this size and importance on piers composed of ordinary cribs.... We have therefore substituted at your suggestion steel cylinder piers.[13]

The steel piers appeared in the final design and bid submitted by the San Francisco Bridge Company, which had erected the wonderful steel bridge across the Pend Oreille on the Nelson and Fort Sheppard, and this company again won the contract. Its bid, which did not appear to have been the lowest, apparently offered the most satisfactory alternatives for a span that was to cost approximately $96,000 for superstructure and another $40,300 for substructure. Again Hugh Cooper supervised the construction of the bridge which consisted of seven piers carrying three 250-foot Petit combination spans and three 150-foot Howe truss spans.

In the hope that he could complete much of the substructure during the river's low-water season, Cooper called his crews to work during the early cold months of 1897, but time ran out on him in May. The rising water shook the timber scaffolds and workmen scrambled from the tottering structure to watch as the falsework for two spans was swept away. Construction was delayed until low water in midsummer. Finally in October the 1,200-foot bridge was done, its Oregon fir and steel superstructure resting on granite slabs atop steel piers filled with concrete, its track sixty-nine feet higher than the normal low-water mark. At either end, there were 500-foot dirt fills along the approaches.

About four o'clock in the afternoon of the first Monday in October, four flatcars loaded with rock and three with coal were nudged onto the bridge by a locomotive to test it. Edward Roberts stood by beaming, as crowds gathered on the riverbank and in the Northport streets overlooking the water, while the brass band played spirited airs. Within a few hours, the first freight train crossed the Columbia River bridge and the next day, the regular passenger trains began using it. After the Columbia flood of 1948, the bridge was to be dismantled and Northport citizens were to persuade its wreckers to pile four of the granite slabs on the riverbank south of the town to mark the location of the old railroad bridge.

With the opening of the Columbia River bridge, the Columbia and Red Mountain Railway was completed. Some minor improvements remained, such as repair of the line where it had settled, a job Roberts turned over to a subcontractor, and the addition of small sidings at strategic points to receive ore deliveries. The railroad had cost a reported $555,400. E. J. Roberts said that it paid from the start. After six months' operation, the Columbia and Red Mountain counted earnings of $27,638, largely from ore delivered in the United States and supplies sent to Canada.[14] An average of forty passengers a day rode the railroad. This was a propitious beginning, much better than the first months of the Nelson and Fort Sheppard although in the fiscal year ending June 30, 1897, it also reported a profit for the year of $62,000.

Knowing that the securities issued for construction of the Spokane Falls and Northern exceeded its actual cost, one is tempted to speculate on the outlay for building and equipping the Columbia and Red Mountain, but $555,400 appears accurate. The Columbia River bridge had cost approximately $136,300 including its substructure, and from prices of the period, two locomotives would have cost $12,000 apiece, a passenger car $6,000, twenty freight cars $1,000 each, all of which totals $186,300. Considering the rough terrain, grading, track laying, and rails must have cost an average of $14,000 a mile, leaving $131,000 for the temporary ferry at Northport, trestles, and all the miscellaneous costs of legal service, telegraph lines, cattle guards and signs, fuel and water stations, terminals, and the other trappings of a railroad. The Columbia and Red Mountain, mile for mile, was Corbin's most expensive link between Spokane and the commerce of the country tributary on the north.

The effect of direct railway transportation was spectacular both for Spokane and Rossland. Some of the result is measurable by statistics but some echoes only in the enthusiasm that glitters in newspaper articles, letters, and legends of the time. In headlong expansion, the Rossland mines virtually doubled their production from 1896 to

1897, turning out mineral, principally gold, valued at $2,097,280 in the latter year. The *Inland Sentinel* declared that the Kootenays yielded five times as much gold and silver as the rest of Canada, turned out half the Dominion's copper, and one-third of its lead. Not all the traffic was metal, for agricultural imports to Rossland in 1896 alone were valued at $826,234, on which Canada collected approximately $187,000 in duties.

During a part of April, 1897, the Columbia and Red Mountain was closed by slides, throwing the stream of speculators, miners, businessmen, and tourists bound for Rossland back to the river steamers, and providing a brief, unintended spurt in fares for Heinze's railway, as the *Trail Creek News* reported:

> The rush of passenger business on the steamers has been very heavy of late since the Red Mountain has been closed by slides. The Lytton has brought in from 100 to 130 passengers every night of late. The great bulk of the arrivals goes right through to Rossland and the Columbia & Western trains have been loaded to the platforms on every trip.[15]

Spurred by Rossland's ore and trade, Spokane revived from the depression years of 1893–94, growing from eleven thousand souls to thirty-five thousand by 1897, not counting waves of itinerants which swept the city. Bank clearances, representing the volume of business transacted, doubled between 1894 and 1897. Because the Coeur d'Alenes were stifled by labor conflict, Rossland's mines were the primary source of Spokane's wealth. The contest between D. C. Corbin and Fritz Heinze, however, was to spiral Rossland to dizzier pinnacles. In 1897 the mines looked better every day, the miners believed they worked the richest diggings in the world, and in the prevailing exuberance, one J. G. Devlin placed notices in the Toronto newspapers, advertising for single girls to come West to find husbands in Rossland, "the safest city in the world," boasting seven thousand residents and only one policeman. Scores of girls answered Devlin's ads with letters while the *Rossland Miner* indignantly denied that women were needed to colonize the tarpaper shack and canvas town.

CHAPTER TWELVE

A SMELTER FOR NORTHPORT

THE CLIMAX OF THE CONTENTION BETWEEN D. C. CORBIN AND F. Augustus Heinze occupied 1897; the denouement, 1898. The year 1897 was one of hell-bent-for-smelter mining in Rossland, its last free-wheeling year, because large, staid companies of British and Canadian investors flushed capital into the district, washed out the Americans, and in 1898 returned the Kootenays to Canada in fact as well as in fief.

Corbin in the last moments of 1896 coupled Rossland by rail with great cities, smelters, and refineries; Rossland dug a million dollars worth of gold in 1896 and in 1897 produced just short of two millions; copper forced its path to prominence so that before 1899 it was to overtake gold as Rossland's biggest money-maker; and Rossland was gamboling through its last year of adolescence, for with the change in the mines' economic structure, the town, too, showed signs of stability and circumspection.

It should not be supposed that the momentary expansion and prosperity were Rossland's alone, for the entire Canadian West benefited, and from 1896–98 Spokane based its economic well-being on lusty Rossland. Within a decade Spokane was to forget Rossland and thrive on lumbering, farming, and the transition of the bigger Coeur d'Alene mines to machine operation with large companies. To understand the transformation of Rossland in 1897 which prepared the way for 1898, one must know more of Fritz Heinze's efforts to forestall Daniel Corbin, the struggle that spiraled the camp toward its giddy zenith.

Canada had chartered Heinze's Columbia and Western between Trail Creek and Rossland in April, 1896, and construction began the following month. Financing the smelter and railway simultaneously had strained the Heinze brothers, and during his stay at the Driard in Victoria, Fritz Heinze had been bombarded with telegrams from Arthur and Otto pleading for decisions on the financial problems of the Montana Ore Purchasing Company. Otto had gone to Europe in the hope of securing loans abroad after he failed to obtain money in New York, and while he visited London and Berlin, a trusted employee gambled and lost approximately a half-million dollars' worth of securities, ruining his dry goods firm and throwing a critical burden on the Heinzes' whole financial structure.

"God only could tell what effect that might have on our western situation," Otto lamented,[1] but the Heinzes kept their troubles to themselves. To the Canadians, said the *Inland Sentinel,* F. Augustus Heinze was "one of the most pushing men in British Columbia," who seemed "to have more money at his back than other people." Reckoning the anticipated value of his federal charter that allowed a railway as far west as Penticton, Fritz himself sailed for London in July, 1896, and the *Inland Sentinel* reported:

> It is generally supposed that his mission is to float the bonds of the Columbia & Western Railway which is being surveyed from Rossland to Penticton. As the tonnage is already waiting for the road there should be no difficulty in securing money for its building.[2]

The Columbia and Western, which E. J. Roberts disparaged as a "switchback," opened its twisting route between Trail Creek and Rossland on July 3, 1896, and made money by the boxcar, posting average profits of twenty thousand dollars a month at the end of the year. Henry B. Smith, the engineer who inspected Heinze's line on behalf of the province, reported that the 11.04-mile track fell 2.20 miles short of its intended terminus, the Le Roi, and because it had to climb 2,020 feet between Trail Creek and Rossland, the line rose 3.46 feet in every hundred.[3] The road's curvature was severe, required ten trestles and four switchbacks, and Smith considered its rail, bought used when the Alberta Railway tore up a roadway, "too light" for heavy freight. He predicted frequent derailments and recommended an engine in front and a second behind each train of cars, limited to sixteen miles an hour for safe operation. He also discovered embankments that had been damaged by tracklayers who shoveled materials from them to fill spaces between ties, damp earth crumbling across the narrow-gauge track, and dangerous timber cribwork filled with sand.

Heinze equipped his gimcrack railway with two twenty-two-ton Hinckley mogul locomotives, one caboose, four boxcars, fifteen dumpcars, and twenty-five flatcars. Of two passenger cars seating eighteen persons each, one was an ornate coach with a frieze of painted cherubs and flowers in gaudy colors, and a ceiling mural of angels, said to have been the private car of Brigham Young. Until it disappeared in 1899, this bedizened coach ran in regular service.

From one hundred to one hundred twenty tons of ore reached Heinze's smelter daily over his railway, barges brought upward of one hundred tons of limerock from Nakusp quarries each day, Washington State and eastern coke came via Spokane Falls and Northern and by river barge, and matte returned by river and rail en route to Butte for refining. To residents of Trail Creek, the smelter seemed large but it was, in reality, rather small, treating a daily capacity of not more than four hundred tons. It ran twenty-four hours a day, and of the two hundred fifty men employed, one hundred did nothing but cut fuel in the forests. By December, 1896, flumes from Stoney and Trail creeks to a generator at the foot of smelter hill supplied electric power for the plant.

The smelter was organized as a New Jersey corporation on July 24, 1896, by Stanley Gifford, one of Fritz's former schoolmates who was also a minor shareholder in the Montana Ore Purchasing Company, and two Heinze minions, George W. Mark and Edwin G. Maturin, with an operating capital of one thousand dollars.[4] The British Columbia Mining and Smelting Company was registered in British Columbia on October 2 of that year.

By this time Corbin was grading his Columbia and Red Mountain toward Rossland, but he was being discounted due to the death of Austin, his older brother, on June 4, 1896. As the *Inland Sentinel* remarked, "It was commonly supposed that it was through Austin Corbin's influence that D. C. Corbin was able to swing his different railway enterprises."

Moreover, the Spokane Falls and Northern had been compelled in July, 1894, to issue scrip to cover coupons falling due on its mortgage bonds, and had not been able to resume cash payments.[5] In what was generally considered an attempt to recoup the fortune spent on the Nelson and Fort Sheppard, Corbin optioned the War Eagle for $800,000 and tried to sell it and the Le Roi, whose owners consented to the arrangement, to British investors. London men came to look at the mines but did not buy, so when his bond expired, Corbin reoptioned the War Eagle for a million dollars, bonded the Iron Mask for half a million, and again tried fruitlessly to peddle them to London purchasers.

Not only that. Corbin blocked the commercial development of certain areas of Rossland which he claimed as bonus lands granted the Nelson and Fort Sheppard under the provincial concession that he might select acreage that did not front on the railway's right of way. Handbills condemning Corbin were circulated in Rossland, a mass meeting convened in protest, but Corbin appealed to the provincial supreme court, and stood his ground. The Heinze camp enjoyed the fact that part of the land was also claimed by the Paris Belle Gold Mining Company, a Washington corporation that included Chester Glass, one of the original directors of the Columbia and Western Railway. In Corbin's opinion the Paris Belle had been formed "purely for speculative purposes," but to preserve his title to an area he and the mining company both claimed, Corbin served writs of eviction on fifteen families living there. Little love was lost, thereafter, between D. C. Corbin and the Canadian citizens of Rossland.

By the time Fritz Heinze returned from England in September, 1896, three other events were preparing the stage for the climax of his struggle with Corbin: organization of yet another railway to cross the southern half of British Columbia, a final decision by the Canadian Pacific to enter the Kootenays without further delay, and a noisy campaign waged by the Le Roi company for another smelter. In retrospect, it appears likely that this last—the clamor for a smelter —was fostered by Corbin who had long declared that he would welcome a plant at Northport. Heinze returned to Rossland with no British capital, only memories of gay times, to find his mantle of monopoly raveling.

The railway, to be called the Vancouver, Victoria and Eastern, was organized by two Canadian promoters, Norman McLean and Donald Mann, to run from Burrard Inlet near Vancouver to Hope on the Fraser River, thence to Princeton, and along the Kettle River valley to Rossland. With the expectation that the railway would reduce traveling time between Vancouver and the Kootenays from three days to twelve hours, the Vancouver, Victoria and Eastern elicited vigorous support in Victoria and in Ottawa, where the company's agent was Dr. G. L. Milne.

Even though the usefulness of water transportation had been curtailed by completion of the Columbia and Red Mountain Railway, the Canadian Pacific bought the Columbia and Kootenay Steam Navigation Company in December, 1896, for $280,000. Van Horne warned the Canadian Pacific directors that "unless your Company occupies the ground, others will, the demand for shipping and traveling facilities being most urgent." Moreover, Van Horne averred in the company's annual report for 1896 that the Canadian Pacific needed

> the immediate construction of a line from Lethbridge to a connection with your Columbia & Kootenay Railway at Nelson, a distance of 325 miles, and anticipating your approval...[we] have already taken steps toward commencement of the work on the opening of spring.[6]

In the meantime, the Le Roi attracted world-wide attention. To speed its rich flow, it had installed the largest compressor plant then operating in Canada, was paying monthly dividends of $100,000, and in the estimate of the *Rossland Miner* dug ore worth $84,000 every twenty-four hours. Once spurned at twenty-five cents a share, sold happily by George Forster at a dollar, Le Roi stock now had soared to $7.50. As the undisputed king of the Rossland camp, the Le Roi produced more ore than Heinze's smelter could handle, so Colonel Peyton invited Heinze, the Canadian Pacific, and D. C. Corbin to tender suitable terms for construction of another smelter.

Simultaneously, the Spokane Falls and Northern and the War Eagle companies enticed the man who had helped design the Trail Creek plant and supervised its construction, E. H. (Ned) Wedekind, to desert Heinze and form a new company that would establish a smelter at Northport. Wedekind formed the Union Smelting and Refining Corporation which intended to smelt the ores of mines within a sixty-mile radius of Northport—this would take in Rossland, the Metaline, the Okanogan, and Kootenay Lake—and was to include Patrick Clark, John Finch, Frank Loring, V. D. Williamson, and others, representing virtually all the American capital invested in major Rossland mines other than the Le Roi.[7] Wedekind optioned ninety acres near the Spokane city waterworks as a likely smelter site, and selected Frank George's homesite at Northport as a second possibility.

As a consequence of these events, F. Augustus Heinze had returned from London to find his pre-eminence in Rossland gravely challenged. He grasped his best opportunity for survival, the projected southern route of the Canadian Pacific, and proposed a railway that conceivably could provide the central section of that southern route. Heinze announced that he would extend his Columbia and Western not only westward to Penticton, but north as well from Trail Creek along the west bank of the Columbia River to a terminus opposite Robson, thus offering a railway between the Canadian Pacific's Columbia and Kootenay and its Shuswap and Okanagan. He also declared his intention of doubling the capacity of the Trail Creek smelter to 750 tons daily, and adding processes for silver and lead ores and a copper refinery. He advocated a second smelter for the Le Roi at his location, Murphy Creek, and as a final stitch in the fabric of his fortune, Heinze negotiated with Dr. Milne to merge the Vancouver, Victoria and Eastern with his Columbia and Western.

Early in the winter 1896–97, Heinze had inquired discreetly at Montreal if the Canadian Pacific opposed his railway to Robson, and had been advised by CPR Vice President Thomas G. Shaughnessy that he was free to build but the Canadian Pacific regarded Rossland as its territory and "would not allow anything to stand in the way of making such rates to Rossland in the future" as it desired.[8] With this admonition, Heinze awarded a contract in December, 1896, to three Butte builders for a 21.6-mile standard-gauge railway from Trail Creek to Robson, to be completed in ninety days.

Heinze next petitioned Ottawa for a cash bonus for his railway from Rossland to Penticton in addition to the land grant allowed by British Columbia. Because the Heinze brothers were pressed for money, one would gather that London investors had proven disinterested in bonds guaranteed by land alone and that they suggested a cash as well as a land subsidy. His projected railway to Robson, however, resurrected old suspicions that Heinze secretly worked for the Canadian Pacific. Citizens of Midway, British Columbia, memorialized Ottawa that he was deliberately stalling development of interior transportation, and the *Spokesman-Review* pontificated:

> There is no question but the Canadian Pacific is the moving spirit... and were that corporation unwilling, the charter for the Columbia & Western Railway would never have been secured by Mr. Heinze.

If, indeed, it was Heinze's covert master, the Canadian Pacific gave him curious support, for it nudged Ottawa to the ungrateful counsel that a railway receiving a cash subsidy should forfeit its land grant. Anticipation of federal money thus punctured, Fritz Heinze and his brothers mortgaged the Montana Ore Purchasing Company in March, 1897, to Richard Lacey for $1,500,000, issuing six per cent bonds for capital to invest in their British Columbia railway and Montana smelter.[9] In a few years, Lacey was to be secretary of United Copper Company and Heinze its president, involved in daring speculation in New York's financial community.

Heinze's petition for cash came before Parliament formally in 1897 at the same time as the charter application of the Vancouver, Victoria and Eastern, and the railway committee saw quickly that the two routes duplicated service to much of British Columbia so that only one could hope for approval. The provincial government feared that both railways might be denied, urged that Heinze and Dr. Milne discuss merging, and it was said that Dr. Milne assented one evening to sell Heinze the VV&E for $55,000 but repudiated the agreement the following morning.[10] When this tale reached the minister of railways, A. G. Blair, he vowed that the Vancouver, Victoria and Eastern would receive no charter, and Heinze no subsidy, from the 1897 session.

Heinze no sooner learned that Canada would give him no money for building his railway than D. C. Corbin's dexterous stroke cut him down, for Corbin had plucked the prize of Rossland. The Le Roi announced that it would build its new smelter at Northport on the Spokane Falls and Northern. With this news, Heinze attempted to persuade Ottawa to impose a duty on ore shipped to the United States, bringing George Turner of the Le Roi to the Canadian capital on the run, only to return to Spokane calmly when he discovered Parliament disinclined to act hurriedly. The ore of the Le Roi now was to fall wholly to Corbin, be shipped over his railway from Rossland to the new smelter, and its matte carried over his Spokane Falls and Northern to a connection with the refinery at Denver, Colorado.

Moreover, James Breen and Herman Bellinger resigned from Heinze's staff to join the new Le Roi Mining and Smelting Company which was to be registered in British Columbia in August, 1897.[11]

Rebuffed in Ottawa, embattled at Rossland, Heinze turned up in Spokane on a hot July evening wearing his heavy black overcoat buttoned to his throat, entering his hotel without a word as the shirt-sleeved gallery on the veranda gaped, fans arrested in the stifling air. Of this behavior, the *Trail Creek News* remarked:

> The fact is that Mr. Heinze is not at all well. He spent the greater part of the winter and spring at Ottawa lobbying.... The strain was great and has left him depressed and worn out.[12]

The Le Roi had settled for Northport after failing to establish a new town of its own, to be called Stevens, on the Spokane Falls and Northern between Kettle Falls and Marcus. The company had even published a newspaper, the *Stevens County Standard,* erected one

building, platted a townsite, chosen the spot for its smelter, and con-
nived to transfer the county seat from Colville to its town before the
county commissioners dismissed an electors' petition to incorporate
the place and Stevens slipped into oblivion.

Everyone naturally concluded that Corbin had swung the Le
Roi to Northport, even though he denied doing more than giving
the company free land, water rights, and special railroad rates, just
as any enterprising businessman would have. Corbin had written a
letter to the *Rossland Miner,* saying in part:

> It appears to be the impression of some of the people ... that I am
> devoting my entire attention, and sitting up nights, in an effort to
> get a smelter located at Northport. As a matter of fact, I have spent
> very little time in trying to induce the building of a smelter there
> and have offered nothing ... excepting a donation of land.[13]

He observed that "the patriotic individuals who are doing most
of the crying" about losing Canada's ore to American smelters were
the ones who supported him when he opened the barren country with
his Nelson and Fort Sheppard Railway. And in retrospect, indeed, it
appears that Jim Breen was instrumental in obtaining the smelter
for Northport. No records relate what kind of arrangement he may
have had with Corbin, but Breen was to receive a royalty of two
dollars a ton on the ore smelted at Northport until the company
would buy him out in 1899 for $300,000. A contemporary Le Roi
manager, Bernard MacDonald, estimated that Breen realized a quarter of a million dollars in royalties and confided that smelting was
profitable for the Le Roi plant only after its payments to Breen expired.

Breen and Colonel Peyton explained their choice of Northport
publicly by reasoning that limestone, coke, coal, and building materials were all cheaper at Northport and that Corbin had given
them a freight rate of seventy-five cents per ton compared to the
two dollars charged by Heinze. Ironically a Canadian, Sol Cameron,
won the contract to build the Northport smelter, and began construction in August, 1897, north of the town on flat land overlooking
the Columbia. On a visit, Eugene Topping reported Northport over-

run with a "thousand opportunists" and sneered that the Le Roi would spend for its plant "the immense sum of $25,000.... The smelter ought to be large enough to roast peanuts for the entire Kootenay country." [14] The Northport smelter actually had not more than half the capacity of Heinze's at Trail Creek which had been enlarged to process approximately six hundred tons a day.

During the construction, the Le Roi suspended its handsome monthly dividends to pay for the Northport project. The smelter blew in January 1, 1898, using eastern coke delivered by the Spokane Falls and Northern, and "ran with a full force of Trail help—they took all of Heinze's best men." [15] Most of the American-controlled mines of Rossland shipped to Northport, where the industry was to prove a mixed blessing: when it ran steadily, as it would for some months, the smelter provided a stable payroll, but in August, 1898, editor Billy Hughes would write, "The smelter fumes are getting in their deadly work on Mr. Walters' orchard.... [It] now looks as if his entire orchard will be ruined." Walters with several others had hoped to establish a fruit-growing district centered at Northport and had been planting toward this end since 1892.

While the Northport smelter was being erected, Heinze's Columbia and Western was laid north from Trail Creek to Robson, and when it was prepared for provincial inspection in October, the engineer Henry B. Smith again recorded his impressions of a Heinze railroad, writing in part:

> From a purely engineering point of view, it would appear that a safer, more desirable, and possibly more economical location would be obtained on the flats immediately above the present construction.[16]

The new section of the Columbia and Western crossed seven timber trestles from 60 to 544 feet long and, although it connected with the Trail Creek-Rossland segment, could not transfer cars directly because the new was standard-gauge and the old, narrow. The older line continued to be profitable, posting net earnings in June, 1897, for the fiscal year amounting to $96,886. Notwithstanding his lucrative railway, further enlargement of the Trail Creek smelter to 730 tons daily capacity, and his charter to build westward from Rossland, Heinze could not shift the pressing legal and financial burdens of his Montana properties so that he could divert money to undertake an extension of the Columbia and Western to Penticton. His slender resources lagged behind his commitments. Moreover, the provincial government from which he received so much encouragement tottered beneath criticism of its handling of land and funds. Heinze floundered, and because perceptive men on both sides of the border now recognized his true situation, no one reached to help him. F. Augustus Heinze had run his course in British Columbia.

D. C. Corbin now owned the direct rail connection with prolific Rossland and the major mines, save the War Eagle, shipped the bulk of their ore to smelters via his railroads. During the two-year struggle between Corbin and Heinze, Rossland reached its greatest expansion. It was short-lived, for stability set in almost as soon as Rossland evolved from camp to town, and the element in its population seeking excitement moved on.

The period 1895–97 embraced the rapid growth of Rossland's mines and the contest to control their output by railway and smelter. Two events anticipated the succeeding period, 1898–1900, when Canadian and British capital would virtually drive out American: the first, the determination of the Canadian Pacific to lay rail to the Kootenays, and the second, the sale of the War Eagle and its associated properties, the Poorman, Iron Mask, and Virginia, in January, 1897, to the Gooderham-Blackstock combine of Toronto for $850,000. George Gooderham belonged to the family of distillers; T. E. Blackstock was a Toronto attorney. A harsh conflict among the War Eagle's stockholders preceded the sale, not to prevent it, but to assure taking the best of three offers, because Americans generally were eager to sell. The fact is that while Canadians hailed their investors as saving the Kootenays from the Americans, the American owners —many from Spokane—had overreached their bank accounts and avoided financial collapse only by selling their Rossland mines.[17]

By the end of 1897 Rossland numbered perhaps six thousand

persons, a perceptible shrinkage had started, the best mines had
been sold and resold, the local smelter could not accommodate all
the district's ore so that much went to the United States, a decline
in silver prices depressed the whole metals market, and many of the
prospectors rushed off to the Yukon. After two years of boom Rossland acquired a rude constancy; and over in Trail Creek, Colonel
Topping acknowledged the new permanence by erecting a small
building as an office for his various pursuits: real estate, mining,
postmaster, and justice of the peace. Its reception room contained
a cabinet of ore samples and a file of mining periodicals.

The forces set in motion by the discovery of precious metals at
Rossland swirled in every direction, so that an increase in the Kootenays' lead industry produced lower freight rates which, in turn, en-
abled farmers and cattlemen in Alberta and British Columbia to
capture the region's market for foodstuffs before 1900. By then there
were more than thirty-two thousand permanent residents in the area
populated a decade earlier by miners and prospectors.

Spokane grew with Rossland. Spokane's population rose to more
than forty thousand by 1898, and its bank clearances increased from
$20,082,553 in 1895 to nearly twice that amount in the first eleven
months of 1898. Observing this, the 1899 *Spokane City Directory*
said:

> The chief cause for the notable increase of the prosperity of the city
> is undoubtedly the development of mineral resources tributary to the
> city. British Columbia has proved to be rich in mineral and the ad-
> venturous people from Spokane who discovered and developed its
> mines are now reaping their reward.

One may speculate that Red Mountain's ores, had they not been
found by prospectors in 1890, would have been discovered later and
the story of their development might have been quite different.
Canada might have been better prepared at some later time to
exploit its mines, and their riches would not have flowed to Spokane
at the moment the city sorely needed succor from the depression
years of 1893–94 with the Coeur d'Alenes stultified by labor war,
agriculture and lumbering on the threshold of their coming eco-

nomic importance. Moreover, Red Mountain might have been dis-covered at a time when Spokane had no D. C. Corbin to tie her to the abundant region that geographically, and for a time econom-ically, was tributary.

CHAPTER THIRTEEN

CANADA
REGAINS THE KOOTENAYS

O NE YEAR OF CHANGE, 1898, ENDED AMERICAN DOMINATION OF THE Kootenays. It was a time of wholesale reversal which was stimulated by profit rather than by patriotism on the part of Toronto and London investors prominent in mining around the world, particularly within the Commonwealth. As the sale of the War Eagle in January, 1897, had anticipated events of 1898, so rumors late in 1897 heralded the coming year of change, for the rumors were that F. Augustus Heinze was negotiating to sell his British Columbia holdings to the Canadian Pacific. One such report, datelined Montreal, appeared in the *Inland Sentinel* and quoted Van Horne as saying the Canadian Pacific "would have preferred to purchase the Trail Creek road ... but we could not come to terms." [1] The Canadian Pacific's southern route was then under construction between Lethbridge and Kootenay Lake.

During the first week in January, 1898, Fritz Heinze revisited CPR Vice President Shaughnessy, perhaps hoping to dicker over a price for his railways and smelter, but Shaughnessy's remarks were brief and to the point. The Canadian Pacific offered $800,000 and no more. This amount, actually, was roughly twice that recommended by the Canadian Pacific's appraisers. Heinze tried to haggle, said the *Toronto World,* adding:

There are no flies on this shrewd American, and realizing that he is master of the situation he asks a cool $1,300,000 for his property and will not take a cent less.[2]

Heinze told reporters that a London company, the British-American, also had offered him $800,000, but no higher bid was forthcoming from the Canadian Pacific. Now the minister of railways, Blair, called Heinze aside to explain that he previously had withheld permission for the Canadian Pacific to build directly into Rossland but he could "not hold the Canadian Pacific at bay any longer." Moreover, the Canadian Pacific openly investigated the cost of erecting a smelter at Blueberry on the Columbia between Trail Creek and Robson. This would be supervised by a thirty-year-old engineer from Colorado, Walter Hull Aldridge, who had advised Shaughnessy that the Trail Creek plant was not worth the price Heinze demanded, and had joined the Canadian Pacific with the understanding that he would manage the Trail Creek smelter when the CPR acquired it. Aldridge's inquiries drew Heinze back to Trail Creek, and, as he and Aldridge had been classmates at Columbia, Heinze proposed that they determine the proper price for his smelter by a gentlemanly game of poker. Aldridge declined, explaining that the Canadian Pacific directorate, plump with Methodists, would never condone it. He suggested arbitrating the price before a reliable third party, Heinze agreed, and they drove by buggy late at night to rouse J. C. S. Frazier, manager of the Rossland branch of the Bank of Montreal. Frazier spent the rest of the night listening to the two men argue, decided by dawn that the Canadian Pacific offer was eminently fair, and went jovially to breakfast with Aldridge and Heinze.[3]

Consequently, on February 11, 1898, Heinze signed a contract with Shaughnessy and R. B. Angus of the Canadian Pacific giving the CPR title to the Columbia and Western Railway and his British Columbia Smelting and Refining Company, holding back certain mining claims and half the 575,000 acres in provincial land subsidies earned by his railway construction.[4] Shaughnessy and Angus agreed to retain half the land for Heinze until 1912 when its tax exemption would expire under the railway charters. Acquisition of the Heinze smelter assumed a nationalistic guise as Shaughnessy was quoted in the *British Columbia Mining Record:*

> The Canadian Pacific Railway was not going into the smelting business in order to make money out of it. The company realized that in order to make the lower grade ores abounding in the Trail district profitable it would be necessary to afford the miners cheaper transportation and smelting rates, and smelting facilities would be, therefore, provided at cost.[5]

The reduction of smelting rates from $11.00 to $7.50 per ton, in the *Mining Record* editor's opinion, continued to allow the CPR a margin of profit. The provincial minister of mines, in his annual report for 1898, believed that lower freight and treatment charges would permit re-examination of claims that had been abandoned simply because costs had been so high.[6] Almost immediately upon assuming direction of the smelter in March, 1898, the Canadian Pacific closed the plant to convert it wholly to electricity, and it was noted that both the Pilot Bay and Hall smelters were also idle due to a lack of markets other than the United States.

Estimates of the price the Canadian Pacific paid Heinze have been varied. Heinze's private secretary, Carlos Warfield, a former treasurer of Silver Bow County, Montana, had been present when the contract was signed, and insisted that Heinze received $1,250,000. Fritz, himself, always mentioned this amount in his discussions of the sale. Otto Heinze pegged the price at $900,000, but he may have set a valuation on the land and taken into account various later settlements such as Fritz's suit in December, 1898, which was to bring him $55,000 more for goods transferred to the Canadian Pacific. The Canadian Pacific said that it paid $200,000 for the smelter and $600,000 for the Columbia and Western, amounting to the $800,000 listed in the company's annual reports.[7] No matter what the true price, F. Augustus Heinze had been bought out of British Columbia, but his legend lived on, enhanced by his occasional reappearance. Heinze never selected his half of the subsidy land despite urgent requests from the Canadian Pacific, and in 1913 the British Columbia government amended its taxation acts to permit the public sale and return to tax rolls of the 575,000 acres, disallowing an appeal by Heinze's estate.[8]

Heinze achieved momentary worldwide notoriety when, with Charles W. Morse, he attempted to corner copper and was destroyed by the men who controlled the Anaconda Copper Mining Company and by H. H. Rogers and William Rockefeller of Standard Oil whose market manipulations against Heinze were a contributing cause of the Panic of 1907.

Heinze represented the second major American influence bought out in the Kootenays—the War Eagle had been the first—the Le Roi was to be third, and D. C. Corbin, fourth. In January, 1898, a former lieutenant governor of the North West Territories, Charles H. Macintosh, began wide-scale negotiations for Rossland mines on behalf of the British-American, a promotional company whose public offering in stock was "one of the largest and most successful in the mining line which had occurred in London since the first days of the Transvaal excitement," according to a dispatch in the *Spokesman-Review*. Rossland mine stocks, at the time, had been "notoriously promoted" in London and were generally discredited by cautious investors, so that the nature of the British-American affected Rossland profoundly within six years.

The British-American was a subsidiary of the London and Globe Finance Company, organized in London in 1895 by Whitaker Wright, a financial adventurer who had promoted similar companies in various parts of the world. Born in the United States, Wright studied abroad and then returned to America as a British mining engineer, spending some years in Pennsylvania, New York, and Colorado, seeming finally to acquire a magic touch in 1881 when he bought the Lake Valley silver mines in New Mexico for $400,000 and in five years profited more than seven million dollars. He was "a man democratic in manner...who wanted nothing to do with small things."[9] In 1894 he became managing director of the West Australian Exploring and Finance Corporation, merged it with the London and Globe in 1897, and successfully quashed those stockholders in the Australian venture who complained that their returns fell far below Wright's promises.

Wright displayed every appearance of a successful tycoon. He was fifty-two years old, persuasive, and handsome, when Macintosh, following a careful personal investigation of Rossland in 1896, approached him as an old schoolmate to finance a company to buy Canadian mining properties. Together they organized the British-American and Wright persuaded Frederick Temple, the Marquis of Dufferin, to be chairman. Temple, a man of impeccable reputation, did not seem to comprehend Wright's deftness in speculative investment.[10] Macintosh, too, apparently did not understand that Wright simply paid the stockholders of one company from the assets of its successor, and he returned to Rossland in January, 1898, announcing that the British-American had optioned the Le Roi and was prepared to buy other useful mines. At his hotel, Macintosh, said a newspaper report, "was practically holding a levee. His rooms are thronged, and everybody in the camp with a mine to sell is sending in his name."[11]

The British-American truly held an option on the Le Roi, granted in London the previous November when Isaac Peyton and George Turner, neither trusting the other, had met Wright during a mission to sell the mining company. After giving the option, however, Peyton and Turner fell out over the selling price and the division of the commission, but there was never a question of the necessity for selling the Le Roi, even though it had now returned twenty-four per cent on its investment and paid dividends of $775,000. Only those closest to the operations knew that its owners were heavily mortgaged and that the ore seemed to show poorer and poorer. The widening chasm between the Peyton and Turner factions reached comic proportions as each side tried to sell the mining company to its own advantage.

Although a California syndicate fronted by Idaho's Judge W. B. Heyburn also bid for the Le Roi, the company apparently had been sold to the British-American on May 13; and Valentine Peyton of Spokane, the largest individual stockholder, caught the Spokane Falls and Northern for Rossland to collect the down payment of a half-million dollars in cash while the newspapers printed front-page estimates of how much money each shareholder would receive at six dollars a share. But further internal arguments deferred the transfer, and Turner seemed to have prevented the sale altogether until June 27, 1898, when the company's secretary, Lyman F. Williams, took the Le Roi's papers and seal from the safe and fled to Rossland. Peyton drove Williams to Mead, a station north of Spokane, to catch a special Spokane Falls and Northern train. They found a sheriff's deputy, acting on an injunction obtained by Turner, detaining the train at gunpoint, but after a few indecisive moments, Austin Corbin II locked the passenger car doors inside and directed the engineer to start. The unhappy deputy hung outside as far as Northport. To Williams' dismay, he discovered he had purloined the wrong seal. Apparently Turner had switched seals in the safe at some earlier time.

Eventually the factions arranged separate sales, the Peyton majority group at $6.00 per share, and the Turner minority at $7.25, with an additional payment for ore and matte on hand and the smelter, so that the British-American finally paid an estimated five million dollars for the Le Roi. This sale restored or established Spokane fortunes, and saved the owners of the Le Roi from possible collapse. The magazine *Mining Truth* commented, with some exaggeration, that after sale of the Le Roi for cash, "a blanket mortgage upon almost all the downtown city was lifted." With the money, in fact, Peyton bought the Seven Gables and the burned frame of the Great Eastern Building and rebuilt them as the Peyton Block, George Turner financed the Columbia Building, Ridpath erected a hotel, and Major J. M. Armstrong and Williams bought the Hyde Block, all downtown construction in Spokane.

In addition to the Le Roi, the British-American also bought the Josie, Number One, Nickel Plate, Great Western, and the Columbia and Kootenai.[12] A new Le Roi company had been organized June 7, capitalized for one million pounds, and its stock sold quickly at five pounds per share, despite warnings like that published by the *Engineering and Mining Journal:*

There is no possible basis for such capitalizations as have been put on them [Wright's stock companies in British Columbia]—$2,250,000 in one case and $2,500,000 each in two others—making $7,250,000 for three groups of undeveloped claims.... There is no probability that they will ever earn respectable dividends on this enormous amount, and the valuation is for the vendors' and promoters' benefit, the public being expected to take care of itself.[13]

Two years after buying the Le Roi, the British-American Company failed, and Wright, apprehended in New York, stood trial in London on a charge of falsifying the Le Roi balance sheets. He was convicted of fraud in January, 1904, and in reviewing his various promotions, the court concluded that Wright had piled securities on securities to an aggregate of $111,000,000! [14] Sentenced to seven years in prison, Wright ended his life in a consultation room of the court by swallowing cyanide of potassium.[15] The Le Roi and the British-American's other properties in Rossland passed to the Canadian Pacific.

But in 1898, no one guessed the future, and when the Le Roi sale finally became fact, his friends entertained Macintosh at an historic banquet in Rossland's Allan Hotel. The menus alone, bearing a likeness of Macintosh in his gubernatorial robes, cost $2.50 each, and the banquet with its toasts and speeches lasted from early evening until nine the next morning. Two of the celebrants, emerging from the hotel, determined to settle an argument about their respective skills at horse racing. In full dress they commandeered milk wagons and raced madly along Columbia Avenue. After several heats the rutted street was littered with cans and the banqueters passed their hats to pay for spilled milk.

With Heinze gone, the War Eagle and Le Roi sold, Daniel Corbin remained alone in Rossland to face his old adversary, the Canadian Pacific. Now that Rossland was virtually a British-controlled district, Corbin revived his proposed railway along the Kettle River, intending to enter the new Boundary mining region already served by two stagecoach lines, and surveyed a route from Marcus through the Colville Indian Reservation to the Kettle. The Boundary camp, discovered in 1895, had emerged as Rossland stabilized, and its extensive low-grade copper deposits were being exploited by Americans, prominent among them Jay P. Graves of Spokane.

Congress authorized Corbin's right of way through the reservation,[16] and on March 19, 1898, the Kettle Valley Railway Company was incorporated in Washington state with a capital of one million dollars by Austin Corbin II, Roberts, and Jay H. Adams, a Spokane attorney.[17] D. C. Corbin's name did not appear among the organizers because he was in Ottawa to support his petition for a Canadian charter.

Notwithstanding the expected Canadian Pacific opposition, Corbin for once seemed to have mustered apologists in Parliament. Blair, the minister of railways, favored his charter, and announced that he had received petitions urging its passage from Rossland, Greenwood City, and Grand Forks, British Columbia. Closure of the Trail Creek smelter for renovation was regarded, said the *Spokesman-Review,* as an attempt by the Canadian Pacific to apply pressure in Rossland against Corbin's road. Not many citizens followed newspaper accounts of Corbin's vicissitudes in Ottawa; they were caught up, instead, by headlines reporting the sinking of the battleship *Maine* and impending war with Spain.

In Ottawa, on March 31, the railway committee approved Corbin's charter 54–48, despite the Canadian Pacific's effort to overthrow it with faked telegrams purporting to be from British Columbia, according to Duncan Ross, editor of the *Boundary Creek Times.* Ross also opined that businessmen of Victoria and Vancouver sided with the Canadian Pacific out of fear of the railway's influence in approaching provincial elections. The charter afforded the Kettle Valley Railway no cash or land subsidies, retained to the governor-general in council authority to fix maximum and minimum tolls and to cancel the charter if the railway company evaded his instructions. Corbin voluntarily proposed a limit of one year for completing fifteen miles of the road that were to lie in Canada, and two years for the entire railway.

Corbin's apparent victory in Parliament was short-lived, for in March, too, the British Columbia legislature had passed and forwarded to the federal government a resolution urging denial of future charters that would divert Canadian traffic to the United States. Consequently on April 15 the House of Commons defeated

the Kettle Valley Railway charter 64–44 with the entire French bloc
in opposition, and one indignant observer denounced the Canadian
Pacific for running special trains to carry members from their Easter
vacations to the session if they promised to vote against Corbin.
Corbin himself remarked that the Canadian Pacific "used all its
resources to defeat me." [18]

A few days after his return to Spokane Corbin said he would
not apply again for a Canadian charter. He knew, but did not dis-
close, that an unpublicized movement of Spokane Falls and Northern shares on the New York Stock Exchange was to end his
proprietorship of his railway system. On behalf of a mysterious
buyer, the Chemical National Bank of New York bought stock in
amounts indicating that it contemplated control of the Corbin lines,
and these purchases attracted notice in several quarters. C. S. Mellen
of the Northern Pacific concluded that the secret buyer must be the
Canadian Pacific, mentioned this to J. P. Morgan whose own men
had noted the transactions, and Morgan directed his people to buy
all the Spokane Falls and Northern stock obtainable to protect the
Northern Pacific's interest in the Spokane area. Mellen smelled the
Canadian railway grasping Corbin stock rather than the Great
Northern because a short time earlier he and James J. Hill had discarded their contemplated joint purchase of the Spokane Falls and
Northern as a feeder. Mellen and Hill notwithstanding, the Spokane
Falls and Northern was making money, reporting net earnings of
$212,747 for the fiscal year ending June, 1896, and $327,041 the fol-
lowing year. Passenger revenue accounted for forty-eight per cent
of its gross income.

After conferring with Mellen, Morgan appealed directly to Corbin who later revealed,

> My agreement with the Morgan interests was to deliver them a ma-
> jority of the capital stock. I was able to transfer some more than
> this...I received what I asked. They were very nice about it.[19]

The *Spokesman-Review* estimated that Corbin received approximately $1,200,000 for his stock, Austin II $300,000, E. J. Roberts

$100,000, and Thomas A. Herrick $60,000, but none of them confirmed this reckoning.

Only after he had corraled a majority of the Spokane Falls and Northern stock at Corbin's price, Morgan learned that the Chemical National had been buying for Jim Hill who was indignant that Morgan, bidding against him, had increased the price on the market. To placate Hill, the Northern Pacific agreed that he should have the stock at the price Morgan had paid for it, and turned over to the Great Northern nearly all the Spokane Falls and Northern's outstanding capital stock and all its outstanding bonds. A contract between the Northern Pacific and the Great Northern on July 1, 1898, provided that "the Great Northern had purchased and the Northern Pacific had sold all of such stocks and bonds." [20] Corbin might not have sold so readily had he recognized Hill's part in the affair, for some years later he did not want it thought he had sold to Hill, explaining, "I really sold the Spokane Falls & Northern to the Northern Pacific and they afterward sold to the Great Northern." Fourteen days after he sold his majority stock, Corbin's new private railway car reached Spokane and was side-tracked, unused, on a spur in the company's yards.

How much money Daniel Corbin realized from the sale of his Spokane Falls and Northern system, including the Nelson and Fort Sheppard and the Columbia and Red Mountain, is difficult to surmise. Corbin refused Hill a detailed statement of the railroad's finances,[21] and the annual statement he gave the Interstate Commerce Commission told little, for while the commission reported that the Spokane Falls and Northern had borrowed $475,551.30 from Corbin and the Land and Securities Investment Company between December, 1891, and June, 1898, it could only record that $294,171.88 had been repaid in cash and $181,379.42 charged off in August, 1898, to "stock assessment," and "this transaction cannot be further explained." [22] Thus Corbin's profit from the sale of his railroads remained his secret.

One knows that the railroad system had cost more than $7,224,859 in securities based on annual statements published in

Poor's Manual of Railroads, that their aggregate capitalization exceeded $4,000,000, and that the Great Northern on April 15, 1898, issued $15,000,000 in capital stock, using a portion of it to buy the Spokane Falls and Northern stock from Morgan. Moreover, when the Spokane Falls and Northern was dissolved as a subsidiary and its assets transferred to the Great Northern on July 1, 1907, the Interstate Commerce Commission learned that the Great Northern had assumed all obligations of the Corbin railways when it began operating them on July 1, 1898. It should be pointed out that in 1898 the commission did not require carriers to submit reports of sale, and a member of the commission's staff appended a wistful note to the railway's annual report for 1899:

> While it is understood that the Great Northern Railway owns a considerable amount of the stock of the S.F. & N.R., I cannot say that there is any arrangement existing for the operating of this line by that company.[23]

When Corbin delivered "some more than" a majority of his railways' capital stock, it is conceivable that he turned over securities worth more than two million dollars at par, that he cashed other obligations of his companies that could have amounted to five millions more, and that he profited from buying stock from small shareholders who may have sold rather cheaply. Corbin did not think more than fifty shares remained outside his control in Spokane at the time. This borders on conjecture, it is true, but Corbin's reputation in Spokane in 1898 was that of a man several times a millionaire.

Spokane's citizens did not discover who had purchased the Spokane Falls and Northern, and Corbin refused to comment, until G. C. Dixon, the Great Northern general agent, remarked at Rossland that his company was the buyer, adding with satisfaction that the Corbin system totaled 217 miles of road with only $3,050,000 bonded indebtedness. Cornelius Shields, former general superintendent of the Chicago Great Western, was appointed manager of the Spokane Falls and Northern, and he immediately cleared the old land disputes at Rossland by giving home owners their lots and ceding half the surface rights on contested ground to the Paris Belle. On August 8, Hill and his directors visited Spokane in private rail-cars, Hill handed Corbin a list of men he wanted as Spokane Falls and Northern officers, and they were elected the same day. At its request, Roberts stayed with the Great Northern until August 13.

Corbin's final gesture as president of the Spokane Falls and Northern revealed a turn of sentiment he rarely indulged. He stopped all train service for the day except for specials to carry his employees and their families on July 25 to a giant $4,000 picnic at Loon Lake. It was said that 775 attended Corbin's unique farewell, boated, swam in heavy woolen bathing suits, consumed forty to fifty kegs of beer, and ate at long wooden tables under open-walled tents. One passenger car bore a banner, "Kindness of Our President." Through the gaiety ran a requiem. For all his gruff manner, his employees respected D. C. Corbin, who moved quietly among them, now sixty-six years old, and for all they knew, at the end of his busy career. Their spokesmen made short, self-conscious speeches and gave Corbin their final gift, a $280 gold watch.

CHAPTER FOURTEEN

CORBIN TRIES NEW FIELDS

After he had sold his railway system, Daniel Corbin might have been expected to seek comparative ease, for he had been occupied for nearly half a century in surveying, real estate, freighting, mining, investing, banking, and railway construction on western frontiers. Neither he nor his family needed money. His daughters had married wealthy Englishmen: Louise, the Earl of Orford, a Walpole, and Mary, Edward Balguy of London. In 1894, Corbin's son, Austin, had married Katherine Benham, the daughter of a pioneer Spokane wholesale grocer, and soon was rearing two daughters. White-haired, punctilious, abrupt, D. C. Corbin was pointed out on city streets as Spokane's richest man, his fortune estimated airily in millions. The raw, struggling village that had been Spokane Falls in 1888, when Corbin first deliberated a railway northward, had grown into a bumptious, prosperous city.

The two Corbins, Daniel and Austin, built homes in 1898 designed by the fashionable Spokane architect Kirtland K. Cutter, on Seventh Avenue, "on the hill" among other elegant residences overlooking the city from heights rising toward a black basalt cliff. Cutter drew houses that fitted into their surroundings, intending that they appear established and permanent. Austin erected a columned mansion in southern colonial style, said to have cost $33,000, a home of cream brick that became a center of Spokane society, renowned for lavish holiday and costume parties.

Daniel Corbin's colonial home, set in five landscaped acres two blocks east of his son's, cost only $17,000. Other Spokane homes exhibited authentic Swiss decor, stained glass in leaded panes, ceiling murals by imported Italian painters, or hand-hewn marble, but D. C. Corbin's house was squarish, utilitarian, and sturdy. From the outside, Corbin's dun brick home appeared large, with a wide veranda on three sides lighted by torches enclosed in latticed iron. Inside, the three-story home seemed to shrink: its rooms were generally small and plain, and the third floor was unfinished. Its doorknobs were commonplace brass, its panels machine-oak, and its windows clear glass glazed in wood. Floors in the family area were hard wood; those in the servants' quarters, kitchen, and pantries, soft wood.[1]

Other than a pillared fireplace of green ceramic tile, ringed with electric lights that screwed into brass petals, Corbin's prosaic house brandished little of the adornment of other Cutter homes. When he furnished it, Corbin set a billiard table near the center of the living room and his rolltop desk in one corner. The Corbin house stood austerely apart from the city, like its owner, who moved from his rooms in the Spokane Hotel into the first house he had owned since his early years in Helena. East of the house, a brick stable sheltered his fine horses. There were no gay parties. Corbin's wife, Louisa, returned from Europe to live in the house for a few months, confined to her wheelchair, but soon left the place and died in France in 1900.

Perhaps this solid structure represented the roots that Corbin's years of roving had denied him. But Daniel Corbin did not plant his house as a retreat. Soon he was busy at new careers. Corbin's prod was that he saw things that needed doing, for as E. J. Roberts learned, "Corbin was a man of vision, level-headed. He carried a notebook in his pocket and figured in it with a sharp pencil."[2] Corbin worked out new ventures in detail in his notebook before undertaking them.

In his younger days, Corbin had faced frontiers to be conquered, but his new enterprises now incubated in a region tamed largely by his own effort. In the seventeen years between 1881 and 1898, Spo-

kane had taken root as the metropolis of its Inland Empire. Railroads spanned this empire from the Cascades to the Rockies, from
the Selkirks on the north to the Blue Mountains on the south, and
two great rivers, the Columbia and the Snake, coursed through the
land tributary to Spokane. Much of Spokane's trade rode D. C.
Corbin's roads in this period, for the city early had battened on
mining and railroads. In 1898, its other great industries, agriculture
and timber, waited at the threshold of their maturity. The first farm
produce reached only local markets. But irrigation flowered, and the
Northern Pacific was selling its farm lands at two to four dollars an
acre, and grazing range for fifty cents, to encourage settement. Much
of the region's early logging produced poles and ties for railroads
or lumber for towns along the tracks, but by 1894 Washington lumber had reached midwestern markets and this flow was to increase,
so that by 1905 Washington led every state in lumber production.
The bulk of commerce in the nineties depended on railroads; and
without Corbin's railways to the Coeur d'Alenes and the Kootenays,
no guessing what manner of flagstop Spokane Falls might have
remained.

Spokane had changed measurably since Corbin first joined it
to Colville by rail. In 1889 there had been six agricultural implement
firms in Spokane Falls, one of them the omnipresent Knapp, Burrell
and Company of Portland, Oregon, who monopolized farm supplies and crop information in the Pacific Northwest for two decades.
Ten years later, despite the intervening depression, Spokane supported seven farm implement companies, five locally owned, and
Knapp, Burrell was gone.

Further citations from the Spokane city directories for 1889 and
1899 reveal the expansion of retail and wholesale trade. In 1889 there
had been six commission companies dealing in produce; in 1899,
twelve. General contractors had increased from two, including Monaghan and King, to six. One express company in 1889 had four com-
petitors ten years later, among them Wells Fargo and Company.
Seven hardware dealers had grown to eleven; seven lumber manu-
factories to twelve; one manufacturer of mining machinery to
three, including the Union Iron Works headed by E. J. Roberts;

four sash and door makers and two sawmills, to nine sash and door manufacturers and six sawmills.

The growth of mining had been staggering. Three mining companies had offices in Spokane Falls in 1889. In 1899, there were 239. In the seven years between 1890 and 1897, 195 mining companies, organized simply to exploit the Kootenay district, staffed main offices in Spokane; and these did not include the Le Roi with its offices at Rossland, the Monarch Gold Mining Company based at Northport, or the Chenango, headquartered at Waneta, British Columbia.[3] The aggregate capitalization of these companies totaled a giddy but meaningless figure, for many paid no dividends, others merged, and a number disbanded. The fact that investors believed the companies worth organizing demonstrates the effect of Corbin's Spokane Falls and Northern system on Spokane, however, and one is more impressed when he considers that these 195 represented nearly two-thirds of the American-controlled companies formed to operate in the Kootenays between 1895 and 1900.

In 1898, money from the mines and general economic recovery coalesced to a glittering promise for Spokane. Local businessmen bought back downtown property that had been mortgaged in 1893 to Dutch investors, and homes rose by the score. Spokane had over-built immediately after its fire in 1889 so that eight years later its business district scarcely had changed, but in 1898 both commercial and residential construction revived. Among the major projects was Peyton's block, erected for $46,000 on the skeleton of the burned Great Eastern Building. The city's architects estimated that fifty new commercial buildings and 450 new dwellings went up in 1898 costing altogether $1,500,000, almost all of them financed from surplus earnings of the community rather than from loans. Although Spokane's population had not grown at all in 1893 or 1894, it rose thirty per cent to an estimated 30,000 by 1895, to 41,822 by 1898, and there was also a large transient populace bound for homesteads, forests, and mines.

Spokane men published two mining journals, the Northwest Mining Association's monthly, *Mining,* and a weekly, *The Spokane Miner and Electrician.* The weekly *New West Trade* reported mercantile news. Supplanting Howard as a principal business street, Riverside Avenue had been paved in 1898 with vitrious brick. The old Loewenberg Brothers wholesale dry goods store, on the southeast corner of Howard and Front, had been remodeled as a notorious variety theater by Dutch Jake Goetz and Harry Baer with their windfall from the Bunker Hill. So Spokane had grown and it bore its emblems of growth. Five years after the Panic of 1893, there seemed no limits to Spokane's bright future.

Not all the grand expectations came true: Spokane could not establish its smelter, and the city lagged in manufacturing, due, its citizens contended, to discriminatory railway freight rates. Nevertheless, Spokane sparkled in 1898.

The time seemed ripe for Daniel Corbin to exploit his forty-acre tract of northside property, the earlier site of the Washington and Idaho Fair. The Fair had mortgaged its grounds in 1890 for a $15,000 loan from Corbin at ten per cent interest, to be repaid within one year. Three years later, when the Fair association patently could not repay his loan, Corbin had sued, the court had ordered the property sold, and Corbin had acquired it for $16,895.86 at a sheriff's sale on July 15, 1893. From the sale's proceeds, the court had paid Corbin $15,166.66 due him in principal and interest, and he had retained the property, so the fairgrounds actually cost him $1,729.20, or $43.23 an acre, a fact not mentioned by State Senator Byron C. Van Houten, who tried to prevent Corbin's acquisition of the grounds, asserting them worth several times $15,000.[4]

The Fair association, organized in 1886, had constructed a racetrack, grandstand, and midway on level ground "twenty chains by thirty chains," bought in 1887 from the pioneer attorney, John J. Browne. The fairgrounds, unused by 1898 except for occasional horse races, lay on the northern fringe of the city's residential area. Corbin razed the wooden stands and midway and platted sixteen blocks as Corbin Park Addition for homesites that sold briskly at $200 a lot and up. The old racetrack, approximately eleven and a half acres, he deeded the city for a park, turning it over formally in 1901 for one dollar. The area evolved as one of substantial family homes typical of the early twentieth century, many of brick, and Corbin Park retains its oval racetrack shape.

A minor real estate venture was not enough to keep Daniel Corbin busy, as he was accustomed to being, and moreover, eastern Washington's farm products were beginning to reach regional markets, offering new profitable opportunities to a man of means. Apples, to mention one crop, were distributed nationally. Like other jealous cities, Spokane sought distinctive products and as early as 1894 had fastened on beet sugar as a possibility. Once again, Corbin saw that he was needed to do what no one else seemed prepared to do.

He inquired and found that Europe had been producing sugar beets profitably from Napoleonic times and that there had been experimental manufacture of beet sugar in the United States in the years when cane was scarce after the Civil War. Several states— Maine, for one—had offered bounties on sugar and California boasted a beet sugar industry comparable to large southern cane milling. But refining was expensive, American labor costly, the work in the fields extremely hard, the McKinley Tariff Act stifling, and except for isolated factories, beet sugar making lagged in the United States until 1897 when the Dingley Act had reversed the McKinley provisions and imposed high duties on imported sugar. Almost overnight, new sugar companies had sprung up in Michigan and other central states, and Colorado had soon joined California as a western producer.

Shortly after passage of the Dingley Act, Colonel Edward H. Morrison entreated Corbin to establish a sugar factory. The husky, imposing Morrison virtually owned Fairfield, a hamlet thirty miles south of Spokane, where he had spent ten years nursing his specialty, a beet sugar seed that won distinction in world-wide competition. Morrison's beets were said to average eighteen per cent sugar compared to twelve to fourteen per cent for midwestern beets.[5] In 1894 Professor Charles P. Fox of the University of Idaho, after soil and climate tests, had pronounced the Spokane area suitable for beet growing; other tests at Washington State Agricultural College bore out Fox's conclusions, and both schools recommended beet cultivation.

As a result, Colonel Morrison had organized the Waverly Beet Sugar Manufacturing Company in February, 1895, intending to build a plant at Waverly, six miles west of Fairfield. His company had included Miles C. Moore, Washington's last territorial governor, and the Spokane attorney George Turner,[6] but Morrison's Chicago associates had withdrawn their financial support, apparently because the Waverly company had rejected their demand for 5,000 acres of free farmland. These reluctant investors probably had been James W. Forsyth and Philip Sheridan, who had bought thousands of acres of Northern Pacific land in partnership with Morrison, using money advanced by Marshall Field, and then had sent Morrison west in 1883 to manage the land sales that were to occupy thirty years.

Morrison's sugar company had continued to exist on paper until he appealed to Daniel Corbin to finance it. Brusque though he was known to be, Corbin was continually solicited to back surefire schemes to increase his wealth, and he seems to have considered a good many of them. In this case, Corbin reorganized the Waverly firm as the Washington State Sugar Company in December, 1899, and although Morrison was not an officer, he was active in promoting the new company.[7] Corbin undoubtedly was encouraged to enter sugar manufacturing not only by the Dingley Act, but by other factors: his own inspection of beet sugar factories, the Spokane Chamber of Commerce's campaign since 1896 to establish a local sugar industry, the open interest of Scottish capitalists who were rebuffed by Washington's denial of land ownership to aliens, and finally by the state legislature's bounty of one cent a pound. The bounty was to be paid for three years on sugar produced by factories in Washington completed before November 1, 1901.[8] With customary thoroughness, Corbin visited Michigan farms and refineries where farmers told him they earned thirty dollars an acre growing beets and where he inspected the most recent machinery. Corbin went to Michigan shortly after the Washington legislature passed its bounty in February, suggesting that he regarded the bounty as his guarantee of profit and pursued the project vigorously after state payments had been approved. Corbin also was interested in irrigation, believing he could combine irrigated land with a sugar manufactory to command his product from field to grocer.

Through Morrison and other agents, Corbin gave free beet seed to farmers for miles around Waverly. He seeded 1,400 acres for his company, a tract Morrison proclaimed "the largest individual beet-growing farm in America," hired French overseers, and Morrison's one hundred Japanese workmen, with a good many Indians, tilled it. Sugar-making machinery was imported from France and Belgium, and fabricated in Chicago. The three-story factory, 96 by 300 feet, required a new plant at Fairfield to make two million bricks. The $500,000 beet factory and outbuildings occupied the only flat area in Waverly, east of the town now grown to perhaps a thousand souls, and was served first by a spur from the Oregon-Washington Railway and Navigation Company, and after 1906, by a spur from the Spokane and Inland electric line. Latah Creek nearby was diverted by a stone-and-earth dam into a flume running between frame beet hoppers that dropped the vegetables into the water to be washed before processing.

The Waverly factory was expected to produce 50 tons of sugar daily during its annual run of 100 to 120 days, working two twelve-hour shifts with approximately 70 persons a shift at a minimum wage of $1.50 a day.[9] It opened in December, 1899, and closed its first season near the end of January, 1900, turning out approximately 4,000 100-pound sacks of sugar in two grades of fineness and a molasses byproduct for distilling alcohol. After this first year, some sugar was produced by allowing molasses-stained sugar to stand in pits for twelve months, then digging it out with heated shovels, re-boiling it, and spinning it white in the centrifuge. Byproduct syrup was fed to horses, pulp to cattle. The Waverly output of perhaps 200 tons in its first season, while it seemed a bountiful harbinger of a new industry for Spokane, totaled a miniscule share of the 80,000 tons of beet sugar produced 1899–1900 in the United States.

During the summer while the factory had been constructed, half a hundred other new buildings had risen in Waverly, many in

Morrison's Addition south of the original town,[10] and to swell the permanent population the factory employed as many as four hundred Japanese and transient Indians in its fields at one dollar a day. The payroll at Waverly was enough to make Spokane envious, had not the sugar and the money flowed to Spokane as the center of its empire.

From its outset, however, the Washington State Sugar Company found farmers reluctant to grow beets. Beets often withered from blight; they demanded backbreaking work to thin, weed, and harvest; they required careful crop rotation. Grains and field peas resisted disease better, needed little attention, and often brought more money. Graves and Hanauer, land promoters, persuaded many Waverly farmers to convert their land to orchards, like those going in near Spokane, Four Lakes, Fairfield, and Valleyford. The state bounty ended after 1903 because Governor Henry McBride, pleading government economy, vetoed a bill to renew it. His veto whittled thousands from the Waverly company's assured income. During the three years that the bounty was paid, the Washington State Sugar Company collected $67,394.02 from it. The 1901 run brought $13,493.96 in bounty for approximately 674 tons of sugar, the close of the 1902 season drew $19,207.60 from the state, and 1903, $39,692.46 in bounty money.[11]

For varied reasons the Waverly factory continued to be hampered by a shortage of beets throughout its years of operation, although the vegetables were growing bigger and more sugary as farmers learned to cultivate them advantageously. Six years after the bounty had been discontinued, faithful Frank George toured the Farmington area, trying to persuade farmers to plant beets, offering higher prices and experienced advisors. But at the same time, grain dealers urged farmers to return to flax to meet demand, and enough farms had been converted to orchards that an apple-packing plant had been raised at Waverly beside the Spokane and Inland tracks. Hay proved scarce after the wet fall of 1909, bringing an attractive $14.00 a ton, and timothy, $18.00. These conditions enticed farmers to abandon beet cultivation. In its 1909 season, as a result, the Waverly factory ran only a few days in December, producing 35,000 sacks of sugar, a total lower than its output six years earlier. Moreover, the farmers now demanded twenty-five cents more per ton for their beets, and Corbin refused to pay it. His experience in growing beets on irrigated land near Rathdrum and Spokane had been proven unsatisfactory by this time, for the gravelly soil yielded beets containing stones that damaged the factory's knives.

After one more disappointing season, when the company "had considerable difficulty in working up sufficient acreage to meet its requirements," [12] the Waverly plant closed forever. In 1916 the industrial committee of the Spokane Chamber of Commerce conducted a campaign to reopen it without success. Corbin consequently sold his plant to a California buyer for $50,000 and the next year, 1917, it was resold to the Gunnison Valley Sugar Company of Utah for $100,000 due to a wartime scarcity of equipment. The Gunnison company, which used ninety railcars to move the Waverly machinery south, ran it for half a century after the Washington State Sugar Company locked its doors. Two fires in the mid-twenties destroyed most of the town of Waverly, and the remaining residents moved across Latah Creek where they built a new community, but Waverly never again witnessed the like of its sugar days. At his death, Corbin held all 5,000 shares of the capital stock of the Washington State Sugar Company. The men who appraised his estate listed the stock as valueless. [13]

Meanwhile, beginning in 1899, Corbin investigated the practicality of irrigating the river valley east of Spokane where a number of snow-fed lakes offered suitable reservoirs. He had been a farm boy himself, and in his study of beet cultivation, he had observed a good deal of recent farm methods, so that he was disposed favorably toward the proposition of W. L. Benham that he finance valley irrigation. Benham painted a rosy picture for water in the valley, fifty-eight square miles, fourteen miles long and from two to six miles wide, with an elevation of 2,100 feet above sea level at the Idaho line sloping to 1,900 feet at Spokane's east city limits, and thus permitting a canal system to deliver water by gravity. With Benham and Austin Corbin II, D. C. Corbin incorporated the Spokane Valley

Irrigation Company, capitalized for a modest $50,000, with the intention of putting 22,000 acres under water. As customary, Corbin had inquired carefully before committing his money: he studied soil analyses and kept three parties of engineers constantly in the field in the spring and summer of 1899.

Benham had been temporarily employed as a real estate salesman for the Spokane Hypotheekbank and had spent several years obtaining water rights to surrounding lakes and perfecting his titles before approaching Corbin. At the time these rights were secured simply by posting the proposed point of diversion and entering a copy of the notice in county records. Benham believed that the valley's entire 40,000 acres could be irrigated from the Spokane River and from Liberty, Saltese, and Newman lakes in Washington, and from Fish (Twin), Hayden, Mud (Hauser), and Sucker lakes in Idaho. He held water rights both from Washington and Idaho, and had acquired the Hayden and Newman lake water rights from the defunct Spokane and Idaho Irrigation Company which surveyed the Spokane Valley in 1894 but built no ditches because its financing by Chicago men fell through.[14]

Benham had been western traffic agent for the Great Northern Railway in Seattle but for several months before settling in Spokane, he had scouted the Pacific Northwest for likely irrigation sites and was pondering one in Montana when the Spokane Valley caught his eye. Irrigation evoked enthusiasm and promised much in Washington, as Benham recognized. As early as 1889 the Northern Pacific had bought two-thirds of a million-dollar irrigation company near Yakima and there were many small districts in south central Washington. Irrigation, with the railroads, farm plows, and fences, was driving out the cattleman. There was intense popular interest in irrigation, attested by the December 12, 1894, editorial in the *Spokesman-Review*:

> Eastern Washington must take hold of irrigation in self-protection. ... It is no less a business proposition that he who gains the eye and ear of the eastern buyer first will find the secret of successfully advertising the fruits and other matchless products of the Pacific Northwest.

The newspaper challenged Inland Empire farmers to make their products as famous as those of California.

At first, Benham anticipated that property owners in the valley would donate rights of way, that he would deliver water, and that all would share the system's profits. Many of the farmers had purchased their land from the Northern Pacific for $2.50 to $15.00 an acre; they were raising truck crops but due to the gravel in its soil they regarded the loamy valley as marginal. There were also stretches of land held by speculators without houses or tilled acreage as far as a man could see.

Daniel Corbin envisioned this grassy, gravelled valley verdant with hundreds of farms, each ten to forty acres, raising vegetables and fruits (beets were to come later) and he thought that "under irrigation this valley alone can support in comfort more people than now reside in Spokane." [15] Pioneer settlers called Corbin and Benham foolhardy, scoffing that when ditches were dug, the "gravelly, loamy soil would not hold sufficient water to help mature a crop." [16] Today, native stone fences and an occasional stone school, house, or church testify to the rocky character of the land. Older residents expected the water to sink through the ground before it reached the fields farthest from Liberty Lake, the first reservoir Benham determined to tap. His second, never built, was to entail a six-foot steel pipe from Twin to water Rathdrum Prairie by gravity.

Despite jibes, during 1899 the Spokane Valley Irrigation Company, using Corbin's money, bought or condemned rights of way and constructed a ditch twenty feet wide at its top that ran west from Liberty Lake a distance of six and one-half miles to an area the company optimistically named Greenacres. To encourage irrigation, the Hypotheekbank sold Benham 500 acres of it at $12.50 an acre. The first unlined ditch served the old Wells farm and adjoining property, 776 acres in all, and although the ditch was finished too late for the 1899 growing season, it carried water that achieved spectacular success for its farms in 1900 and encouraged the whole valley to re-evaluate irrigation. The canal did lose a lot of water by seepage but it delivered enough to help the crops.

By the end of 1900, Greenacres contained sixteen miles of ditches watering 1,400 acres and had been platted as ten-, twenty-, and forty-acre farms. Now Benham claimed he was offered bonuses by land-owners who wanted early water delivery, and that he could sell an irrigated acre for $500. The company was aided in its efforts by the Washington legislature's passage in 1899 of an act authorizing con-demnation of private land for canal rights of way, and containing a provision that if a ditch had been surveyed "on the shortest route practicable" superior courts could not deny access to the land but could only rule on its value and damages from ditchwork.[17]

At this point, in October, 1901, Daniel and Austin Corbin II withdrew from the Spokane Valley Irrigation Company, perhaps because their attention was diverted to a proposed new railroad from Spokane to a connection with the Canadian Pacific. Whatever their reason, Benham replaced the Corbins with men close to the Great Northern: W. J. Footner, St. Paul, who had been vice president and general manager of the Great Northern Express Company but who died before becoming active in the irrigation company; F. E. Ward, St. Paul, general superintendent of the Great Northern; and Ar-thur A. Hawley, Seattle, an investor and property owner who was instrumental in modernizing his city's electric and transit systems.

The new directors formed a subsidiary, the Spokane Valley Land and Water Company, to buy and sell property.[18] The firm began acquiring open tracts to develop as irrigated farmland and quickly overreached its resources, partly because its extended ditch, meander-ing through the valley to take in as much area as practicable, was first dug on too high a grade and had to be reconstructed in 1903 with a headgate added at Liberty Lake. The original water contracts, given in perpetuity, called for fourteen inches of water during the growing season but this proved one-third of what was needed and everything had to be redone on a scale bigger than anticipated. The company pressed ahead, regardless, opening Greenacres' 3,000 acres in 1902, receiving an Idaho state permit for 1,440 cubic feet per second of water from Spirit, Fish (Twin), Hayden, Sucker, and Mud (Hauser) lakes, and reaching an agreement with the Washing-ton Water Power Company in 1904 fixing a location and amounts of water for drawing from the Spokane River behind Post Falls dam.

Irrigated land that had been priced at $50.00 an acre in 1902 had risen, once it had been shown sufficient water could be carried through the ditches, to an average price of $200 an acre by 1905. But the company's money went out faster than it came in. Some was dissipated in lawsuits with lake resort and shoreline owners suing to maintain water levels, and these disputes were to convince irrigation companies that they should rely on the river for water rather than lakes.

In 1905 the first of several rivals, the Spokane Canal Company, took Benham's unexploited rights to water from Newman Lake to develop its Otis Orchards project. Thus the gravelly valley bloomed with water delivered by a network of canals, ditches, and aqueducts, while the coming and going of real estate salesmen and right-of-way agents created a constant traffic. To save money, the Benham company lined its canals with concrete mixed with native unwashed aggregate that did not last as long as the pay-out period.

Despite general good times and rapidly expanding irrigation projects, Benham's company fell deeper into debt, so he retired in 1904 and turned it over to James C. Cunningham and Cyrus Happy of Spokane. Cunningham, who held the major interest, in 1905 urged Daniel Corbin to refinance the company, and when Corbin agreed, Happy joined the competing Spokane Canal Company. Corbin returned to irrigation partly because his Waverly factory needed a constant supply of beets and he hoped to plant as many as 20,000 acres of irrigated beets in the valley over several years. He had been experimenting with beet-field irrigation on a small valley plot and concluded the area was capable of high yield. Corbin therefore bought 3,488⅙ of the Spokane Land and Water Company's 5,000 shares of capital stock and spent, it was declared, $850,000 paying off the company's obligations.[19]

By this time perhaps fifteen thousand acres were under irrigation in the Spokane Valley and forty miles of main ditches, some owned by companies other than Corbin's, using water from wells or seven lakes lying in an irregular horseshoe around the valley at higher elevations than its floor so the water flowed by gravity without pumps, requiring only locks to maintain lake levels.[20] The Corbin canals and laterals, then and later, were engineered with such precision that a small flow of water would reach the entire system by gravity, and in the opinion of one observer, not one spade of dirt or one inch of concrete had been wasted in their construction.[21]

With Corbin's return to the irrigation company, Benham's cronies from the Great Northern left it but two Spokane realtors who managed its land sales, Cunningham and Fred B. Grinnell, stayed. Under Corbin's direction, the company bought more land and ran a canal from the Spokane River to serve the area north of the river. The canal became known locally as the "Corbin ditch," although much of the distribution system was not ditch but a weathering three-by-five-foot wooden aqueduct that crossed the valley on frame trusses and dipped beneath roads in square concrete ducts.[22] The company instituted a series of expansions: in 1908 it opened East Farms Number One, near the Idaho border; in 1909, East Farms Number Two, crossed by the Spokane International Railway which Corbin built; and in 1910, East Farms Numbers Three and Four. With water from the Corbin ditch, the company in 1911 opened West Farms Irrigated Tracts and joined the Peyton Investment Company in platting Pasadena Park irrigated farms.

Under irrigation the Spokane Valley was blossoming, not only with vegetables and fruits but with commercial endeavor. When the canals approached specific areas new districts were being platted, palpable testimonials to D. C. Corbin's success with irrigation in the face of predictions that he would fail. During 1908 Hanauer and Graves formed Valleyview Addition, and platted Fruitvale the next year, Frederick W. Suksdorf and the Spokane Orchard Company platted Spokane Bridge additions, Peyton Investment Company opened Grandview Acres, Warren Truitt and Harry Salmons platted Fairacres, and the Modern Irrigation and Land Company laid out a district they hopefully named Opportunity. Orchard Avenue was organized in 1909 by the Orchard Avenue Irrigation Company, Pinecroft by the Spokane and Inland Empire Railway and Liberty Lake

Orchards by the Union Trust Company (Corbin was a director) in 1910, Pinecroft First Addition by the Washington State Real Estate Association in 1911, and Otis Orchards by the Otis Orchards Company in 1912. Thus the pattern of the Spokane Valley's agricultural development was established by Corbin's demonstration that its soil could be irrigated and by his determination to build the canals to do it.

Corbin's hope that he could raise beets in quantity in irrigated fields to maintain his limping Wavery factory did not materialize, although he devoted 700 acres near Corbin, Idaho, and 400 more in East Farms to beets, using Japanese field hands and a steam plow that worked with headlights through the nights. In 1910, the last year of his Waverly plant's operation, a steam tractor was photographed hauling fourteen wagonloads of beets in tandem to the Spokane and Inland loading dock.

The irrigated Spokane Valley continued to flourish and Daniel Corbin remained active in its promotion for the rest of his life. He was not to see its population rival that of the city, as he had forecast, for by 1920 the valley's was only 5,912 but he did see its melons, vegetables, and fruits achieve renown. A former federal reclamation engineer from the Yakima project, R. K. Tiffany, was hired in 1918 by Corbin's executor, the Union Trust Company, to manage the Spokane Valley Land and Water Company with the intention of combining its units and extending service.[23] Tiffany found the Corbin Ditch thirty-four miles long, connected with fifty-four miles of lateral canals, carrying water for 12,000 acres but serving half that number, and estimated that no less than 32,000 acres of the valley might be successfully irrigated.

Corbin's estate held 878⅓ shares of the company's capital stock, and as the valley underwent its greatest population surge of the twenties, this stock with the land, water rights, and equipment that Tiffany had consolidated, were sold in 1922 to the newly organized Spokane Valley Farms Company, which established West Farms, containing 5,000 acres, that same year.[24] The new firm included a noted New York bell maker, William R. Meneely, whose bells hung in Independence Hall, and a corporation lawyer, Rush Taggart, Jr., who represented the Pennsylvania Railroad, Western Union, and American Telegraph and Cable Company, among others.[25] Both men were to figure in the disposal of other Corbin properties. The new owners of the irrigation system inaugurated an extensive renovation of the old Corbin ditch and its laterals, excepting the Liberty Lake canal, completing their renewal program in 1930.

Among the areas to be opened by Spokane Valley Farms lay 4,230 acres on the south side of the river, and on both sides of Sprague Avenue near the old Spokane Bridge, that were to be named Corbin Addition to Greenacres in memory of D. C. Corbin, the man whose vision and energy first brought practical irrigation to the valley of the Spokane.

CHAPTER FIFTEEN

CORBIN'S LAST RAILROAD

Notwithstanding his sojourn in agriculture, D. C. Corbin regarded himself as a builder of railroads. Corbin had always been serious about business, energetic and purposeful, and now that he was nearing seventy, the prospect of retirement repelled him. He could not sit idle while others were busy in the broadening commerce of what Corbin regarded as his country.

Consequently, not two years after he sold his stock in the Spokane Falls and Northern system, while he was promoting his beet sugar factory and paying for valley irrigation canals, Corbin joined George Turner, now United States Senator from Washington, in organizing a rail connection directly between Spokane and the Canadian Pacific. Possibly the Canadian company approached Turner, for Turner played a prominent role in negotiations with the Canadian Pacific during the formation of the new company which was incorporated in December, 1902, as the Spokane and Kootenai Railway.[1] Turner had personal motives for supporting such a railroad, for he was then a director of the Sullivan Group Mining Company, formed to develop a large deposit of low-grade lead, silver, and zinc ore in the Fort Steele mining district of British Columbia, east of Kootenay Lake. The company sorely needed transportation, an improved separation process, and a smelter. E. J. Roberts, who had been chief engineer on the Spokane Falls and Northern, was investigating the Sullivan Group on behalf of his current employer, Charles Sweeny, president of the Empire State-Idaho Mining and Developing Company, and could testify to the vast ore bodies at hand.

Reconnaisance for the projected railroad had been completed in the spring, 1902, and an imposing roster of Washington men had been induced to form the corporation two days before Christmas. They included Corbin and Turner, of course; Jacob Furth, president of the Puget Sound National Bank and of the Seattle Electric Company, owner of Tacoma's street railways, and an organizer of the Puget Sound Electric Railway; former governor John H. McGraw, Seattle; and Charles S. Bihler, former assistant chief engineer of the Northern Pacific, Tacoma. Capitalized for three million dollars, the Spokane and Kootenai was to be financed by "interests friendly to the Canadian Pacific," and the Canadian company, Corbin's old adversary, openly supported his new venture.

Spokane's merchants greeted Corbin's plan enthusiastically, predicting prosperity for it and for themselves in consequence of it. They believed, said the *Spokesman-Review,* that "the chief aim in the construction of the new line is to furnish terminal rates for Spokane." The Canadian Pacific "has had a jealous eye on the trade of Spokane for years ... to get some of the wheat business of the Palouse and the ore traffic of the mines." Terminal rates had been a rallying cry for Spokane businessmen for some years, for they were convinced that the Northern Pacific and Great Northern had treated Spokane shabbily when these transcontinental carriers had adjusted their rates to meet water competition at coastal terminals.

Doubtless the Canadian Pacific expected profitable commerce with the bright Inland Empire but, more to the point, James J. Hill had announced extension of his Great Northern immediately into central British Columbia, using the old Vancouver, Victoria and Eastern charter, and the Canadian Pacific reacted swiftly to his encroachment. Corbin observed publicly that competition motivated the CPR, explaining that the Canadian road could have entered Spokane anytime in the past ten years but stayed out of Hill's territory until he invaded theirs. Roberts recalled afterward that the Guggenheim's American Smelting and Refining Company was interested in the railway "to tie together the mining country," because their smelters exercised a virtual monopoly on ore processing.

If Spokane could not reasonably expect terminal rates from a direct connection with the Canadian Pacific, it could look toward lower charges, for as a condition of its charter to build through Crow's Nest Pass, the CPR in 1897 had agreed to decrease its rates in certain western areas and had voluntarily extended these reductions to other districts, resulting in Canadian freight rates substantially below those for shipping similar goods over United States lines.

All these reasons for direct service to the Canadian Pacific aside, the new railroad was to cross northern Idaho which offered an attractive and expanding freight business in its own right, even though the Northern Pacific and the Great Northern traversed it with their main lines and catheterized it with spurs. The railroad and the commerce would benefit each other, for the road needed the business, and the companies needed the railroad. Once again, Corbin, by building a railroad, provided impetus to the development of the region.

Idaho's panhandle showed many signs of progress. The Northern Pacific sold off nearly all its remaining timber lands in northern Idaho and northeastern Washington in sales that wound up in April, 1902, charging an average price of $2.50 an acre, the Weyerhaeuser syndicate had begun buying timber lands and mills in the area as early as 1900, and Sandpoint, Idaho, already was reputed the largest producer of cedar poles and piling in the Pacific Northwest, shipping 4,000 carloads a year.[2] The Humbird Lumber Company at Sandpoint averaged a monthly payroll of $6,000, and there were also large mills at Coeur d'Alene, Harrison (which floated logs to the Spokane-bound railroad), Priest River, and Bonners Ferry.

In addition to its lumber industry, now penetrating midwestern and eastern markets, northern Idaho sustained a mining sphere that had weathered several rushes and seemed on the brink of stability. When quartz had been located as early as 1884, a year after lime deposits were found, mining camps had been opened around Lake Pend Oreille. Chicago investors had erected the Weber mill in the

middle nineties, but it closed due to a faulty process, and the buildings about it were periodically boarded or reopened as enthusiasm
for the surrounding mines waned and waxed. Active mines in 1902
included the Blue Bird, Keystone, Little Joe, Black Jack, Black
Hawk, Keep Cool, Conjecture, Cashier, Rainbow, Crown Point,
Pearl, Brown, Perry, McCarter, and more—picturesque names for
fortunes lost and riches found.[3] Lakeview, Idaho, had its boom in
1889 and was believed reviving, as was the Chloride district on Pend
Oreille's south shore, which had dwindled after stamp mills had
been erected in 1890. Such a knowledgeable promoter as Jim Wardner had sunk thousands of dollars in Pend Oreille mines beginning
in December, 1888. A $250,000 smelter had been erected at Sand-
point, serving the mining districts with lake tugs and steamers.

Furthermore, agricultural development was encouraging, if not
widespread, in northern Idaho. Bonners Ferry, the site of a river
ferry in 1864, now produced not only poles, ties, and lumber, but
vegetables, fruits, beef, hides, and dairy products. Corbin's own investigation showed that the region between the Spokane River and
Rathdrum might be brought into farm production by irrigation,
and his surveyors crossed this area as they started to study a railroad
route.[4] So no matter what other motives lay behind the plan for a
new railway from Spokane to the Canadian Pacific, there would
be an opportunity to embrace the commercial attractions of northern
Idaho.

The Spokane and Kootenai accomplished little beyond studying a route, however, and apparently its major difficulty lay in financing the road in the face of opposition from the major United
States railroads serving Spokane.[5] Corbin went to London to seek
capital but on his return he proved evasive, discussing with reporters
instead the overcapitalization of trusts and "undigested stocks" on
the eastern market. Nothing was done to build the Spokane and
Kootenai, although the newspapers continued their wistful forecasts
that Corbin would not fail, recalling,

> Spokane got its first metropolitan impetus from the building by Mr.
> Corbin of his pioneer narrow gauge railroad line into the Coeur

d'Alenes in 1886....Mr. Corbin's next undertaking was the construction in 1889 of the Spokane Falls & Northern.... This enterprise was the key that unlocked for Spokane the treasure vaults of
the Kootenai country.[6]

In March, 1904, D. C. Corbin concluded that his company would
never function with its directors. Bihler, the former Northern Pacific
man, was now a partner in a contract to build a power dam at Post
Falls for the Washington Water Power Company, and Turner had
demonstrated himself an implacable juridical foe of big railroads
as a territorial judge 1884–88. Moreover, he was out of the Senate
after 1903. So Corbin gathered about him his proven associates of the
Spokane Falls and Northern and set about reorganizing the railroad
to the Canadian Pacific. He asked the citizens of Spokane to donate
land for a terminal and right of way within the city limits, but later
waived these demands, and he called on the two Chapins and James
Sherwood to join his railway.[7] Corbin asked advice from Edward
Roberts and Roberts, as soon as he learned Corbin needed him, quit
Sweeny and rejoined Corbin. With his loyal coterie about him,
Corbin wrote a construction and traffic contract with the Canadian
Pacific that provided the CPR would pay one-eighth of the construc-
tion cost in return for an option on fifty-two per cent of the capital
stock at a price to be determined not later than January, 1917.

Corbin completed his arrangements with the Canadian Pacific
on January 4 and 5, 1905, in talks with Sir Thomas G. Shaughnessy,
now president of the Canadian line, went from Montreal to New
York where he "concluded arrangements with JKO [Sherwood]
and company," and on January 18 in Spokane, "Organized the
Spokane International Company, and adopted articles of incorporation. Commenced survey of line in city and terminal grounds."
This was all recorded in his precise hand in his pocket datebook.
The initial surveys were supervised by E. G. Tabor under Roberts'
guidance, and because certain northside property owners anticipated
fat profits from land they believed the railroad would need, Roberts
wrote Tabor to "make some more surveys on the south side to divert
attention until everything possible is acquired by purchase." [8]

The Spokane International Railway absorbed the assets of the

Spokane and Kootenai, consisting mainly of preliminary survey maps. Its articles of incorporation, filed in Spokane County on January 18, 1905, listed as trustees: Corbin and his son, Austin; the attorney, Albert Allen, who helped Turner draw the papers, and Allen's son, Frank; George H. Martin and Albert H. Sperry, Corbin's men; James Monaghan, Chester Chapin, Alfred Chapin, and J. K. O. Sherwood, familiar names from the days of Corbin's management of the Spokane Falls and Northern. Turner was not listed; neither was Roberts, although in his letter of resignation, Roberts wrote Sweeny that he had "a substantial interest in the scheme."

Customarily, railroad companies anticipated opportunities to exploit the country they crossed, and the Spokane International was no exception, listing among its purposes the construction and operation of branch lines and of telegraph and telephone lines, the manufacture and sale of electric current, ownership of mines, woodlands, and oil lands, and the sale of their products, and building and operating steamboats and ferries on inland lakes and navigable streams.

Corbin contracted to construct the Spokane International's railroad for $30,000 in capital stock at par value for each mile and $30,000 in bonds at par a mile. On completion of the road's 139.8 miles, consequently, he was to be paid $8,400,000 in securities. This would include all of the company's $4,200,000 in capital stock, and all of its first-mortgage bonds, also amounting to $4,200,000, issued in July, 1906, to return five per cent over a fifty-year period. For actual cash, the railroad maintained an open account with Corbin commencing in November, 1905, and was to borrow on notes from individuals and from the Canadian Pacific.[9]

Under Roberts the surveyors plotted a new route from Spokane to Post Falls that ran south of the old Spokane and Kootenai line, and then proceeded almost directly north to the Canadian border to meet the Canadian Pacific at Eastport, Idaho. The surveys were approved during the summer of 1905 and construction was begun immediately. As terminal grounds in Spokane, Corbin bought seventeen acres on the north bank of the river—all of River Front Addition between Washington and Division streets—obtaining by condemnation certain parcels the Great Northern had purchased

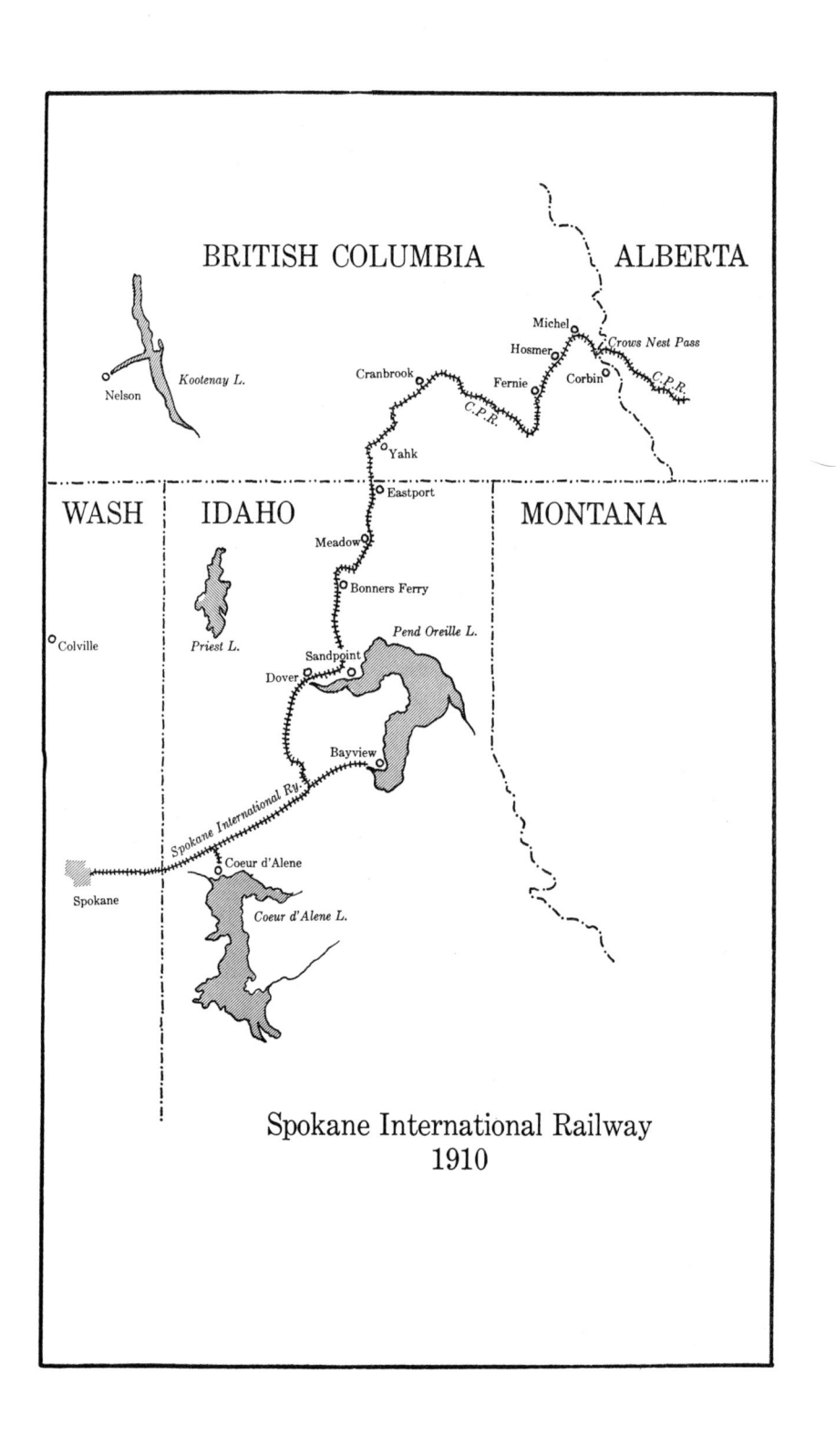

Spokane International Railway
1910

to thwart him. As he previously had done to level ground for the Spokane Falls and Northern depot, Corbin blasted away rock outcroppings through which Division Street had been cut and used the rock for fill, spending approximately $600,000 to acquire and clear his terminal area.

At Bonners Ferry a sawmill ran all winter within a mile of Corbin's proposed crossing of the Kootenai River, preparing timbers for a bridge of five 150-foot spans built of wooden trusses resting on rock piers. In June, 1906, the Spokane International erected a two-story brick depot on Washington Street in Spokane, costing $18,000, and a year later invested $60,000 in three brick buildings to be used as roundhouse and shops on forty acres of triangular area at Greene Street and Trent Avenue, northeast of Spokane's baseball diamond, Recreation Park.

The Spokane International opened for business on November 1, 1906, after Lord Shaughnessy had prodded his own crews to lay their section of the line from Yahk, British Columbia, to Eastport by July 31. As completed, the railroad left Spokane at an elevation of 1,900 feet above sea level, ascended the valley of the Spokane to its summit at 2,325 feet, and then crossed a high plateau, descending to the valleys of the Kootenai and Moyie rivers which it followed to the international boundary. A single track 139.8 miles long, it served the stations of Spokane, Millwood, West Farms, and Otis Orchards in Washington, and Coeur d'Alene Junction, Corbin Junction, Clagstone Junction, Dover, Sandpoint, Bonners Ferry, and Meadow Creek in Idaho. Not only did the Spokane International meet the Canadian Pacific at Eastport, but it connected with the Great Northern at Bonners Ferry, at Spokane with the Northern Pacific and other transcontinental railroads, with the Spokane, Portland and Seattle, and with the Oregon-Washington Railroad and Navigation Company.

Corbin posted the costs of building and equipping the Spokane International in his personal ledgers, so the actual construction expense was never made public. His meticulous notebook, however, itemizes the major costs as totaling $3,634,400, and a similar total was to be accepted as accurate by the Washington State Equalization

Board in 1911 after examinating Corbin's records.[10] One is again tempted to speculate in an area Corbin curtained with reticence, for the one-eighth of the expenses borne by the Canadian Pacific, loans from individuals and the CPR, and cash advanced by Corbin together total almost three and one-half million dollars, indicating that these were the sources of cash for meeting the railroad's bills for construction and equipment.[11] In evaluating the Spokane International in 1926, the Interstate Commerce Commission was to report:

> Nothing is known of the cost of the construction of the carrier's property except amounts shown for the cost of additions and betterments made...since June, 1907. Corbin constructed the property and kept the records concerning the construction in his personal books. Since his death his heirs have not been able to locate the books. No ascertainment or determination was possible from the records obtainable....[12]

So long as there were men with the Spokane International who remembered D. C. Corbin, they related with fierce pride how the old man refused his records to the inspectors, and office legend held that he had snapped to an ICC inquisitor, "That's none of your damned business!"

Four years after opening its main line, the Spokane International extended to Bayview, on the southern tip of Lake Pend Oreille, and to Coeur d'Alene, via the Coeur d'Alene and Pend Oreille Railway, organized March 29, 1910. The company issued $544,000 worth of capital stock, first-mortgage bonds in the same amount, and these securities, totaling $1,088,000, were paid over to Dan Corbin for building the railway at the rate of $25,000 in stock and $25,000 in bonds for each mile. Corbin again refused to divulge the construction costs, but sixteen years after it was built the Interstate Commerce Commission estimated the Coeur d'Alene and Pend Oreille's cost of reproduction at $413,477, and the railroad probably was completed for a good deal less than that, for its terrain was not difficult and all its rolling stock belonged to the Spokane International.

The Coeur d'Alene and Pend Oreille trackage ran 9.34 miles

from Corbin Junction to Bayview and 11.61 miles from Coeur d'Alene Junction to Coeur d'Alene, so that without intervening Spokane International track it did not form one continuous line, and was completed on July 1, 1910, opening for traffic under a fifty-year lease to the Spokane International. Its primary purpose was to serve the mills, for the value of wood products flowing from Idaho now passed ten millions of dollars, triple the worth of 1904 production, and lumber accounted for almost half the total industrial output of the state. With the access to Pend Oreille and Coeur d'Alene lakes afforded by the Coeur d'Alene and Pend Oreille, the Spokane International could pick logs from the huge booms and deliver them directly to a number of mills. Moreover, the Spokane Portland Cement and the Washington Brick and Lime companies incepted limestone quarries and kilns near Bayview, and the town also enjoyed a decade of popularity as a summer resort with a steamer plying between it and Sandpoint. At Bayview, Corbin moored his private launch, *Viking*.

Throughout its operation, the Spokane International was to be a freight carrier without significant passenger mileage. The railway pulled one passenger coach a day, as a courtesy, for Edward Roberts guessed that on the average run "there were ten passengers—eight on passes," which probably was an exaggeration but indicated the company's attitude toward human cargo. The Spokane International abandoned its Spokane passenger station in October, 1915, converted it to a warehouse, and delivered its few riders to a union station shared with the Oregon-Washington Railroad and Navigation and the Chicago, Milwaukee and St. Paul companies. After the Canadian Pacific exercised its stock option and took control, the Spokane International fell into disrepair, rattling over rusting track with depreciated equipment, a museum-piece railroad.

Its profits during Corbin's management are as veiled as its costs, for under Corbin the Spokane International paid no dividends, and on occasion borrowed from the Canadian Pacific to meet interest on notes or passed interest that fell due. Between its opening in November, 1906, and June 30, 1917, the Spokane International reported gross earnings of $8,955,492 but claimed to have spent $9,118,530 in the same period. Of this total expenditure, however, more than eight million dollars was represented by the securities paid Corbin to build and equip the railway, and $39,206, improvements to the property after the construction period.[13] Roberts concluded that the Spokane International rewarded Corbin with generous personal profit but was unproductive for other shareholders, and the ICC was to discover in 1921 that all the railway's capital stock and first-mortgage bonds were outstanding. In the eighteen years between grading the first mile of the Spokane Falls and Northern and the opening of the Spokane International, conditions had changed from the heady risk of embarking into new country to the predictable development of a region whose course had been set. Roberts never expressed the same fondness for the Spokane International as for the old twisting Spokane Falls and Northern, and his attitude without doubt mirrored Corbin's.

Athough it did not deliver the desired terminal rates, the Spokane International solidified Spokane's position as hub of the Inland Empire by linking it with the burgeoning farm and lumber industries of northern Idaho. By 1916, when the Canadian Pacific bought its agreed fifty-two per cent of capital stock, the railway was operating two or three freight trains daily, and in the fall, 1916, enjoyed its biggest business in its history, hauling Palouse wheat to the Canadian Pacific, fruit from the Spokane Valley, lumber from Idaho's mills, and through passengers to Calgary. By this time, the Spokane International also was delivering a sizeable tonnage of coal from Canadian mines controlled by D. C. Corbin.

Corbin announced in Spokane on November 13, 1916, that negotiations with Lord Shaughnessy had resulted in purchase of the Spokane International by the Canadian Pacific and the Soo Line— the Minneapolis, St. Paul and Sault Ste. Marie Railway.[14] The Spokane International was in debt to the CPR more than a million dollars at the time, and among the obligations the Canadian road assumed with its purchase was the unpaid salary of the superintendent, amounting to $15,000. Corbin had expected to retire immediately but Shaughnessy persuaded him to remain in charge until May 1, 1917. Among Corbin's last acts as president of the Spokane International was payment of $51,775 in delinquent taxes, the amount of assessments he had withheld for five years on the ground that the levy was excessive, which he settled only after two Spokane whole-sale liquor dealers, David Holzman and Jacob Schiller, bought his delinquent tax certificates from Spokane County and set about collecting them at fifteen per cent interest. The Washington State Equalization Board had estimated the railway's terminal property, alone, would sell in 1911 for more than the line's original construction cost. In answer to questions about the terms of his sale, Corbin said, "I think the price is satisfactory to both the sellers and the purchasers, and do not feel it would interest the public." [15]

In 1905, when Corbin had first consulted him about resurveying a route for the Spokane International, Edward J. Roberts told Corbin about a coalfield near the Michel River in British Columbia dis-covered by two prospectors who had been grubstaked by Roberts' landlord at Wardner, Al Page, the hotel keeper. Roberts argued that the coal meant "freight from the start" for the new railway, for there was no lack of demand: the smelters required increasing amounts, and the Great Northern was buying large quantities of coal from the Crow's Nest mines. On July 30, Roberts and Corbin set out on horseback, despite Corbin's seventy-three years, riding an overgrown trail to see Page's coal deposit. As they bowed their backs so low branches would not knock them from their mounts, Corbin called down imprecations on those who had enticed him on this goose chase. But about half a mile up what soon was named Coal Mountain, they entered a clear area and seemed to see coal every-where. Regaining his breath, Corbin said, "Well, I'll be damned!" [16]

Roberts followed a stream downhill on foot to estimate the grade for a railway, then rejoined Corbin who was sitting on the CPR tracks several miles distant, holding the horses. In the next few months, Corbin escorted a number of visitors from the East to see the coal fields and each asked Roberts the same question, "Can you build a railroad into here?" Roberts invariably answered that he could. On Christmas Day, 1905, Lord Shaughnessy agreed that the stock and bonds of the Spokane International system should be increased to pay for a fourteen-mile mountain road from the Canadian Pacific, which cost $420,000 in securities, was named the Eastern British Columbia Railway, opened in September, 1908, and in Roberts' opinion "was the best fourteen miles of mountain railroad you ever saw!"

The Eastern British Columbia was a subsidiary of the Corbin Coal and Coke Company, Ltd., which Corbin organized in Washington on August 8, 1908, including among its directors those of the Spokane International, as well as Al Page, who told Roberts about the coal in the first place, and J. A. Harvey of Cranbrook, British Columbia, where the principal company offices were maintained.[17] The coal line was sold to the Canadian Pacific with the Spokane International system.

Lying about fifteen miles east of Fernie, British Columbia, Corbin's coalfields comprised approximately fifteen-thousand acres of the northern fringe of a basin where both the Crow's Nest Pass Coal Company, Colonel Baker's firm augmented by Montreal capital, and the Hosmer mines, owned by the Canadian Pacific, were operating. Corbin's coal seams were forty feet wide at the outcrop, considered of "tremendous width," and could be worked from the surface, although during 1908 the Corbin company began driving the first of a series of tunnels and erected a $100,000 colliery at McGillivray, British Columbia, junction of the Eastern British Columbia with the Canadian Pacific. The deeper Corbin dug the better his coal looked, a "mass of phenomenally large size—as much as 300 feet in width underground... being mined with a steam shovel."[18]

In the next few years, the Corbin coal enterprise expanded so rapidly that the capitalization was increased from the original one million to two million dollars and then to ten million, and its investment in the colliery grew to $315,000. A workmen's town was established, Corbin, British Columbia. The company used two locomotives run by a compressed air plant to pull twenty freight cars at one time, the engines performing merely as brakes on the descent, and dumped coal along the Canadian Pacific tracks to be loaded, producing 10,080 Canadian tons (2,240 pounds) for sale in Canada and 114,790 for sale in the United States in 1910, amounts average for the output in three succeeding years. Throughout its life, the Corbin company's principal market was the United States where it sold to steam plants, industrial customers, and the Spokane International as late as 1934. Unlike the Crow's Nest and Hosmer companies, Corbin produced no coke, selling coal principally in Canada to the Trail [Creek] smelter. The output of the Crow's Nest region as a whole in 1910 was 1,250,000 tons but this was soon to decline as the Great Northern converted to oil-fired boilers.

Corbin's luck with his coal company added luster to his legend, for he had organized and built a railway despite the opposition of the major United States railroads serving Spokane, and as a by-product of such contention, developed a magnificent coal mine. But in March, 1913, his magic failed. The honeycombed prime seam collapsed of its own weight and friction started a fire deep in an abandoned level called Number Two South. For three months the Corbin company tried to erect an effective concrete-and-stone stopping to isolate the fire from other tunnels but finally, after consulting British Columbia government advisors, consented to seal off this portion of the mine, closing it on June 3. In Roberts' opinion, "It was a calamity the coal field was so big. If the fire had waited another six months, we'd have made a million dollars!"

For years afterward the fire continued to burn deep in the earth, requiring careful watching. Despite the misfortune, production continued from mines Three, Four, Five, and Six, and from stripping a surface cut known as the "Big Showing," where steam shovels worked on four benches of a coal quarry estimated to contain a million tons. The Corbin Coal and Coke Company dug from sixty to seventy thousand tons annually after 1913, continuing to sell most of it in the United States. In 1918 production passed 98,000 tons, the company's greatest after the fire, but in the next year, the yield fell to 45,249 tons as a result of labor stoppages connected with a statutory reduction of work hours and union organization. In 1920 the two big copper smelters of the Boundary district closed, further reducing the coal market.

After his father's death, Austin Corbin II operated the coal company with some of the faithful old group, including James Sherwood, and with the same eastern investors who had purchased the valley irrigation system, Meneely and Taggart. They added to the company William Weaver Heaton, a widely known New York broker and a member of the board of governors of the New York Stock Exchange. But Corbin coal never matched again its production of the wartime years 1918–19, due partly to lessening demand for industrial coal and partly to passage by Congress of the Fordney-McCumber Tarrif Act, aimed at equalizing the cost of American and imported products. The colliery burned in 1928 and was replaced the following year by a plant costing $175,000.

Much of the Crow's Nest region reduced its output after 1920. The Canadian Pacific closed its Hosmer mines as a result of labor strife in 1935 and the Corbin colliery operated only fifteen days in January and twenty in September of that year. Most of the workers' time was spent gathering loose coal from the Big Showing for the school, hospital, hotel, and company officers' homes at Corbin. Except for this brief reopening, the Corbin mines were shut down by a union dispute on May 21, 1935, and thereafter lay unused. Austin Corbin finally liquidated the company, sold its machinery, and concluded its dissolution in 1942 with the sale of 849 tons of equipment as scrap to the War Time Salvage Board.[19] Consolidated Mining and Smelting leased the Corbin property in 1943, using trucks and steam shovels for stripping, even renovating some of the old buildings, to replenish short stockpiles at its Trail and Kimberley smelters.

At his death, D. C. Corbin held 6,200 shares of his coal company stock, valued at par at $620,000 and estimated as worth $124,000 by his appraisers. Austin Corbin II was to leave no coal stock as a part of his estate.

With his retirement from the Spokane International, Daniel Corbin had closed his career as a railroad builder. Surely he realized that he could not have much time left, but he remained active in coal mining, irrigation, real estate, and the stock investments that he had gleaned in the twenty-nine years since he came first to Spokane Falls. In his three decades in the city, Corbin had laid seven railroads, diverting to Spokane the first rich flow of the region's two considerable mining districts, and had delivered, as well, an irrigated valley to the city's east. No man of his time had molded Spokane as had D. C. Corbin, who viewed its high buildings and long streets from his tall-backed, rung rocking chair on the wide porch of the austere house at the head of Stevens Street.

CHAPTER SIXTEEN

LAST DAYS AND LEGACY

Many men retire after the age of sixty-five; but brisk D. C. Corbin when he was past that age undertook four notable careers: those of sugar manufacturer, irrigator, coal merchant, and railroad builder, and each had buttressed the physical and economic development of Spokane, his adopted city. The breadth and direction of the city's expansion for half a century to come had been fixed, in large measure, by irrigation of the valley. When Corbin retired as president of the Spokane International, Spokane was served with five transcontinental and an even dozen branch or feeder railways, a metropolis of 157,626 persons, the axis of an area of 150,000 square miles that yielded one-ninth of the nation's wheat crop, a third of the world's lead ore, and produced annually $350,000,000 in new wealth from mines, forests, and fields.

Corbin had found Spokane Falls in 1888 a town of seven thousand, thriving with the substance of his chippy railway to the Coeur d'Alenes. Soon he was to revive Spokane after depression by capturing for it the mineral outpouring of Rossland, and during the city's most accelerated growth period early in the twentieth century, 1900–10, he bestowed on it the commerce of northern Idaho, irrigated farmland, and coal and sugar industries.

Despite his varied works, Corbin lived a quiet, ordered private life, peopled mainly with business associates. He had "kept his figure," a neighbor's daughter was to recall, and had remained notoriously punctual, so that at five o'clock sharp each workday evening his coachman drew Corbin's paired bay cobs and buggy to the Old National Bank Building, the erect old man stalked out, spanked the reins, and whirled home to his lonely house on the hill.

To the end of his days, Corbin commanded his domain. He was not above ordering E. J. Roberts, in a kingly manner, to summon the mechanic, Lew Schwartz, running a pile driver on the Moyie River, so Schwartz could fix a leaky hot-water faucet in the Corbin house. Schwartz's son, who remembered such an occasion, also recalled that Corbin "liked to be talked up to." Roberts, too, related that Corbin liked to be talked up to, but the old man had treated newspapermen, and a good many others, with brusque impatience, and had been reflected in the public press as an unceremonious authoritarian, as he was. Even his son, Austin, who in later life attempted to emulate his father's stern image, remained subservient so long as Daniel Corbin lived.

To the residents of Spokane in the second decade of the twentieth century, however, D. C. Corbin was an anachronism, limning the city's past, the man who had built the first railway to the Coeur d'Alenes, who had tied Rossland and Nelson to Spokane, who had irrigated the valley, who had put a railroad up the center of Idaho's panhandle. These deeds seemed in the distant past to many. The city had acknowledged its debts to Corbin formally on January 19, 1915, when the Chamber of Commerce had selected him, from several candidates, as its first honorary member. The occasion was the Chamber's annual banquet which Corbin did not attend. Except when his name added luster, as in the case of his appointment as a trustee of Spokane College, Corbin's advice was seldom sought in civic affairs and he was not one to offer it.

After 1907, when Corbin had married his housekeeper, Anna Louise Larson, he was socially ignored in Spokane, and treated with some coolness even by Austin, his son, although the Corbin family in the East received the new Mrs. Corbin cordially. A native of Sweden brought to the United States as a child by her father, a railroad contractor, she had been prepared for her marriage to Corbin by attending eastern schools, including Columbia University, and by travel in Europe, and her previous marriage had been quietly dissolved.

Death came before Daniel Corbin showed any inclination toward retirement. In the spring of 1918, he slipped, fell, and fractured his right leg on the polished terrazzo of his tenth-floor suite in the Old National Bank Building. The broken leg aggravated an intestinal disorder that had troubled Corbin as his years crept upon him. Dr. James M. Neff, called from Chicago, advised Corbin to put his affairs in order and operated.[1] Pneumonia set in and shortly after noon on June 29, 1918, D. C. Corbin died in Sacred Heart Hospital.

He had provided for his family well: to Anna, he left his home and bonds, principally Liberty, Spokane International, and Union Pacific; and to Louise's children (for Louise, his daughter, had died in 1909), Corbin left generous trusts. Two-thirds of the remainder of his $679,564 estate went to Austin, his son, and one-third to Mary Balguy, in trust, as well as provision for her child by her first marriage to Kirtland Cutter. The boy's name had been Corbin Cutter; after the marriage had been sundered, he became Corbin Corbin, taking his grandfather's name. D. C. Corbin's personal possessions, such as watches, guns, and desks, were bequeathed to Austin. Corbin's body was incinerated and the ashes placed in a $35.00 urn at Austin's direction, for, as Austin was to explain in his own will, "I have a prejudice against expensive funerals." [2] It was commonly believed that Anna kept her late husband's ashes in her kitchen until they were placed in the Fairmount mausoleum.

The legacy D. C. Corbin left Spokane was its secure place as Queen City of its Inland Empire, one of the notable inland cities of the West, folded in a fabric of commerce patterned by Daniel Chase Corbin.

NOTES

In ANNOTATING THIS STUDY OF D. C. CORBIN I HAVE ATTEMPTED TO guide readers to my sources without a shower of little numbers flecking the text. Some may wish for more notes; some, fewer, although these latter, I suspect, have already contrived to ignore the annotation. For those who peruse the notes, I believe the references will be more useful with the following explanation of what they contain—and what they do not.

In general, my annotation has been restricted to sources for direct quotations, unpublished matter, and mention of persons, organizations, or studies that illuminated a specific aspect of Corbin's career.

Five collections are cited by parenthetic identifications following individual notes: Hauser, Magnuson, National Archives, Reed, and Roberts, in alphabetical order.

The Hauser papers comprise seven file drawers of personal, business, and political correspondence, beginning in 1853, of Samuel T. Hauser, and may be examined in the library of the Historical Society of Montana, Helena.

The Magnuson acknowledgements refer not to personal memorabilia but to a collection of newspapers and miscellaneous documents concerning the Coeur d'Alene mining district, which have been preserved by Richard G. Magnuson of Wallace, Idaho. Magnuson has compiled a detailed index of early newspapers which he allowed me to use at my convenience.

The National Archives of the United States of America are, doubtless, familiar to many readers. I cite them simply to indicate the location of documents mentioned in the notes.

The Reed papers include letters, notebooks, and personal records of Simeon G. Reed, indexed by the Works Progress Administration and deposited in the archives of Reed College, Portland, Oregon.

The Roberts papers consist of several packets of business records, maps, photographic glass plates, and notebooks of Edward J. Roberts, filed with the Eastern Washington State Historical Society, Spokane, and miscellaneous letterbooks in the Roberts family's possession. While valuable for this study and for their bearing on later Coeur d'Alene mining history, the Roberts papers do not represent an unbroken record of Roberts' career, and I filled in many gaps by personal interviews with him.

The reader may also wish to know that several early newspapers on microfilm repose in the Bancroft Library on the campus of the University of California, Berkeley, including issues of the *Northport News, Stevens County Miner,* and the *Kettle Falls Pioneer.*

Mrs. Ray Evans of Northport provided me with 1920–30 issues of the *Northport News* which she saved from destruction when the newspaper cleaned its offices some years ago. The Colville *Statesman-Examiner* holds scrapbooks and back issues containing detailed historical articles sifted by its former editor, J. C. Harrigan. Bound copies of the periodical, *Mining Truth,* and its successors, belong to the Northwest Mining Association, Spokane.

Because I did not propose to pelt the reader with notes like raindrops, I ought to explain the sources that provided continuity for broad sections of this book. The chapters on D. C. Corbin in the Coeur d'Alenes are drawn generally from the *Spokane Falls Review,* Magnuson's collection, the Hauser papers, official correspondence in the National Archives, and *Poor's Manual of Railroads.*

The Spokane Falls and Northern discussion emerges largely from interviews with E. J. Roberts, from his papers, the *Spokesman-Review,* the Colville *Statesman-Examiner,* and the National Archives.

Much of the parliamentary material concerning Corbin's railways into Canada was published at the time in the *Inland Sentinel*, one of the British Columbia papers contained in the magnificent collection of the provincial archives in Victoria, and in the *Rossland Miner* and *Trail Creek News*, stored in the library of the *Trail Daily Times*.

My dependence on Spokane County platbooks and the annual reports of the British Columbia Minister of Mines seems implicit in the chapters dealing with Corbin's irrigation and coal enterprises without annotation.

In summary, therefore, the notes do not contain the thread of continuity to Corbin's career month by month. The notes do indicate the sources of direct quotations (unless the sources seem obvious from the context), information not readily available in many libraries, and credit to persons or organizations who helped me or whose research supplied detail for specific portions of the Corbin study.

CHAPTER ONE.
NEW HAMPSHIRE TO MONTANA

1. *Spokesman-Review* (Spokane), November 8, 1908.

2. Harvey M. Lawson, *History and Genealogy of the Descendants of Clement Corbin* (Hartford, Conn.: Case, Lockwood and Brainard Co., 1905), pp. 229–30. The National Archives did not locate a record that Corbin held a government contract as a surveyor but reported that certain records are incomplete.

3. The author is indebted to R. E. Dale of the Nebraska State Historical Society staff for the information on Corbin in Nebraska from his research in periodicals, and from census records, August, 1856, in the *Nebraska and Midwest Genealogical Record*, XVI, 34.

4. D. C. Corbin, "Recollections of a Pioneer Railroad Builder," *Washington Historical Quarterly*, I (January, 1907), No. 2, p. 43.

5. *Montana Post* (Helena), May 5, 1866.

6. Organized in 1862 by Charles D. Woolworth and Guy C. Barton, the Woolworth and Barton forwarding company followed Union Pacific construction across the southwestern plains, handling freight consigned to New Mexico, Colorado, Utah, and Montana. Woolworth and Barton operated from the end of the track, using mule and cattle trains, and moving their portable warehouses as the railroad extended westward. Woolworth managed an eastern office at 254 Broadway, New York, while Barton supervised operations from

his office at St. Joseph, Missouri. There were agents in Boston, Cincinnati, St. Louis, Denver, and—when Corbin reached Montana—in Helena. The company sold in 1868 to Megeath, Miller and Company of Omaha. See J. Sterling Morton, succeeded by Albert Watkins, ed., *Illustrated History of Nebraska* (Lincoln: Western Publishing and Engraving Co., 1905–13), I, 586–87; *Rocky Mountain News* (Denver), February 3, 1866, and January 21, 1867.

7. Hubert Howe Bancroft, *Works* (San Francisco: The History Co., 1890), XXXI, 797; Michael A. Leeson, ed., *History of Montana, 1739–1885* (Chicago: Warner, Beers and Co., 1885), pp. 271 and 1217.

8. The mill process is described in Robert George Raymer, *Montana, the Land and the People* (Chicago: Lewis Publishing Co., 1930), I, 441.

9. Letter from A. M. Esler to S. T. Hauser, March 15, 1867 (Hauser).

10. Letter from Mrs. Anne McDonnell to author, February 2, 1952; *Montana Post* (Helena), October 30, 1868. Corbin's house was later moved to a different location and occupied by the fourth territorial governor, Benjamin F. Potts.

11. *Montana Post* (Helena), February 26, March 19, and March 26, 1869.

12. Letters from D. C. Corbin to Hauser, August 26, 1871, and September 13, 1876. The latter outlines Corbin's stock ownership. On several letters in 1871, Corbin has written his name in ink on the bank's letterhead (Hauser).

13. Letter from Corbin to Hauser, September 18, 1871 (Hauser).

14. Letter from Corbin to Hauser, June 10, 1876 (Hauser).

15. Letter from Corbin to Hauser, June 20, 1876 (Hauser).

16. E. W. Knight's bond, dated September 1, 1876, is in the Hauser papers; letter from Corbin to Hauser, September 13, 1876 (Hauser); Leeson *History of Montana, 1739–1885*, p. 1228.

17. Letter from Corbin to Hauser, September 13, 1876 (Hauser).

18. Hauser was involved in many pursuits and invited Corbin to join him in several. At this time, Hauser was a partner in Davis, Hauser and Co., driving cattle from Washington and Oregon to Montana over the old Mullan road, but the *Northwest Tribune* (Spokane), April 29, 1881, reported that not half his herd completed one trip, a number of cows running off with buffalo herds. The *Montana Post* (Helena), May 5, 1866, said that the San Francisco Chamber of Commerce had awarded Thomas Page of Walla Walla a $10,000 contract to clear the Mullan road and make it passable but apparently it was deteriorating too rapidly to permit any substantial improvement.

19. Letter from Corbin to Hauser, November 25, 1884 (Hauser).

20. Letter from T. F. Oakes to Hauser, February 12, 1884 (Hauser).

21. Letter from A. Raht to Hauser, February 25, 1885 (Hauser).

CHAPTER TWO.
CORBIN'S FIRST RAILROAD

1. H. K. Hines, *An Illustrated History of the State of Washington* (Chicago: Lewis Publishing Co., 1893), p. 387. Glidden was educated at a Meth-

odist seminary in New Hampshire, had been in the iron business in Ohio until 1865, moved to St. Paul in 1876, and arrived in the Coeur d'Alenes in 1885, for a time maintaining a store at Thompson Falls, Montana Territory, as well as his Tiger mine.

2. Letter from A. M. Esler to S. T. Hauser, January 12, 1886 (Hauser).

3. Letters from Esler to Hauser, January 12, 29, and February 2, 1886 (Hauser).

4. Letter from Esler to Hauser, January 29, 1886 (Hauser).

5. Letter from Esler to Hauser, March 16, 1886 (Hauser).

6. Letter from Esler to Hauser, April 11, 1886 (Hauser) in which Esler mentions writing to Corbin.

7. Letter from Oakes to Hauser, April 27, 1886 (Hauser). Browne appears to have been relieved to turn over the Coeur d'Alene project to Corbin and Hauser. He was president of a projected new railway, the Spokane and Columbia Railroad, to build from Spokane Falls to the Little Dalles of the Columbia River, in which the magazine editor E. V. Smalley was prominent.

8. D. C. Corbin, "Recollections of a Pioneer Railroad Builder," *Washington Historical Quarterly,* I (January, 1907), No. 2, p. 44.

9. Articles of incorporation, July 1, 1886. (Record group 49, records of Division "F," railway right-of-way files, Act of 1875, National Archives); charter, June 6, 1886, secretary of state, Montana. In an interview in the *Spokesman-Review* (Spokane), November 8, 1908, Corbin said he intended first to call his line the Montana and Coeur d'Alene Railroad and Navigation Company, and, "This little railroad started me on my life's work."

10. Letters from Corbin to Hauser, May 14 and June 16, 1886 (Hauser). Merle W. Wells, historian and archivist, Idaho Historical Society, wrote the author on September 27, 1960: "For practical purposes, Corbin's statement that Idaho lacked a railway incorporation law is accurate. At least the restrictions on corporations in Idaho law very likely made it impractical to corporate a very extensive railroad business." Wells also pointed out that the statute did not specifically mention railroads.

11. The Washington and Idaho was incorporated in Washington Territory July 5, 1886. The W&I had studied its route so that it was able to begin surveying a section of the line on August 30, 1886. Appellant's Brief, Washington & Idaho v. Coeur d'Alene Railway & Navigation Company, Supreme Court of Idaho, January, 1889, p. 4 (Magnuson).

12. Letter from Esler to Hauser, June 25, 1886 (Hauser).

13. *Morning Oregonian* (Portland), July 6 and October 19, 1886; *Wallace Free Press,* April 25, 1891.

14. Letter from Esler to Hauser, August 9, 1886 (Hauser).

CHAPTER THREE.
OPENING IDAHO'S MINES

1. Letter from Corbin to Hauser, August 15, 1886 (Hauser).

2. Letter from Corbin to Hauser, July 27, 1886 (Hauser).

3. Letter from Corbin to Hauser, August 27, 1886 (Hauser).

4. Cost account records of the Spokane and Idaho (Hauser).

5. Articles of incorporation, Spokane County, Wash., miscellaneous book B, p. 218; *Spokane Falls Review,* October 24, 1886.

6. William S. Shiach, John M. Henderson, and Harry B. Averill, *An Illustrated History of North Idaho* (Chicago: Western Historical Publishing Co., 1903), p. 770.

7. Letter from Corbin to Hauser, July 15, 1886 (Hauser). The laws of 1875 gave railways the right to use earth, stone, timber, and other native materials for construction along their rights of way.

8. Letter from George H. Earl, secretary, Coeur d'Alene Railway and Navigation Company, to commissioner, General Land Office, February 9, 1893, mentions that original station grounds were approved September 22, 1886. (Record group 49, records of division "F," railway right-of-way files, Act of 1875, National Archives.)

9. Letter from George C. Chandler, acting secretary of the interior, to commissioner, General Land Office, January 25, 1893, says the line, in its entirety, lies on unsurveyed public lands. (National Archives.) Shiach, Henderson, and Averill, *op. cit.,* p. 999, explains that the Northern Pacific claimed nearly all south-fork land within its forty-mile limit. The role of the Department of the Interior is described by Secretary John W. Noble in a letter to the commissioner, General Land Office, March 21, 1892: "Heretofore railroad companies desiring to secure the right of way over the unsurveyed lands of the United States have been permitted to file a map of location for the approval of this Department, without waiting for survey, but it was required that immediately upon survey ... the company must file another map showing the line of route. ... No rights followed the approval of the map over unsurveyed public lands, the same being furnished presumably as a matter of information." (National Archives.)

10. Letter from Corbin to Hauser, October 17, 1886 (Hauser).

11. Letter from Corbin to Hauser, December 26, 1886 (Hauser).

12. Quoted by Shiach, Henderson, and Averill, *op. cit.,* p. 995.

CHAPTER FOUR.
THE NORTHERN PACIFIC TAKES OVER

1. Articles of incorporation, July 6, 1887, on file in Shoshone County, Idaho, which maintains its records alphabetically by company.

2. *Spokane Falls Review,* August 19, 1887.

3. *Wallace Free Press,* October 1, 1887, and March 10, 1888; William S. Shiach, John M. Henderson, and Harry B. Averill, *An Illustrated History of North Idaho* (Chicago: Western Historical Publishing Co., 1903), p. 1032; *Report on the Internal Commerce of the United States for the Year 1890,* Executive Document No. 6, Part 2, House of Representatives, Second Session,

Fifty-First Congress, p. 507, discloses that the Coeur d'Alene Railway and Navigation Company was then 31.53 miles long with the following stations and equipment:

> Mission, water tank and ore building.
>
> Kingston, depot.
>
> Wardner Junction, one freight and passenger depot, two ore platforms.
>
> Osborne [sic], freight and passenger depot.
>
> Wallace, one freight and passenger depot, one water tank, one engine shed, and one engine shop.
>
> Burke, one passenger depot.

4. Appellant's brief, Washington & Idaho v. Coeur d'Alene Railway and Navigation Co., Idaho supreme court, January, 1889, pp. 8–9 (Magnuson).

5. *Spokane Falls Review,* March 19, 1887. The author has not located a record of sale in Kootenai, Shoshone, or Spokane counties. Monaghan recalled that the steamer line had been sold to Corbin in 1886. See J. Orin Oliphant (ed.), "The Early History of Spokane, Washington, Told by Contemporaries" (typescript, State Normal School, Cheney, Wash., 1927), p. 17.

6. William W. Howard, "Spokane Falls and Its Exposition," *Harper's Weekly,* XXXIV (1890), 689–706.

7. One such warning, a letter from E. B. Nash of the Omaha and Grant Smelting and Refining Company, to Hauser, March 2, 1888 (Hauser), reads in part: "There seems to be a feeling...that Mr. Wardner, as a middle man, is getting more money out of the business than he is entitled to."

8. The code book, agreement for sale dated March 5, 1887, and a telegram from Wardner to Reed, April 20, 1887, are in the Reed collection. Wardner had filed on the water rights to the Bunker Hill and Sullivan soon after the claims were staked.

9. Letter from Horace Cutter, cashier of the First National Bank of Spokane Falls, to Reed, May 7, 1887 (Reed). The Reed papers also contain a long letter of explanation to Laidlaw and Company.

10. Letter from Goldsmith to Reed, June 6, 1887 (Reed).

11. Letter from Reed to Hauser, November 4, 1887 (Hauser).

12. Helena and Livingston articles of incorporation, May 5, 1888, filed with the secretary of state, Montana. In a letter to Hauser, July 13, 1888, Corbin wrote, "I *suppose* A. C. Seligman is treasurer of the new reduction company, but I do not know" (Hauser).

13. Report of trustees' meeting in Seattle, July 16, 1888. (Record group 49, records of Division "F," railway right-of-way files, Acts of 1875, National Archives.)

14. *Spokane Falls Review,* July 14, 1888.

15. Spokane Falls & Idaho v. J. J. Costello, in Kootenai County, Idaho, case file No. 162; *Spokane Falls Review,* April 4, 1888.

16. Shoshone County deeds, book R, p. 441.

17. *Spokane Falls Review,* January 29, 1890.

18. *Spokane Falls Review,* May 10, 1888.

19. J. M. Porter in *Mining Truth* (Spokane), March 1, 1924.

20. George L. Shoup in *Report of the Secretary of the Interior, 1890* (First Session, Fifty-First Congress), III (Reports of the Governors), 850.

CHAPTER FIVE.

TWO WEEKS TO START A RAILROAD

1. *Spokane Falls Review,* January 1, 1889.

2. Articles of incorporation, Spokane County, miscellaneous book B, p. 341.

3. *Spokane Falls Review,* April 18, 1888.

4. Richard F. Steele, *An Illustrated History of North Washington* (Chicago: Western Historical Publishing Co., 1904), p. 132; *Colville Miner,* April 12, 1888. By 1892 the smelter had gone into receivership and Moore had become a collector of customs in Alaska. Benjamin P. Moore was the son of J. S. Moore, a New York financier, who apparently put up the money for his son's smelter, according to the *Spokane Falls Review,* July 12, 1889.

5. *Spokane Falls Review,* May 18, 1888.

6. *Spokane Falls Review,* February 12, 1889.

7. The Canadians spelled the name Kootenay, while the Americans spelled it Kootenai, and the spellings were frequently intermixed in newspaper stories. The Canadians also wrote Okanagan, the Americans, Okanogan. The three remaining mining districts were the Coeur d'Alenes, of course, the Silver Creek in the Cascade Mountains, and the Seven Devils, 250 miles southeast of Spokane Falls in central Idaho. See John R. Reavis, *The City of Spokane* (Spokane: Clough and Graves, 1891), pp. 31–36.

8. *Spokane Falls Review,* November 7, 1888.

9. *Spokane Falls Review,* February 9, 1889.

10. *Spokane Falls Review,* February 13, 1889.

11. *Spokane Falls Review,* March 2, 1889.

CHAPTER SIX.

CONSTRUCTION TO COLVILLE

1. J. P. Crittenden and Charles B. Helffrish, comp., *New York Securities* (New York: New York Securities, 1893), II, 212 and 464. The Securities Company was capitalized for $500,000. Sherwood was its president, the Chapin cousins, directors. The Land and Securities Company was capitalized for $250,000, and Sherwood was also its president. A. C. Chapin was secretary-treasurer.

2. For a Skinner biography, see Nelson W. Durham, *Spokane and the Inland Empire* (Chicago: S. J. Clarke Publishing Co., 1912), II, 787. Skinner

became a leading Spokane contractor, and may have been associated, before coming to Spokane, in a hoop factory at Ronceverte, West Virginia, with D. C. Corbin. The department of archives and history, West Virginia, could find no record of such a factory in answer to an inquiry by the author. See also Emmett Holmes, "Some Historical Facts and Other Remembrances of the Construction and Operation of the Spokane Falls & Northern" (MS, Spokane Public Library, 1941).

3. Quoted in *Spokane Falls Review*, February 27, 1889. Although the *Herald* talks of bonds, the railroad bonds were not issued until July, 1889, so the newspaper doubtless meant stocks. See Crittenden and Helffrish, *op. cit.*, p. 963.

4. Letter from Newbery to Secretary of the Interior, June 28, 1889. (Record group 49, records of Division "F," railway right-of-way files, Act of 1875, National Archives.) In this letter, Newbery is transmitting amended maps of the first two sections of the railway. The right of way approved in 1888 remained in force until it was forfeited formally by the Great Northern in 1914. The date of the survey is from Roberts' notebooks showing locating time (Roberts).

5. *Colville Miner,* March 15, 1889.

6. Letter from James T. Maher, Great Northern right of way, land and tax commissioner, to commissioner, General Land Office, August 9, 1926 (National Archives).

7. *Spokane Falls Review,* May 23, 1889. Representative pay scales are contained in Roberts' records of time certificates, showing an assistant engineer receiving $90.00 to $125 a month, a leveller $75.00 to $90.00, a chainman $40.00, a team and teamster $75.00, an axman $35.00, a rodman $45.00, and a cook (invariably listed as "Jim Chinaman") $50.00 (Roberts).

8. Specifications, March 22, 1889, Baldwin Locomotive Works. The same misspelling of Spokane appears on the blueprints where it has been lined out and corrected. Engines were classified by wheel arrangement and cylinder diameter, so the code classification of these engines was 8–30–D. Blueprints and specifications furnished the author by A. R. Kilgore, sales promotion manager, Baldwin-Lima-Hamilton Corp.

9. These are lots 1, 2, 3, and 4, block 2, River Front Addition to Spokane Falls.

10. *Stevens County Miner* (Colville), June 21, 1889.

11. *Spokane Falls Review,* October 26, 1889, publishing an account date-lined Colville, October 19.

12. Roberts' tables of cost (Roberts).

CHAPTER SEVEN.
EYES ON CANADA

1. F. W. Howay, W. N. Sage, and H. F. Angus, *British Columbia and the United States* (Toronto: Ryerson Press, 1942), p. 233.

2. Roberts' notes of locating time (Roberts).

3. *Spokane Falls Review,* December 13, 1889. In *Poor's Manual of Railroads, 1890* the Spokane Falls and Northern lists its projected route from Marcus to the Coast, 320 miles, and from Colville to Metaline, 40 miles.

4. *Spokane Falls Review,* November 3, 1889; *Poor's Manual of Railroads, 1890.* See also George F. Brimlow, ed., "Marias Pass Explorer John F. Stevens," *Montana Magazine of History,* I (Summer, 1953), 41, quoting a letter of Stevens' which says in part: "During the summer season of 1889 I was employed in making the final location surveys of the Spokane Falls & Northern Railway...from Spokane north to the international boundary.... At the conclusion of this work late in the fall of that season I was idle in Spokane for some time." Stevens found Marias Pass in 1890, the next year took charge of Great Northern surveys to Puget Sound, and in the course of these, located Stevens Pass in the Cascade Mountains.

5. Mollie E. Cottingham, "A History of the West Kootenay District of British Columbia" (MS, University of British Columbia, 1947), p. 140, quoting the *Nelson Miner,* March 17, 1894.

6. *Vancouver Telegram* quoted in the *Spokane Falls Review,* July 6, 1890.

7. *Spokane Falls Review,* July 29, 1890. According to the *Review,* March 18, 1888, the wagon road had been constructed by Wardner, Monaghan, and King, and sold shortly after to Dr. Wilbur A. Hendryx, owner of the Blue Bell Mine in British Columbia, who operated it as a toll road under a charter from Idaho Territory.

8. *Spokane Falls Review,* January 27, 1888.

9. *Inland Sentinel* (Kamloops, B.C.), October 5, 1889. What was in 1889 called Sproat's Landing became Robson, B.C.

10. *Spokane Falls Review,* January 11, 1890.

11. British Columbia Legislative Journal, January 23, 1890.

12. Sylvia L. Thrupp, "A History of the Cranbrook District in East Kootenay" (Master's thesis, University of British Columbia, 1929), pp. 53–56; *Inland Sentinel* (Kamloops, B.C.), January 8, 1897; *Colonist* (Victoria, B.C.), February 30, 1894; Fred J. Smyth, *Tales of the Kootenays* (Cranbrook, B.C.: The Courier, 1942), p. 69, says Galbraith was in financial straits and sold to Baker for $21,000 in 1884.

13. Letter from Wilson to Robson, January 18, 1890, printed in the British Columbia Legislative Journal, 1890.

14. *Ibid.* The Crow's Nest and Kootenay Railroad Company had been chartered April 28, 1888, to provide an all-weather route between Kootenay Lake and the Canadian Pacific.

15. Moved by Baker, seconded by Mr. Duck. British Columbia Legislative Journal, February 27, 1890.

16. Thrupp, *op. cit.,* p. 88, quoting a personal interview with N. A. Wallinger, Cranbrook, B.C.

17. Telegram printed in British Columbia Legislative Journal, 1890.

18. *Inland Sentinel* (Kamloops, B.C.), March 8, 1890. The records of the

House of Commons were mostly destroyed by fire in 1916, and a Department of Transport search for pertinent records turned up none, so the account of the committee's action is taken largely from the *Inland Sentinel*.

19. U.S. Public Law 105, 1890, approved May 8, 1890. (Record group 49, records of Division "F," railway right-of-way files, Act of 1875, National Archives.)

20. Quoted in *Spokane Falls Review,* March 28, 1890.

21. Thrupp, *op. cit.,* p. 76; and letter from Clara Graham, Roberts Creek, B.C., August 14, 1959, to the author, which reads in part: "When the building of the British Columbia Southern Railway was being planned, Colonel Baker, who was very much behind the project, contrived to have it run through his farm. In spite of the fact that that course did not present the best grade nor shortest route, Cranbrook eventually became an important railway divisional point and the CPR, in return, received a generous portion of the townsite."

22. British Columbia Legislative Journal, 1890.

CHAPTER EIGHT.
RAILS REACH THE COLUMBIA

1. Roberts' notes show the land was purchased September 19, 1891. What was formerly Meyers Falls is today Kettle Falls, Washington, and the site of old Kettle Falls is covered by the back-water from Grand Coulee Dam.

2. *Spokane Falls Review,* January 13, 1891; "Kettle Falls—Boom and Bust," *Spokesman-Review* (Spokane), magazine section, March 13, 1949. The Kettle Falls and Columbia Valley Railway and Navigation Company had been capitalized for $2,500,000 by William H. Reid, a wealthy seed merchant of Rochester, N.Y., and his associates. They expected to reach Spokane over the Washington Central road. The *Review,* April 2, 1890, reported that the Washington Legislature had memorialized Congress to appropriate $50,000 to remove obstructions from the Columbia River at Little Dalles to make it navigable 280 miles upriver to Revelstoke.

3. Register, General Land Office, in a letter to commissioner, General Land Office, April 21, 1891 (record group 49, records of Division "F," railway right-of-way files, Act of 1875, National Archives). The grant was forfeited by the Great Northern in 1926.

4. This booklet is described in detail, and the author has relied on this description, in the *Spokane Falls Review,* March 19, 1890.

5. *Spokane Falls Review,* May 3, 1890.

6. *Inland Sentinel* (Kamloops, B.C.), September 26, 1891.

7. *Spokane Falls Review,* July 16, 1890. Corbin did not erect his proposed hotel.

8. *Spokane Falls Review,* August 13, 1890. Loon Lake formerly had a bay called Corbin Bay but this is now called Moose Bay.

9. Abstract of title No. 6303, Colville Abstract Company. In Roberts'

ledger, April, 1892, he lists 500 shares of stock in the Northport Townsite Company at ten dollars par each, and lists the holdings as: Corbin, 300 shares; Roberts, 100 shares; Farquhar, 50 shares; and A. Downs, 50 shares (Roberts).

10. J. C. Harrigan, personal interview; Mrs. Ray Evans, personal interview.

11. *Northport News,* n.d., quoted by Richard F. Steele, *An Illustrated History of North Washington* (Chicago: Western Historical Publishing Co., 1904), p. 138.

CHAPTER NINE.

BACKWARD TO NELSON

1. Thomas I. Oakshott, "Fort Shepherd" (MS, Eastern Washington State College, Cheney, n.d.), pp. 1–4. The fort's name, which was generally spelled Sheppard, appears to have been corrupted from that of John Shepherd, governor of the Hudson's Bay Company 1856–58. Fort Sheppard was constructed to replace Fort Colville when the latter was judged in United States territory, and ironically, later surveys indicated that Fort Sheppard, too, was on American soil.

2. British Columbia, *Sessional Papers, 1891,* p. cxvi.

3. British Columbia, *Sessional Papers, 1891,* p. cxvi; British Columbia, *Statutes, 1891,* chap. 58.

4. *Inland Sentinel* (Kamloops, B.C.), April 5, 1890. John Mara, Moses Lumby, and others in interior towns had raised private capital to survey and charter the Shuswap and Okanagan in 1884, but stepped aside when the Canadian Pacific consented to build the line. To encourage the railway, the provincial government in 1890 guaranteed interest on its securities for twenty-five years at four per cent, and $1,250,000 was floated for the railroad, completed in 1892. There had been talk that the line would be extended eastward into the mining country. Robson had helped frame a charter that gave forty per cent of the Shuswap and Okanagan's revenue to the province.

5. *Inland Sentinel* (Kamloops, B.C.), October 29, 1892. The Columbia and Kootenay railroad commenced operation May 31, 1891, and the Canadian Pacific officially assumed its operation under lease in April, 1892. The C&K had been subsidized by a grant of approximately 200,000 acres of land from the province, and $112,000 from the federal government. See *Inland Sentinel,* March 19, 1892, and Edward Lloyd Affleck, *Sternwheelers, Sandbars, and Switchbacks, A Chronicle of Steam Transportation in Southeastern British Columbia* (Vancouver: mimeographed by Affleck, 1958), p. 20.

6. *Poor's Manual of Railroads, 1896,* pp. 1028–29. The route was subsidized by Canada at $11,000 per mile (60–61 Vic. C. 5, 1891) with provision for federal control of its rates and a stipulation that freight rates would be reduced west of Fort William. The Canadian Pacific voluntarily reduced rates to certain other western stations. See John Murray Gibbon, *Steel of Empire* (New York: Bobbs-Merrill Co., 1935), p. 344, and Harold A. Innis, *A History*

of the Canadian Pacific Railway (Toronto: McClelland and Stewart, Ltd., 1923), pp. 183–84.

7. Robert Edgar Cail, "Disposal of Crown Land in British Columbia, 1871–1913" (MS, University of British Columbia, 1956), gives the total as 580,780 acres but acknowledges that sources disagree on the figure. *Poor's Manual of Railroads, 1897,* p. 890, reports 614,400 acres.

8. The committee records were reported burned in 1916. This report is based on the *Inland Sentinel* (Kamloops, B.C.), June 25, 1892, and the *Nelson Miner,* June 11, 1892.

9. William Duryea of Nyack, N.Y., was associated with his family in the Glen Cove (N.Y.) Starch Company, since amalgamated with National Starch Company, and was an official and director of various companies with property or investments in Canada and the Pacific Northwest, including the Spokane Falls and Northern Railway and The Securities Company. It is possible that he became acquainted with these enterprises through J. K. O. Sherwood, whose home was in Glen Cove. See Duryea's obituary, *New York Times,* April 28, 1907, and *Directory of Directors of the City of New York* (New York: The Audit Company, 1898–1905).

10. Roberts' time certificates and reconnaissance notes (Roberts). These are fragmentary rather than complete. The name Troup, for the steamer captain, came into use several years after completion of the Nelson and Fort Sheppard.

11. Canada, *Statutes, 1893,* Chapter 57.

12. *Inland Sentinel* (Kamloops, B.C.), April 26, 1898.

13. Copies of the bids are among Roberts' papers.

14. This is the same Hugh L. Cooper later famous as the builder of the Keokuk Dam for the United States and the Dneiper River dam for Russia.

15. *Nelson Miner,* November 25, 1893.

16. Keefer's report, December 21, 1893, may be found in British Columbia, *Public Works Report, 1893.*

17. *Nelson Miner,* December 23, 1893. The first train reached Nelson on December 19.

18. *Colville Index,* June 14, 1894; *Nelson Miner,* June 9 and 23, 1894. This was afterward regarded as the severest winter on record in British Columbia.

19. *British Columbia Law Reports,* IV (1896), 151. The lien was reported in detail in the *Nelson Miner,* February 10, 1894, as $328,044.55 and in the Law Reports as $318,000. Justices Crease and McCreight wrote the supreme court opinion pointing out the conflict between provincial and federal law. For the reader who wishes to find these reports, British Columbia records misspell the contractors' names as Larsen and Welsh.

20. D. C. Corbin, "Recollections of a Pioneer Railroad Builder," *Washington Historical Quarterly,* I (1907), No. 2, pp. 45–46.

21. *Nelson Miner,* December 14, 1895. The *Nelson Miner* published reports of Corbin's effort to reach the waterfront on February 16, April 13, May 25, and June 11, 1895.

CHAPTER TEN.
RACE TO RED MOUNTAIN

1. Stories of the discovery at Trail Creek vary. See William A. Carlyle, *Report on the Trail Creek Mining District* (Victoria: Provincial Bureau of Mines, 1896), Bulletin No. 2, pp. 15–16; Lance H. Whittaker, *Rossland, the Golden City* (Rossland: Rossland Miner, Ltd., 1949), foreword and pp. 1–2; Fred J. Smyth, *Tales of the Kootenays* (Cranbrook: Courier, 1942), pp. 6 and 21; *Trail Creek News,* January 8, 1897; and *Spokesman-Review* (Spokane), June 28, 1895.

2. Bourgeois and Moris's offer amounted to showing Topping the location. Carlyle, *op. cit.,* p. 15, points out the men "were forbidden by law to strike more than one claim on the same vein."

3. Whittaker, *op. cit.,* p. 3; *Trail Creek News,* January 15, 1897. Topping pops up in newspaper reports from various mining areas as in *Spokane Falls Review,* January 22, 1889, he is quoted as a representative of Lemon and Hume criticizing Northern Pacific station facilities at Kootenai, Idaho. His name occurs in a number of mining deeds in the records of Shoshone County, Idaho, principally in the gold districts.

4. Frances Macnab, *British Columbia for Settlers* (London: Chapman and Hall, Ltd., 1898), p. 283.

5. Letter from Department of National Revenue, Canada, to the author, December 4, 1959.

6. Letter from Corbin to commissioner, General Land Office, July 30, 1894. (Record group 49, records of Division "F," railway right-of-way files, Act of 1875, National Archives.)

7. Articles of incorporation, Spokane County, miscellaneous book B, p. 341.

8. *Engineering and Mining Journal,* Vol. 98 (1918), pp. 880–81. Material on Heinze also drawn from *Dictionary of American Biography* (New York: Charles Scribner's Sons, 1930), VII, 507; Report of the Minister of Mines, 1898, British Columbia; Sarah McNelis, "Life of F. Augustus Heinze" (MS, University of Montana, 1947); Sarah McNelis, "F. Augustus Heinze: An Early Chapter in the Life of a Copper King," *Montana Magazine of History,* II (1952), pp. 25–32; "The Story of Heinze, a Tale of Copper—and Brass," *Current Literature,* 44 (1908), pp. 34–36; J. C. Harrigan, personal interview.

9. Personal interview, E. J. Roberts.

10. The Colville reservation had been established July 2, 1872, on the west bank of the Columbia River between the Okanogan River on the south and the Canadian border on the north. It originally included the Colville valley but sixty or so white settlers there objected, so the Indians were pushed back onto approximately 4,000 square miles of generally poor farm land. See Hubert Howe Bancroft, *Works* (San Francisco: The History Co., 1890), XXXI, 381.

11. Robert Edgar Cail, "Disposal of Crown Lands in British Columbia,

1871–1913" (Master's thesis, University of British Columbia, 1956) writes: "Before legal safeguards ... timber was regarded more as a nuisance than as an asset. But the necessity for securing revenue established a pattern of thinking that was to see the reckless alienation of millions of acres of land to railway promoters between 1883 and 1900."

12. *Nelson Tribune,* October 10, 1896; F. W. Howay and E. O. S. Schole-field, *British Columbia from Earliest Times to the Present* (Vancouver: S. J. Clarke Publishing Co., 1914), II, 485–86.

13. *Inland Sentinel* (Kamloops, B.C.), February 11 and March 17, 1896. Perhaps this is the place to point out that Heinze hoped to conclude an arrangement with Colonel James Baker that would improve his bargaining position with the Canadian Pacific, and explains some of the reason for his jaunty confidence. McNelis, MS, *loc. cit.,* p. 37, quotes a telegram from Spokane Falls [sic] from Chester Glass to Heinze, April 23, 1896: "Canadian Pacific likely to get cash subsidy from Dominion government for Crow's Nest railway. Think option got from Baker we could force Canadian Pacific to terms and perhaps give them a part of land grant and retain coal and oil lands and getting special freight agreements and other concessions. Speedy action required." This would indicate that Heinze had discussed the subject with Baker and that Glass believed their talks had reached a point where Heinze might conclude negotiations to his great advantage.

CHAPTER ELEVEN.
TWO RAILROADS TO ROSSLAND

1. British Columbia, *Statutes,* 1893, Chapter 61.

2. Letter from Corbin to commissioner, General Land Office, July 30, 1894. (Record group 49, records of Division "F," railway right-of-way files, Act of 1875, National Archives.)

3. *Inland Sentinel* (Kamloops, B.C.), January 25, 1895. Corbin's federal charter, 58–59 Victoria, Chapter 60, permits either narrow- or standard-gauge construction.

4. Letter from agent T. D. Rockwell to commissioner, General Land Office, July 22, 1895 (National Archives).

5. Resolution of trustees, Columbia and Red Mountain Railway, July 30, 1895 (National Archives).

6. Canada, *Statutes,* 1895, Chapter 60, section 10, assented to June 28, 1895.

7. *Statutes at Large,* vol. 29, p. 44; public law 38, 1896 (National Archives). *Spokesman-Review* (Spokane), March 8, 1896, printed the text.

8. *Interstate Commerce Commission Reports: Decisions,* 133, 308–310. Possibly the delay between granting the right of way and this arrangement was due to Austin Corbin's death June 4, 1896, which may have dictated reconsideration of financing.

9. W. P. Hughes, "Northport 27 Years Ago," *Northport News,* May 4, 1923. The "others" mentioned in the last sentence of the newspaper were E. G. Tabor, Roberts' assistant, and Harry J. Skinner, who built depots and trestles. Roberts' notebooks show that Stewart and Welch and Burns and Jordan were given subcontracts for grading and clearing portions of the roadbed.

10. British Columbia, *Public Works Report, 1896.* Smith's report is dated December 16, 1896.

11. Letter from Corbin to the Secretary of the Interior, August 24, 1897 (National Archives).

12. *Statutes at Large,* vol. 29, 501–02.

13. Letter from A. J. Tullock, Missouri Valley Bridge and Iron Works, to Roberts, December 27, 1896 (Roberts).

14. Interstate Commerce Commission, *Twelfth Annual Report, 1898,* p. 378: Columbia and Red Mountain for the year ending June 30, 1897, reported twenty-nine per cent of its revenue from passenger service compared to forty-eight per cent reported by the Spokane Falls and Northern.

15. *Trail Creek News,* April 30, 1897; *Spokesman-Review* (Spokane), April 21, 1897.

CHAPTER TWELVE.

A SMELTER FOR NORTHPORT

1. Sarah McNelis, "Life of F. Augustus Heinze" (MS, University of Montana, 1947), pp. 53–54, 58–59.

2. *Inland Sentinel* (Kamloops, B.C.), July 24, 1896.

3. British Columbia, *Public Works Reports, 1896.* Smith's report is dated June 8, 1896. The railway used twenty-eight-pound rail, little worn but bent, that fell within the empirical formula but was too light in practice for ore trains.

4. Certificate of organization, secretary of state, New Jersey. The capitalization was $2,500,000.

5. *Poor's Manual of Railroads, 1897,* p. 266: From July 1, 1894, to July 1, 1897, the Spokane Falls and Northern issued scrip in lieu of cash for coupons falling due on and between those dates.

6. Canadian Pacific Railway, *Annual Report, 1896,* pp. 9–10.

7. *Spokesman-Review* (Spokane), December 31, 1896; *Trail Creek News,* January 8, 1897. The author can find no record that this company actually was organized in Washington or British Columbia.

8. *Trail Creek News,* August 27, 1897, quoting Shaughnessy. The Canadian Pacific had once considered erecting a smelter at Robson, but according to Shaughnessy, abandoned its plan "because Rossland ores were so little understood."

9. Silver Bow County, Mont. The mortgage was filed for record March 8, 1897. See also Robert George Raymer, *A History of Copper Mining in Montana* (Chicago: Lewis Publishing Co., 1930), p. 29.

10. *Trail Creek News,* June 18 and July 16, 1897; F. W. Howay and E. O. S. Scholefield, *British Columbia from Earliest Times to the Present* (Vancouver: S. J. Clarke Publishing Co., 1914), II, 486.

11. British Columbia Register of Companies reports the documents were destroyed August 25, 1912. W. P. Hughes, "Northport 27 Years Ago," *Northport News,* January 30, 1925, says Bellinger was paid $1,000 a month by the Le Roi Company.

12. *Trail Creek News,* July 23, 1897.

13. *Rossland Miner,* May 25, 1897; letter from E. J. Roberts to W. B. Heyburn, June 8, 1903: "As I understand it, Mr. Corbin for the Northport Townsite Company, promised to convey to the smelter company a certain right and interest in the water rights which both he and myself held individually for the Northport Townsite Company" (Roberts).

14. *Trail Creek News,* August 6, 1897.

15. *Northport News,* January 20, 1925.

16. British Columbia, *Public Works Reports, 1897.*

17. John Spencer Church, "Mining Companies in the West Kootenay and Boundary Regions of British Columbia, 1890–1900, Capital Formation and Financial Operations" (Master's thesis, University of British Columbia, 1961), pp. 20–24, expresses the view that the Canadian Pacific and British capital prevented annexation of the Kootenays to the United States.

CHAPTER THIRTEEN.
CANADA REGAINS THE KOOTENAYS

1. *Inland Sentinel* (Kamloops, B.C.), December 7, 1897.

2. Quoted in *Trail Creek News,* January 8, 1898.

3. Lance H. Whittaker, *Rossland, the Golden City* (Rossland: Rossland Miner, Ltd., 1949), pp. 53–54.

4. *Daily Province* (Vancouver) July 6 and 27, 1907. To draw a fine point, the Canadian Pacific did not buy but leased the Columbia and Western in perpetuity. See Harold A. Innis, *A History of the Canadian Pacific Railway* (Toronto: McClelland and Stewart, Ltd., 1923), p. 142. *Poor's Manual of Railroads, 1898,* p. 873, prints an extract from the CPR report for 1897 regarding its lease of the Columbia & Western.

5. *British Columbia Mining Record,* IV (1898), No. 13, p. 13.

6. Quoted by Harold A. Innis, *Settlement and the Mining Frontier* (Toronto: Macmillan Co., 1961), p. 291. Before Heinze built his smelter, the average cost of hauling and treating Trail Creek ore had been $21.00 a ton, and the minister of mines in 1897 estimated treatment could be profitable at $7.00 a ton. According to the *Spokesman-Review* (Spokane), March 3, 1898, and *Inland Sentinel* (Kamloops, B.C.), March 18, 1898, the War Eagle signed with the Canadian Pacific smelter for treatment at $7.50 per ton.

7. *Poor's Manual of Railroads, 1898,* p. 873. The Canadian Pacific annual report for 1899 says the company created and sold a £960,000 four per cent consolidated debenture stock to buy the Columbia & Western bonds. In a letter to the author, September 23, 1960, from D. B. Wallace, manager, department of public relations, Canadian Pacific Railway Company, one sentence reads: "The price that the Canadian Pacific paid F. Augustus Heinze for the Trail smelter was $200,000, and for the Columbia & Western Railway as then built, with part of the land grant, $600,000, making a total of $800,000."

8. *Colonist* (Victoria), February 6, 1916.

9. Bernard MacDonald in the *Spokesman-Review* (Spokane), January 29, 1904; *Times* (London), January 27, 1904.

10. Papers of the Le Roi Mining Co., Ltd., folder No. 57676, Registrar of Companies Office, Bush House, London, available on microfilm reels 345–46 from Bancroft Library, Berkeley. The directors of the British-American on January 14, 1900, included: the Marquis of Dufferin; Wright; Walter James Ruegg, Rodborough Manor, N. Stroud; Henry Herbert Andrew, Toledo Steel Works, Sheffield; and Robert Edward Leman, 50 Lincolns Inn Fields, W.C. The company was nominally capitalized at £1,000,000, divided into 200,000 shares at £5 each. On January 11, 1901, the company reported all shares sold and £999,946 received.

11. *Spokesman-Review* (Spokane), January 16 and May 8, 1898; *Trail Creek News,* January 8, 1898.

12. British Columbia, *Report of the Minister of Mines, 1898,* p. 1092. Only the Le Roi was producing at the time.

13. *Engineering and Mining Journal,* 86 (1900), pp. 121–22.

14. *Times* (London), January 27 and 29, 1904; *Daily Province* (Vancouver), December 6, 1951.

15. Report of inquest published in the *Times* (London), January 29, 1904.

16. *Statutes at Large,* vol. 30 (1898), p. 475.

17. Articles of incorporation, Spokane County, book E, p. 410, as the Kettle River Valley Railway.

18. *Spokesman-Review* (Spokane), April 21, 1898.

19. Quoted in *Spokesman-Review* (Spokane), July 8, 1898.

20. Letter from Great Northern Railway Company to the author, January 30, 1952, also states that the railroad has no records or correspondence now on file bearing on its purchase of the Spokane Falls and Northern system.

21. Letter from Great Northern Railway to the author, January 30, 1952, says in part: "The financing of that company [Spokane Falls and Northern] was largely a personal matter with Mr. Corbin and upon acquisition of control by the Great Northern Railway Company Mr. Corbin retained the books and data in connection with its building and refused to give them up or furnish any information concerning the construction."

22. *Interstate Commerce Commission Reports: Decisions,* 133, 331–33.

23. Spokane Falls and Northern, annual report to ICC, 1899 (National Archives). This report carries a file number, indicating that the ICC wrote

the railway about it, but the correspondence has been destroyed under congressional authorization.

CHAPTER FOURTEEN.
CORBIN TRIES NEW FIELDS

1. The house was remodeled for apartments during the forties. After the second Mrs. Corbin's death on April 25, 1950, it was purchased for the city by the late George F. Jewett to be a part of Pioneer Park, and its remaining furniture sold at public auction. The author is indebted to Wirth V. McCoy, former director, Spokane Art Center, for describing the original design of the house and its furnishings, based on McCoy's inquiry over a period of years.

2. One such notebook belonging to Corbin is in the Eastern Washington State Historical Society, Spokane.

3. Based on John Spencer Church, "Mining Companies in the West Kootenay and Boundary Regions of British Columbia, 1890–1900, Capital Formation and Financial Operations" (Master's thesis, University of British Columbia, 1961), Appendix A. Church says that 295 of 1,039 companies organized to operate in the Kootenays between 1895–1900 were capitalized in the United States.

4. Mortgage dated April 10, 1890, orders of the court, and record of sale, in Spokane County civil case 6344, Corbin v. Washington & Idaho Fair Association.

5. Leonard Fulton, "Agriculture-Cooperative-Lumber," *Early History of Fairfield* (Fairfield, Wash.: History Committee of the Town and County Study, mimeographed, 1960), pp. 21–27.

6. Articles of incorporation, Spokane County, book B, p. 350. The company was organized February 28, 1895.

7. Articles of incorporation, Spokane County, book G, p. 371. Organized December 28, 1899, the company was capitalized for $500,000 and included D. C. Corbin, Austin Corbin II, and George H. Martin, Corbin's auditor. Among its stated purposes was the development of real estate and operation of electric railroads.

8. Washington, *Session Laws, 1899,* chapter XVII. The bill, approved February 21, 1899, required that factories pay not less than four dollars a ton for beets, authorized the president of the state agricultural college to determine the quality and quantity of production for purposes of paying the bounty, and set a limit of $50,000 on state funds that might be paid as sugar bounties in a year.

9. Personal interview with J. A. Stuart, Waverly, who worked in the sugar factory as a young man.

10. Morrison's Addition was platted May 25, 1899. See Spokane County plats, book D, p. 52.

11. Washington, *Session Laws, 1903,* House Bill 380; letter from Auditor, state of Washington, to the author, March 5, 1963.

12. *Spokesman-Review* (Spokane), September 25, 1910.

13. Spokane County probate 11494.

14. *Spokesman-Review* (Spokane), June 25 and July 28, 1901; George L. Kimmel, "Irrigation in the Spokane Valley" (MS, Rosebush papers, Eastern Washington State Historical Society, *circa* 1925), n.p.

15. *Spokesman-Review* (Spokane), July 14, 1900.

16. George L. Kimmel, "Greenacres and Corbin Addition" (MS, Rosebush papers, Eastern Washington State Historical Society, *circa* 1925), n.p.

17. Washington, *Session Laws, 1899,* chapter CXXXI, approved March 14, 1899.

18. Organized April 2, 1901. Articles of incorporation, Spokane County, No. 49606.

19. Corbin notebook, Eastern Washington State Historical Society, entry in December, 1905, shows his holdings. See also *Spokesman-Review* (Spokane), October 1, 1916.

20. *Spokesman-Review* (Spokane), June 25, 1909: the Modern Land and Irrigation Co. in 1905 developed the 3,000-acre Opportunity project using wells and electric pumps.

21. Personal interview, Eldon Thomas, manager, Spokane Valley irrigation district 10.

22. Plans and specifications, Spokane Valley irrigation district 10, January 30, 1923, loaned by Eldon Thomas. In Idaho a multiple-truss trestle was anchored to cliffs along the river and often needed repairs due to weathering.

23. Letter from O. W. Lindgren to the author, March 24, 1963. Lindgren was a surveyman for Tiffany. *Spokesman-Review* (Spokane), March 28 and 31, 1920.

24. Spokane County probate 11494. The appraisers listed the stock as valueless but the bonds, par value $14,000, as worth $9,240.

25. *Spokesman-Review* (Spokane), April 27, 1958. Spokane Valley Farms was incorporated April 26, 1922, by Meneely and Taggart of New York, and H. T. Davenport, B. L. Jenkins, and George H. Greenwood, all of Spokane, with a capitalization of $1,300,000. See Spokane County, articles of incorporation No. 669809. For Meneely, see obituary, *New York Times,* December 10, 1951, and for Taggart, *Who's Who in America,* XI (1920–21), and *Who Was Who 1897–1942,* which reports Taggart's death September 28, 1922.

CHAPTER FIFTEEN.

CORBIN'S LAST RAILROAD

1. *Spokesman-Review* (Spokane), December 24, 1902; Spokane County articles of incorporation No. 73285.

2. *Newport Miner,* December 22, 1900 and March 9, 1901; Richard F. Steele, *An Illustrated History of North Washington* (Chicago: Western Historical Publishing Co., 1904), p. 795. Corbin's notebook in the Eastern Wash-

ington State Historical Society archives indicates that Frederick Weyerhaeuser called personally on Corbin in 1905.

3. These are listed in the *Kootenai County Republican* (Rathdrum), October 11, 1901, but do not constitute a complete roster of Pend Oreille lake mines.

4. *Kootenai County Republican* (Rathdrum), May 23, 1901, places one survey party six miles south of the international boundary and a second between Rathdrum and the Pend Oreille River.

5. This is the reason advanced in a letter from Roberts to Charles Sweeny, February 18, 1905 (Roberts).

6. *Spokesman-Review* (Spokane), March 18, 1904.

7. *Spokesman-Review* (Spokane), March 17, 1904; Spokane County, articles of incorporation, book H, p. 423.

8. Letter from Roberts to Corbin, February 16, 1905 (Roberts). This letter contains a discussion of the kind of locomotives, rail, etc., the railway should consider.

9. *Poor's Manual of Railroads, 1909*, p. 725; Interstate Commerce Commission, Valuation Docket No. 73 (1926), pp. 187–88. The docket shows that Corbin drew a salary of $59,000 as president of the railway from November, 1905, to November, 1916. The stock of the Spokane International was listed on the New York Exchange in 1909, according to the *Spokane Daily Chronicle,* September 21, 1909.

10. *Spokesman-Review* (Spokane), September 12, 1911: The Washington State Board of Equalization, using information supplied by the Public Service Commission, estimated the cost at $3,530,958. The entry in Corbin's notebook carries no date. See also ICC, Valuation Docket No. 73, (1926), p. 189.

11. ICC, Valuation Docket No. 73 (1926), p. 187, reports: cash advanced by Corbin, $813,830; notes due individuals, $949,540; notes to CPR $1,139,421; to which may be added an approximation of one-eighth of the cost, $429,000, for a total of $3,331,791. The valuation report, p. 187, also indicates that Corbin put in $241,093.80 not covered by his contract with the Spokane International. The cost of construction per mile could vary widely, as shown by Roberts' estimates for construction along the Moyie and Kootenai rivers: one mile below the falls on the Moyie he estimated at $40,000, while six miles along the Kootenay averaged $3,000 a mile for engineering and supervision, clearing and grubbing, bridges and culverts, and river-crossing spans. Roberts figured forty-five miles in the river areas cost $323,000, anticipating a maximum grade down the Moyie of 1.25 per cent. These were estimates, it should be emphasized, rather than tabulations of actual cost. (Roberts.)

12. ICC, Valuation Docket No. 73 (1926), p. 189.

13. *Ibid.,* p. 176.

14. *Ibid.* The Coeur d'Alene and Pend Oreille was included in the sale to the Canadian Pacific, and was abandoned in December, 1938.

15. *Spokesman-Review* (Spokane), November 14, 1916. Letter from sec-

retary, Canadian Pacific Railway Company, to the author, March 18, 1963: "It has not been possible to locate any correspondence between this Company and Mr. Daniel C. Corbin."

16. This is Roberts' story as he told it to the author. Certain details are corroborated by Corbin's notebook, Eastern Washington State Historical Society, on the page dated July 30, 1905.

17. Spokane County, articles of incorporation, No. 210616; *Poor's Manual of Railroads, 1909,* pp. 1004 and 2124.

18. Adam Shortt and Arthur G. Doughty, general eds., *Canada and Its Provinces* (Toronto: Publishers Association of Canada, Ltd., 1913), X, 576.

19. British Columbia, *Report of the Minister of Mines, 1942,* p. A131.

CHAPTER SIXTEEN.
LAST DAYS AND LEGACY

1. Doctor Neff charged the Corbin estate $13,266.38 for his travel and services. See Spokane County probate 11494.

2. Spokane County probate 39995.

BIBLIOGRAPHY

BOOKS AND PAMPHLETS

Affleck, Edward Lloyd. *Sternwheelers, Sandbars, and Switchbacks, A Chronicle of Steam Transportation in Southeastern British Columbia.* Vancouver, B.C.: mimeographed by Affleck, 1958.

Bagley, Clarence B. *History of King County, Washington.* 3 vols. Chicago: S. J. Clarke Publishing Co., 1929.

Bancroft, Hubert Howe. *Works* (Vol. XXXI, *History of Washington, Idaho, and Montana, 1845–1889*). San Francisco: The History Co., 1890.

Beal, Merrill D., and Wells, Merle W. *History of Idaho.* 3 vols. New York: Lewis Historical Publishing Co., 1959.

Boughton, Jennie. *Spokane from Memory.* Spokane: privately printed, 1941.

Burt, William P. (ed.). *Fifty Years of Progress.* Wallace, Idaho: Miner Publishing Co., 1937. A special edition of the *Wallace Miner,* December 16, 1937.

Campbell, Marius R. *et al. Guidebook of the Western United States, Part A. The Northern Pacific Route.* Washington, D.C.: Government Printing Office, 1915. U.S. Geological Service bulletin 611.

Carlyle, William A. *Report on the Trail Creek Mining District.* Victoria, B.C.: Provincial Bureau of Mines, 1896. Bulletin No. 2.

Chapin, Gilbert Warren. *The Chapin Book of Genealogical Data.* 2 vols. Hartford, Conn.: Chapin Family Association, 1924.

Clark, Victor S. *History of Manufacturers in the United States, 1860–1914.* 2 vols. Washington, D.C.: Carnegie Institute of Washington, 1928.

Crittenden, J. P., and Helffrish, Charles B. *New York Securities.* New York: New York Securities, 1893.

Dorman, Robert (comp.). *Steam and Electric Railways of Canada, 1836–1937.* Ottawa: Robert Dorman, 1938.

Durham, Nelson W. *Spokane and the Inland Empire.* 3 vols. Chicago: S. J. Clarke Publishing Co., 1912.

Edwards, Jonathan. *An Illustrated History of Spokane County.* Place of publication unknown: W. H. Lever, 1900.

Fairfield, Wash., History Committee of the Town and Country Study. *Early History of Fairfield.* Fairfield, Wash.: History Committee of the Town and Country Study, 1960.

Fuller, George W. *A History of the Pacific Northwest.* New York: Alfred A. Knopf, 1931.

———. *The Inland Empire.* 4 vols. Spokane: H. G. Linderman, 1928.

Gibbon, John Murray. *Steel of Empire*. New York: Bobbs-Merrill Co., 1935.

Glasscock, C. B. *War of the Copper Kings*. New York: Grosset and Dunlap, 1935.

Glazebrook, G. P. de T. *A History of Transportation in Canada*. Toronto: Ryerson Press, 1938.

Glover, James N. *History of Spokane*. Spokane: mimeographed from *Spokane Daily Chronicle* newspaper articles, 1917.

Gosnell, R. E. *A History of British Columbia*. Chicago: Lewis Publishing Co., 1906.

Graham, Clara. *Fur and Gold in the Kootenays*. Vancouver, B.C.: Wrigley Printing Co., 1945.

Graham, Thomas. *Stevens County Fifty Years Ago*. Spokane: typescript of articles in the *Statesman-Examiner* (Colville, Wash.), 1929.

Greenough, W. Earl. *Coeur d'Alene Mining Region, 1846–1946*. Mullan, Idaho: privately printed, 1947.

Hamilton, James McClellan. *From Wilderness to Statehood, A History of Montana, 1805–1900*. Portland, Ore.: Binfords and Mort, 1957.

Haney, Lewis Henry. *A Congressional History of Railways in the United States, 1850–1887*. Madison, Wis.: University of Wisconsin, 1910. Bulletin of the University, No. 342.

Hanford, C. H. *Seattle and Environs, 1852–1924*. 3 vols. Chicago: Pioneer Historical Publishing Co., 1924.

Hines, Rev. H. K. *An Illustrated History of the State of Washington*. Chicago: Lewis Publishing Co., 1893.

Holbrook, Stewart H. *The Columbia*. New York: Rinehart and Co., 1956.

Hook, Harry H., and McGuire, Francis J. *A History of the Early Settlement and the Spokane Falls of Today*. Minneapolis: Frank L. Thresher, 1889.

Howay, F. W. *British Columbia, the Making of a Province*. Toronto: Ryerson Press, 1928.

Howay, F. W., Sage, W. N., and Angus, H. F. *British Columbia and the United States*. Toronto: Ryerson Press, 1942.

Howay, F. W., and Scholefield, E. O. S. *British Columbia from Earliest Times to the Present*. 4 vols. Vancouver, B.C.: S. J. Clarke Publishing Co., 1914.

Hult, Ruby El. *Steamboats in the Timber*. Caldwell, Idaho: Caxton Printers, Ltd., 1952.

Husband, Joseph. *The Story of the Pullman Car*. Chicago: McClurg, 1917.

Illustrated History of the State of Idaho. Chicago: Lewis Publishing Co., 1899.

Ingalls, Walter Renton. *Lead and Zinc in the United States*. New York: Hill Publishing Co., 1908.

Innis, Harold A. *A History of the Canadian Pacific Railway*. Toronto: McClelland and Stewart, Ltd., 1923.

———. *Settlement and the Mining Frontier*. Toronto: Macmillan Co., 1936.

Interstate Commerce Commission. *Twelfth Annual Report (1898)*. Washington D.C.: Government Printing Office, 1898.

————. *Reports: Decisions, Volume 133.* Washington, D.C.: Government Printing Office, 1908.

————. *Valuation Docket No. 73. Spokane International Railway Company et al.* Washington, D.C.: Government Printing Office, 1926.

Johnson, Emory R. *Government Regulation of Transportation.* New York: D. Appleton-Century Co., 1938.

Johnson, Kate. *Pioneer Days of Nakusp and the Arrow Lakes.* Nakusp, B.C.: privately printed, 1951.

Knopf, Adolph. *Ore Deposits in the Helena Mining Region, Montana.* Washington, D.C.: Government Printing Office, 1913. U.S. Geological Survey bulletin 527.

Lawson, Harvey M. *History and Genealogy of the Descendants of Clement Corbin.* Hartford, Conn.: Case, Lockwood and Brainard Co., 1905.

Leeson, Michael A. (ed.). *History of Montana, 1739–1885.* Chicago: Warner, Beers and Co., 1885.

Macnab, Frances. *British Columbia for Settlers.* London: Chapman and Hall, Ltd., 1898.

McCulloch, H. L., S.J. *Life of John Robert Monaghan.* Spokane: Shaw and Borden, 1906.

Miller, C. H. (Joaquin). *The State of Montana.* Chicago: Lewis Publishing Co., 1894.

Mineral Resources of the United States, 1887. Washington, D.C.: Government Printing Office, 1888.

Morton, J. Sterling, succeeded by Watkins, Albert (ed.). *Illustrated History of Nebraska.* 3 vols. Lincoln: Western Publishing and Engraving Co., 1905–13.

Northwestern Industrial Exposition. *The City of Spokane Falls.* Buffalo, N.Y.: Matthews, Northrup and Co., 1890.

Northwest Mining Association. *Yearbook and Program, February 11–17, 1918.* Spokane, Northwest Mining Association, 1918.

O'Connor, Harvey. *The Guggenheims.* New York: Covici-Friede, 1937.

Official Northern Pacific Railroad Guide. St. Paul: W. C. Riley, 1892.

Oregonian's Handbook of the Pacific Northwest. Portland, Ore.: The Oregonian Publishing Co., 1894.

Oregonian Souvenir. Portland, Ore.: Lewis and Dryden Printing Co., 1892.

Ormsby, Margaret A. *British Columbia: a History.* Toronto: Macmillan Co., 1958.

Osborne, Lucy Eugenia. *Alfred Clark Chapin, March 8, 1848–October 2, 1936.* Portland, Me.: privately printed, 1937.

Pyle, Joseph Gilpin. *Life of James J. Hill.* 2 vols. New York: Peter Smith, 1936.

Progressive Men of the State of Montana. Chicago: A. W. Bowen and Co., circa 1900.

Quaife, M. M. *Early Days of Rock Island and Davenport.* Chicago: R. R. Donnelly and Sons Co., 1948.

Ransome, Frederick Leslie, and Calkins, Frank Cathcart. *Geology and Ore*

Deposits of the Coeur d'Alene District, Idaho. Washington, D.C.: Government Printing Office, 1908. U.S. Geological Survey professional paper 62.

Raymer, Robert George. *History of Copper Mining in Montana.* Chicago: Lewis Publishing Co., 1930.

———. *Montana, the Land and the People.* 3 vols. Chicago: Lewis Publishing Co., 1930.

Reavis, John R. *The City of Spokane.* Spokane: Clough and Graves, 1891.

Report on the Internal Commerce of the United States for the Year 1890. Washington, D.C.: Government Printing Office, 1891. Executive Document 6, Part 2, House of Representatives, Fifty-First Congress, Second Session.

Rickard, T. A. *Bunker Hill Enterprise.* San Francisco: Mining and Scientific Press, 1921.

———. *A History of American Mining.* New York: McGraw-Hill Book Co., Inc., 1932.

Rossland . . . A Residential City. Rossland, B.C.: Board of Trade, 1951.

Ruffner, W. H. *A Report on Washington Territory.* New York: Seattle, Lake Shore and Eastern Railway Co., 1889.

Schoenberg, Wilfred P., S.J. *Gonzaga University, Seventy-five Years, 1887–1962.* Spokane: Gonzaga University, 1963.

Shiach, William S., Henderson, John M., and Averill, Harry B. *Illustrated History of North Idaho.* Chicago: Western Historical Publishing Co., 1903.

Shortt, Adam, and Doughty, Arthur G. (general eds.). *Canada and Its Provinces.* 23 vols. Toronto: Publishers Association of Canada, Ltd., 1913.

Shoup, Gov. George L. *Report of the Secretary of the Interior, 1890.* Washington, D.C.: Government Printing Office, 1890. Vol. III, Reports of the Governors. Fifty-First Congress, First Session.

Slater, John B. *Natural Resources of Stevens County, Washington, and the Famous Mining Region of Trail Creek, B.C.* Spokane: Spokane Printing Co., 1895.

Spokane County, Wash., Planning Commission. *Domestic Water Suppliers in the Suburban Area.* Spokane: mimeographed by Spokane County, 1961.

———. *Domestic Water in the Spokane Valley.* Spokane: mimeographed by Spokane County, 1954.

Smyth, Fred J. *Tales of the Kootenays.* Cranbrook, B.C.: The Courier, 1942.

Steele, Richard F. *Illustrated History of North Washington.* Chicago: Western Historical Publishing Co., 1904.

Steele, Richard F., and Rose, Arthur P. *Illustrated History of Stevens, Ferry, Okanogan, and Chelan Counties.* Chicago: Western Historical Publishing Co., 1904. Identical in content to *Illustrated History of North Washington.*

Stahlberg, John A. (ed.). *Montana, A State Guide Book.* New York: Viking Press, 1939.

Stevens, Horace J. *Copper Handbook, 1901.* Hougton, Mich.: Stevens, 1902.

Strahorn, Robert E. *Montana Territory.* Helena: Montana Legislature, 1879.

Swallow, George C., and Trevarthen, J. B. *Reports of the Inspector of Mines and Deputy Inspector of Mines for the Six Months Ending November 30, 1889.* Helena, Mont.: State of Montana, 1890.

Thompson, Slason. *Cost, Capitalization, and Estimated Value of American Railways* (3d ed.) Chicago: Gunthorp-Warren Printing Co.,1908.

Trail, a Half Century, 1901–1951. Trail, B.C.: Trail Golden Jubilee Society, 1951.

United States Beet Sugar Association. *Beet Sugar Story.* Washington, D.C.: U.S. Beet Sugar Assn., 1959.

Van Duyne, Cornelius, and Ashton, Fred W. *Soil Survey of Stevens County, Washington.* Washington D.C.: Government Printing Office, 1916. U.S. Department of Agriculture, 15th report of field operations of the Bureau of Soils.

Wardner, James F. *Jim Wardner of Wardner, Idaho.* New York: Anglo-American Publishing Co., 1900.

Wharton, J. E. *History of the City of Denver.* Denver: Byers and Dailey, 1866. This volume also contains a city directory compiled by D. O. Wilhelm.

Whittaker, Lance H. *Rossland, the Golden City.* Rossland, B.C.: Rossland Miner, Ltd., 1949.

Wilson, Alfred W. G. *Copper Smelting Industries of Canada.* Ottawa: Canada Department of Mines, 1913. Mines bulletin 209.

UNPUBLISHED SOURCES

Cail, Robert Edgar. "Disposal of Crown Lands in British Columbia, 1871–1913." 2 vols. Unpublished MS, University of British Columbia, 1956.

Church, John Spencer. "Mining Companies in the West Kootenay and Boundary Regions of British Columbia, 1890–1900, Capital Formation and Financial Operations." Unpublished master's thesis, University of British Columbia, 1961.

Cottingham, Mollie E. "A History of the West Kootenay District in British Columbia." Unpublished master's thesis, University of British Columbia, 1947.

Dunnigan, Loretta. "A History of Coeur d'Alene, Idaho, to 1910." Unpublished master's thesis, Gonzaga University, 1956.

Flucke, A. F. "A History of Mining in British Columbia." Unpublished MS in provincial library, Victoria, B.C., *circa* 1954.

Holmes, Emmett. "Some Historical Facts and Other Remembrances of the Construction and Operation of the Spokane Falls & Northern Railway." Unpublished MS in Spokane Public Library, 1941.

Kimmel, George L. "Greenacres and Corbin Addition." Unpublished MS in Rosebush papers, Eastern Washington State Historical Society, Spokane, *circa* 1925.

———. "Irrigation in the Spokane Valley." Unpublished MS in Rosebush papers, Eastern Washington State Historical Society, Spokane, *circa* 1925.

Le Roi Mining Company, miscellaneous records. Folder 57676, registrar of companies office, Bush House, London. Microfilm reels 345–46, Bancroft Library, Berkeley, Calif.

McNelis, Sarah. "Life of F. Augustus Heinze." Unpublished master's thesis, University of Montana, 1947.

Oakshott, Thomas I. "Fort Shepherd." Unpublished MS, Eastern Washington State College, n.d.

Oliphant, J. Orin. "Early History of Spokane, Washington, Told by Contemporaries." Unpublished MS, Eastern Washington State College, 1927.

Thrupp, Sylvia L. "A History of the Cranbrook District in East Kootenay." Unpublished master's thesis, University of British Columbia, 1929.

Wilson, Fred L. "Early Recollections of the Coeur d'Alene and St. Joe Rivers." Unpublished MS, Coeur d'Alene Public Library, n.d.

ARTICLES

Brimlow, George F. "Marias Pass Explorer John F. Stevens," *Montana Magazine of History,* I (1953).

Brougham, W. F. "A Typical Mining Town," *Canadian Magazine,* XIV (1889), 19 ff.

Corbin, Daniel C. "Recollections of a Pioneer Railroad Builder," *Washington Historical Quarterly,* I (1907), No. 2, pp. 43–46.

Fitzsimmons, James. "Columbia River Chronicles," *British Columbia Historical Quarterly,* I (1937), 20–34.

Fowler, S. S. "Early Smelters in British Columbia," *British Columbia Historical Quarterly,* III (1939), 183–201.

Gibbons, William H. "The Forests and the Wood-Using Industries of Washington," *West Coast Lumberman,* October, 1927.

Hacking, Norman. "Steamboat Days on the Upper Columbia and Upper Kootenay," *British Columbia Historical Quarterly,* XVI (1952), 1–51.

Howard, William W. "Spokane Falls and Its Exposition," *Harper's Weekly,* XXXIV (1890), 689–706.

Johansen, Dorothy O. "Simeon G. Reed, Pioneer," *Bulletin of the Business History Society,* X (1936), No. 3, pp. 37–43.

Lewis, Sol H. "History of Railroads in Washington," *Washington Historical Quarterly,* III (1912), 186–197.

McNelis, Sarah. "F. Augustus Heinze: An Early Chapter in the Life of a Copper King," *Montana Magazine of History,* II (1952), 25–32.

Nesbit, Robert C., and Gates, Charles M. "Agriculture in Eastern Washington," *Pacific Northwest Quarterly,* XXXVII (1946), 279–302.

Spears, John R. "Corbin Game Park," *Annual Report of the Board of Regents of the Smithsonian Institution to July 1891,* pp. 417–23.

Stewart, William R. "Captains of Industry—F. Augustus Heinze," *Cosmopolitan,* November, 1903, pp. 289–92.

"Story of Heinze, a Tale of Copper—and Brass," *Current Literature,* XXXXIV (1908), 34–36.
Turnbull, Elsie G. "Rossland Camp," *Pacific Northwesterner,* VI (1962), 9–14.

NEWSPAPERS AND SPECIALIZED PERIODICALS

Avant Courier (Bozeman, Mont.)
British Columbia Mining Record (Victoria, B.C.)
Coeur d'Alene Press
Coeur d'Alene Sun (Murray, Idaho)
Chewelah Miner
Colville Index
Colville Miner
Colville Republican
Colonist (Victoria, B.C.)
Daily Province (Vancouver, B.C.)
Engineering and Mining Journal (New York)
Evening Leader (Great Falls, Mont.)
Froid Tribune (Froid, Mont.)
Helena Daily Herald
Helena Independent
Helena Weekly Herald
Inland Sentinel (Kamloops, B.C.)
Kootenai County Republican (Rathdrum, Idaho)
Lower's Golden Claim (Trail Creek, B.C.)
Mining Truth (Spokane, Wash.)
Montana Post (Helena, Mont.)
Morning Oregonian (Portland, Ore.)
Nebraska City News
Nelson Miner
Nelson Tribune
Newport Miner (Newport, Wash.)
New York Times
New York Tribune
Northport News (Northport, Wash.)
Northwest Tribune (Cheney and Spokane, Wash.)
People's Press (Nebraska City, Neb.)
Railroad Gazette (Chicago)
Rocky Mountain News (Denver, Colo.)
Rossland Miner
Spokane Daily Chronicle
Spokane Falls Review
Spokesman (Spokane, Wash.)

Spokesman-Review (Spokane, Wash.)
Statesman-Examiner (Colville, Wash.)
Stevens County Miner (Colville, Wash.)
Times (London)
Trail Creek News
Wallace Free Press
Wallace Miner
Wallace Press
Wyoming Telescope (Nebraska City, Neb.)

DICTIONARIES, DIRECTORIES, AND MANUALS

Biographical Directory of Railway Officials of America, 1887. Chicago: Railway Age Publishing Co., 1887.
Butte City Directory. Butte, Mont.: R. L. Polk and Co., 1895.
Dictionary of American Biography. New York: Charles Scribner's Sons, 1928.
Directory of Directors of the City of New York. New York: Audit Co., 1898–1905.
Poor's Manual of Railroads. New York: Poor's Manual Co., 1885–1930.
Spokane City Directory. Spokane, Wash.: R. L. Polk and Co., 1887–1950.

INDEX

259